I0441852

Peter Steyn was raised in a white, working class suburb in Johannesburg, a city housing some 5 million people, at a time when South Africa was in the grip of apartheid, often teetering on the brink of civil insurrection. His life seemingly normal, his father an Afrikaner, his mother an English South African, in a country still bearing the scars of the Anglo Boer War, evident in the toxic rift between English and Afrikaans white South Africans. Racism was the norm amongst most white South Africans, as a small child he submitted to the thinking at the time. His views changing radically, he later harboured a loathing of racism, a vocal supporter of the first true democratic elections in South Africa which saw the ANC become the first 'black' government of the country. Disappointment set in when the 'new improved' government showed its hand, corruption and racism of a different hue taking hold. He now lives on the north shore of Auckland, New Zealand, with his family.

The wonderful people of South Africa, who have always, and continue to deserve better, virtuous governance untainted by widespread corruption. Timothy Scott RIP, you were a special South African, a man amongst men. Stephen Glynn RIP, my brother-in-law, but more like my brother, always going above and beyond for your staff, both black and white, and everything in between. Andrew Feinstein, who exposed and continues to expose wrongdoing by international arms manufacturers and dealers, at great risk to himself, continues to inspire through tireless, thankless work.

Peter Steyn

SUPPING WITH SATAN

AUSTIN MACAULEY PUBLISHERS™

LONDON · CAMBRIDGE · NEW YORK · SHARJAH

Copyright © Peter Steyn 2024

The right of Peter Steyn to be identified as author of this work has been asserted by the author in accordance with sections 77 and 78 of the Copyright, Designs and Patents Act 1988.

All rights reserved. No part of this publication may be reproduced, stored in a retrieval system, or transmitted in any form or by any means, electronic, mechanical, photocopying, recording, or otherwise, without the prior permission of the publishers.

Any person who commits any unauthorised act in relation to this publication may be liable to criminal prosecution and civil claims for damages.

The story, experiences, and words are the author's alone.

A CIP catalogue record for this title is available from the British Library.

ISBN 9781035830022 (Paperback)
ISBN 9781035830039 (ePub e-book)

www.austinmacauley.com

First Published 2024
Austin Macauley Publishers Ltd®
1 Canada Square
Canary Wharf
London
E14 5AA

An enormous debt of gratitude to my family who endured my grumpy times while I would sit and reminisce, dredging up many old memories, searching for the 'right' material for my book. Dale Smithdorf Waters and Greg Waters who insisted that I re-write the manuscript to inject life into my story, providing encouragement for months and years, giving me the fortitude to see the book through and find a publisher willing to take a risk on a new writer. To the Scott family, who played a huge role in my social and political awakening in my late teenage years, I am eternally grateful.

Table of Contents

Prologue

A fine haze of fresh smoke slowly started to invade the air in the lounge, which would begin each day to chill at the very moment when the legion of mighty Jacaranda trees, now bare, would cast dancing, speckled shadows through the large window. There was a Jacaranda tree standing sentry in front of each home, imposing, when one looked up or down the road, as far as the eye could see. I sat in the bay window in the lounge of the old house in the late afternoon, bathing in the glow of the final rays before the sepia sunlight would surrender to the mighty trunks of the trees and neighbouring roofs, as the world slowly grew a little colder, and suddenly darker.

Our maid, Julie, a slightly built, leathery 'old' Zulu woman of about 45 would kindle the small flames in the glossy maroon coloured ESSE heater, quietly cursing, in her own language, isiZulu, the thing for creating so much smoke while taking too long to burn bright, convinced that Mum would go off like a packet of crackers because the house was icy when it should have been warmed ages ago.

When Mum did arrive home each day, anyone within earshot would be tortured yet again by her repertoire of deep sighs, as she remonstrated with her own exhaustion, following another tedious day stabbing away at a typewriter, a walk to the city bus terminal at van der Bijl Square, a long bus ride which stopped 'a hundred' times before her Royal Oak Street drop-off, then the walk down the steep Royal Oak Street in her stiletto heels. From this vantage point, I could see the gate, looking like it was once part of a picket fence at the front of our garden, before the fence was replaced by a patterned, whitewashed precast wall. I could see on the other side of the front garden, the driveway, as I would sit each day patiently, praying fervently to God that 'today' would be the day I would get that puppy.

A barrage of vows and promises to God would accompany my daily pleadings as I would frequently remind him of the lessons at Sunday School pontificating his omniscience and benevolence. Mum would arrive at the gate, resplendent as always, every bit the Jackie Kennedy O'Nassis look-alike, immaculately dressed in tweed or chiffon, perfect jet black hair, immaculate make-up, matching Italian leather shoes and handbag, she would check the mail box for contents, her poker face not betraying the fact that bundled in a little blanket under her arm was the most beautiful, fluffy, mischievous puppy you could wish for. "No such luck!" I realised yet again.

More likely though, the puppy would arrive by car with Dad, who drove to and from work each day, since his job demanded that he sometimes visit Orlando power station in Soweto, a satellite town housing hundreds of thousands of black people. Day in and day out, Mum's poker face betrayed nothing, other than constant exhaustion, and every day Dad's powder blue Hillman Vogue transported only Dad, his briefcase and his heavy, concealed Taurus 38 Special revolver, for protection against the hordes in the township.

So began my part in God's downfall, since I never did get the puppy. Some years later I received a dying little dog from my Ouma (Grandmother), which had been attacked by another of her dogs. The poor girl had had all her fur shorn, and stitches across a number of ugly lesions where her intestines had been pulled from her body. Ouma had pushed everything back inside her, holding her together on her lap, as they were driven to the vet. The vet recommended euthanasia, which Ouma would not hear of. The vet stressed that he had no staff at his practice on that particular night to keep her under observation.

Following Ouma's insistence, he conducted a lengthy surgical procedure and suggested that the dog could be given a regimen for pain relief, but stressed that she would probably not make it through the night. Reluctant to take her home to be left to the mercy of the other dogs, 'Twiggy' was brought to our home that night and handed to me to take care of during her final hours. Obviously in immense pain and frightened out of her wits, a show of the whites of her eyes and bared teeth leaving no doubt that the unfortunate little creature did not want to be handled or touched in any way.

"If anyone will look after her, it's you…" said Ouma, and through red, swollen, tear-filled eyes she begged me: "Please take good care of her," telling me what the vet had said, and then saying her final farewells to the little dog she had loved so much. Remembering that God had provided the opposite when I had asked—no, begged for a puppy—I decided not to give him the option of providing the opposite of that which I had wished for in my prayers, so I concealed from him the fact that I now had a dog and explained to Twiggy that It would be solely my responsibility to stay up all night watching over her.

I thought that if I didn't let her sleep, well, then she couldn't possibly die, perfect logic for a seven-year-old. Every time she seemed to be drifting off, I would gently coax her eyes open with an offer of a little sliver of chicken, or a drink of warm milk from a syringe. I sang quietly to her, and as the night wore on it became more and more difficult to keep her awake. I lay on the floor with the little dog by my side. She curled into a ball wrapped in an old towel and a blanket, me fighting hard to ward off the overpowering seductiveness of slumber.

I gazed in wonder at the beauty of the pressed steel ceiling, thinking how they all differed in design and complexity from room to room. My bedside lamp, not very bright, cast shadows accentuating the two-dimensional nature of the patterned ceiling and cornices. I imagined the workmen on ladders measuring up each room, and then reporting to the ceiling factory to 'make' a suitable ceiling to snugly fit into each space, including the little scullery and pantry which prided themselves in being as beautiful as their larger counterparts, the lounge, passage, dining room and bedrooms.

The houses on this section of Highland Road had been built in about 1932, the floor plans being almost identical for most. I thought about the ceilings and rooms in the neighbouring homes until sleep finally swept over me. I was relieved when I awoke suddenly, startled, afraid, but Twiggy hadn't died that night. She survived, growing stronger by the day, and with much love and nurturing, she became the most delightful furry companion one could have hoped for, enjoying her few remaining years much loved by my little sister and me.

The sparkle in her hazel eyes, the apparent delight on her face, and the unabashed swishing of her bushy miniature Toy Pom tail became a feature of my world each and every day as she waited at the front door for my return from school., Then turning circles, yelping with joy, she would finally leap into my arms to be cuddled while my face was licked.

Julie would be reprimanded if the house was still cold when Mum walked through the door, and I did not notice it at the time, but it was usually on Mondays that Julie was called to account for the cold in the home. Hindsight might reveal that Monday for Julie was a living nightmare each and every week. Her first task of the day, every day, was to bring piping hot coffee to each family member, still in bed, at one or two minutes before 7.00 which was waking time for us.

She would see to it that breakfast cereal or porridge was served at a time which suited each individual's time schedule. Monday was 'wash day', when she would wash, in a machine, a full week's laundry for the entire family. Mum had taught her that 'delicates' and woollen garments were to be hand washed in 'Lux', a gentle cleanser to be used in lukewarm water. These would then be laid out on a towel to dry in the sun, never hung on a wash line.

All else was washed, wrung and hung on the line to be dried in the sun. Between washing and drying, the beds needed to be made up, carpets vacuumed, house dusted and cleaned after the weekends' activities. Julie was expected to prepare supper, clear the table, wash all dishes by hand and after cleaning the kitchen in preparation for Tuesday, she could be heard locking up at about 7.30 each evening.

Tuesday… was not much better for the hapless Julie as ironing replaced washing, and all other chores remained. Wednesdays, Thursdays and Fridays promised little to no relief for the poor woman, as Mum's boundless morning energy and enthusiasm led to lists of instructions for daily projects involving washing of curtains, bedding, cleaning of windows, unpacking and cleaning out the pantry or fridge, and cleaning of Dad's multitude of boxing trophies. It seemed like there were hundreds of trophies from his youth and then the days when he had been a South African national champion; her 'to do' list inexhaustible.

Saturdays and Sundays provided a small measure of relief, when Julie was granted time off once the lunch dishes had been washed, dried, packed away and the kitchen was cleaned yet again. One weekend a month was for Julie a 'treat', or so Mum said, as she dressed up, late on Friday afternoon, in her finery, laden with bags containing all sorts of basics and perhaps little treats, she made her way out of the gate and it seemed that she would be on her way home to 'Zululand' to see her children.

Whether she travelled by train or bus was never discussed, nor how long the trip would last, or indeed how much time she actually spent with her children. Her rural home would probably have been some 500 km from Johannesburg, and Julie was expected to report for work bright and early on Monday morning. So, it's most likely that she travelled through Friday and Sunday nights sleeping at home only on Saturday evening. Julie was granted annual leave for two weeks coinciding with time when the family would enjoy a beach holiday each year during the coldest weeks of winter in Johannesburg, at a budget family hotel, Skipper's Cabin at Shelly Beach in 'winterless' Natal.

Julie's room at the back of our garden was part of an 'outbuilding', a coal shed and adjacent, her dark bedroom with no electricity, running water or toilet. A toilet attached to the main house was for her use, about a 20 metre walk from her room. She relied on candles for light, a paraffin burner for cooking, a single outdoor tap running only cold water for her drinking, cooking and washing. Julie's eyes were often bloodshot, I later concluded, as a result of binge drinking (cheap to make, home-brewed 'Mageu', made of cold maize meal porridge with yeast)—to keep warm in the winter perhaps, or to take the edge off a life of desperate misery?

Her situation was not uncommon, and although not consciously aware of it at the time, today I reflect on how kind Julie (and the same of subsequent maids employed by my family) was to me and my younger sister when we were children. The maternal instinct and genteel nature of these uneducated tribal women was a marvel, particularly in the face of such horrid, adverse living conditions.

Payment of maids was a subject all on its own, discussed in certain social circles. Mum boasted how little our maid had required in the initial interview. In truth these women, our maid in particular, lived on slave wages, the argument presented by Mum being that she was provided with free accommodation, and ate the same meal as us at supper time. Mum provided her with a bag of maize meal for the month.

Furthermore, she would point out to anyone who sought to contradict her logic that replacing a maid was the easiest thing in the world, since there were frequently women knocking on the door seeking employment. These women had little to no recourse for ill treatment in the workplace, and could be dismissed instantaneously at the whim of employers, in the absence of a legal infrastructure demanding due process, conciliation, mediation or arbitration, or even rudimentary employment contracts.

It was not unusual to hear of a maid or gardener being dismissed because the employer felt that the employee was 'cheeky' or was perhaps accused of taking sugar or tea bags from the pantry. Later, comments would follow: "It's amazing how long our milk, tea, or sugar lasts since I fired her," to be met with nodding of heads and peals of laughter from friends when the inevitable discussion of 'maids' came up in 'white' social settings.

A fish spawning in water is the most natural thing in the world, the young having absolutely no need to understand the nature of water, it's chemical make-up or how food is produced. Instinctively the young do understand survival of the fittest, the very essence of nature's food chain. So, it was with me, as a young child, that I was neither aware of racial prejudice, nor was I concerned about racial or indeed, any injustice, since I was being taught by my parents and society about self-preservation and survival.

Mum and Dad and other adults would explain that a kaffir[1] working in the suburbs was lucky to have a roof over her head and food in her belly. Furthermore, these people were to be treated with disdain, since they were without question, dirty, stupid, dishonest and in almost every way inferior to us. I recall a perennial joke told at braais[2]; about the only good kaffir being a dead one. These tenets, like the young fish bent only on survival and not understanding the chemical composition of water, I held to be true, until such time as I started to meet and talk to enlightened people whose aspirations extended way beyond superficial survival and the denigration of those in a society whose laws ensured that the 'Great unwashed'[3] would remain so in perpetuity.

---

[1] Kaffir is a term used by many white people in Southern Africa to refer to or describe black people. The notoriety of the word evolved over time to the point it had been used in a highly derogatory context, often with adjectives, sometimes expletives, added to emphasise disdain or even hatred, e.g., stupid Kaffir, fucking Kaffir or kaffir bastard. The term was, by and large, quite acceptable in polite society in white suburbia, and when casually dropped into conversation to this day is a thermometer to test those in attendance for the degree of intolerance harboured for non-white people. Until 1994, systemic racial segregation and racism was enshrined in statute books. Post 1994, use of the word was deemed to constitute hate speech, and is now punishable in a court of law in South Africa. In more recent times, the word used in hushed tones, and only in 'trusted company' amongst people of like mind, who cling desperately to the jaundiced white supremacist views of their forebears.

[2] 1Braai, or barbeque, outdoor event, involving large gatherings of friends or family, cooking meat on an open fire, a tradition amongst white South Africans normally accompanied by consumption of alcoholic beverages, chatter and much laughter.

[3] Definition of the (great) unwashed, Webster Dictionary

Old-fashioned + humorous: ordinary or common people who do not have a lot of money, power, or social status.

The common, lower classes; the hoi polloi.

For some it may seem surprising that conscription was accepted almost without question by South Africa. However, there were many reasons for men to accept their military conscription. On a broad scale, it is a well-documented psychological phenomenon that in any society the majority of people will obey the structures of authority, even if they have misgivings.

Psychologist Stanley Milgram[4] showed empirically that within an institutional environment people will comply with orders even if they believe such orders to be wrong or suspect, simply because someone in authority tells them they must. Milgram stated that "our compliance with the imperatives of others is tied to particular institutions and locales in our day-to-day activities," indicating that the more commonplace the authority the more likely it is to be obeyed. In the case of a government, obedience is as a rule endemic and so it would be expected that whether or not other motivations existed, the majority of people would comply with military service requirements.

By the 1960s, military service was becoming more acceptable to the whole spectrum of white South African society, and had not yet acquired the later stigma of being an instrument of racial repression. For most men, obedience to conscription was not a conscious decision but simply something that had to be done, a kind of rite of passage to manhood that became as naturally part of a white South African male's life as going to school or getting a job. For some, the idea of being able to serve their people and country helped them accept their duties, while a wish to follow in the footsteps of their forebears could also have played a part.[5]

This disparaging term was coined by the Victorian novelist and playwright Edward Bulwer-Lytton in his 1830 novel *Paul Clifford.*

[4] 1 Stanley Milgram, Obedience to Authority, an Experimental View (London, 1974), p. 68

47 Milgram.69

[5] Graeme Callister Department of History, University of Stellenbosch

Scientia Militaria, South African Journal of Military Studies, Vol 35, Nr 1 2007. doi: 10.5787/35-1-29

1. Army Daze. 18 January

"Staan op, staan op!"[6] screamed the beast, my mind accelerating into a state of murky confusion, senses jolted awake. The first thing that struck me was cheap deodorant—'Mum for Men'—I knew the sweet smell instantly. I smelled him before I saw him as the lights went on, his 'mum' now competing furiously with the heavy body odour of four drowsy occupants of the stuffy train compartment, the inevitable result of a three-day train ride into the heart of the Karoo Desert, stifling heat during the day, with very little respite after dark. There was also the stale cigarette reek of the little silver ashtray beneath the window, overflowing with 'stompies'[7], remnants of the night before, when Albert, Peter, Keith and I had sat chatting, as we had each night before that, chatting smoking, sneaking the odd Castle Lager to the compartment, like this was the last supper.

The light went on, revealing the face and arms of the beast, which were well tanned, the very same colour as his uniform. He was tall, slender yet muscular, a trimmed black moustache underlining his nose, and a weathered green beret carefully sculpted and fitted onto his head, tipping forward at just the correct angle, proudly hosting a silver springbok head above the green, yellow and black 'balkie', neatly lined up directly above his left eye, identifying him as an infantryman. Two stripes adorning the sleeve of each upper arm, and a rasping voice, seemingly incapable of normal conversation—only the barking of instructions—left no doubt that this was the dreaded 'Korporaal', a demonic automaton, one year in the making.

"Maak laat julle fokken gou uitklim!"[8]. Lucidity, voiced like a four-pound hammer smashing down on us, we literally threw our belongings into suitcases and bags, having been completely unprepared for this onslaught. "Thursday

---

[6] 'Get up, get up!'

[7] Cigarette butts

[8] 'Make sure you climb off fucking fast!'

morning you'll arrive" they'd told us, our naïve 'civilian' minds anticipating an early breakfast on the train, as we would gently roll into the station in Oudtshoorn, while we carefully packed our things at the end of a long journey, ready to take on this new adventure.

No, this was not the morning that we knew, this was the middle of the night, when respectable people were at the height of their slumber. ***"Klim uit, Klim uit… Maak of julle fokken haastig is jou klomp dom fokken takhare!"***[9] they were to be heard screeching from down the carriage corridor. A monster or two had been unleashed in every carriage which had been stealthily orchestrated to erupt all at once to maximise effect. There were more to be seen adorning the platform, all moustachioed, the entire length of the train, spread out to make it seem that there were lots more of them. Hands behind their backs, chests puffed, deadpan, they stared at the train, all the same colour as their slightly faded brown uniforms. 'Robots Inc' fleetingly darted through my mind, now vacillating between murkiness and fearful.

Having been literally bundled off the train, we milled around the platform and within seconds our ears were once again assaulted. **"Staan stil, en klim in julle rye!"** barked an apparently middle-aged man with the South African Coat of Arms insignia etched brightly in yellow onto the sleeves of each of his upper arms; for a fleeting moment, my thoughts turning to humour as my mind processed this instruction—"Stand still and climb into your rows," I translated this directly into English—thinking that this was both grammatically incorrect and entirely contradictory, as the tiniest of smirks on my face must have betrayed this thought.

The gravity of the situation made itself known as the rotund Sergeant-Major Jones waddled over to me, the 'Rollie Fingers Moustache', years in the preparation, taking on a life of its own as he facetiously enquired of me: *"Mannetjie, lyk ek vir jou soos 'n doos?"*[10] Not succumbing to the obvious temptation, it was decision time, and I decided that the joke was over, the time to be serious had arrived, as I took in the bold name 'JONES', proudly emblazoned above the right-hand chest pocket on his uniform in upper case bold, black lettering. Never make assumptions, lesson for the ages, to be learned again and again, as I responded politely in English, quite simply: 'no Sir' assuming

---

[9] "Get out, get out… Pretend you're in a fucking hurry you bunch of fucking ignorant long-haired hippies!"

[10] *Little man, do I look like a cunt to you?*

that he was English: *"NO SIR?… NO SIR?"* His face reddening, looking more and more as though the bulging eyes and facial veins appearing like blue river deltas on his temples would explode, launching his beret into the night sky. He kept repeating the words. I felt like Oliver Twist standing meekly before the dreaded Mr Bumble.

In his finest descriptive—nay, colourful—Afrikaans he explained in no uncertain terms that we were not to speak fucking English in his army camp, since this was the language of the fucking enemy, the communist African National Congress (ANC) who were guided by no less than the fucking devil himself, deviously going about his business having infiltrated the English universities through fucking communist demons. He cursed as whores, the women at these universities for abiding such fucking evil, communist miscreants as he saw before him. Never mind, the army would soon fucking rectify matters, instilling into the very fibre of this new intake, Christian National values, as he glared at me.

"Verder, is ek nie SIR nie, dis wat soldate in die Amerikaanse weermag hulle offisiere noem. Hierdie is nie fokken Amerika nie, en 'Ek' is nie 'n offisier nie, ek's 'n Sa' Majoor—ek werk vir my fokken geld."[11]

Expletives being nothing new to me, this did however, seem a little 'over the top'. Not only did I hear his words screamed into my face like a banshee, I could smell them, and the vitriol of which they were borne, as his tirade took place about 2 inches from my face, which I was unable to back away any further from without causing me to stand on the toes of the fellow behind me. He had definitely had garlic and a few drinks the night before.

A most uncomfortable silence ensued, lasting a good few moments as he paced and glared while all averted their eyes. Ending the silence, a much older rival army made its presence known—a vast invisible army of crickets, whose din quickly blanketed the night air. Their sound synthesised with the sense of smell coming from the dust and wild desert flora, reminding me that I was in the heartland of the Karoo, Southernmost tip of the African continent, a sprawling expanse of sand stretching for hundreds of kilometres in every direction.

---

[11] 1. In addition, I am not a' Sir', that's what soldiers in fucking America call their officers. This is not fucking America, and 'I' am not an officer, I'm a Sar' Major, I work for my fucking money.

It all reminded me that the backdrop for my world, for the foreseeable future, was the jagged mountains, dust, thorn trees, snakes, spiders, ants, scorpions and extremes in weather, ranging from bitter cold which could cause death, to unimaginable heat which, like it's irreconcilable relative, could also take life. All of this would make itself clearer to me over the ensuing weeks.

Bundled into the back of a Samil (South African Military) trucks, we were treated to a 'ROOF RIDE', not as in the 'roof' of a house, but a 'roof' pronounced 'ruwif'. The 'roof' was a 'green' national serviceman, and it was to be our first ride in the trucks, the drivers throwing their vehicles about with sadistic glee, over bumps and around corners, making the ride as uncomfortable and unpleasant as possible. We held on for dear life. Darkness still prevailed as the trucks sped, diesel engines whining as the drivers mercilessly barrelled along the gravel road separating the fenced army camp and the vast parade grounds.

They slowed as guards carrying what appeared to be AK 47 Assault Rifles opened the enormous diamond mesh gates. We had learned from the train episode about speedy disembarking, and following the rantings of Sergeant Major Jones, 'climbing' into squads and spacing out had been the very next lesson. It seemed everything was 'climbed' into, out of or onto, including the mess, barracks, the passage, parade ground etc. I never did quite understand.

Muster under the bright lights on an enormous concrete 'square', surrounded by high fences with barbed wire rolls atop, revealed that we were standing next to a large fuel depot, guarded for 24 hours on rotation. The word 'Alcatraz' flashed briefly through the recesses of my mind.

That fateful day had arrived, when studies completed, I could no longer defy the South African government's decree that all white males would report for two years of military service; that time-honoured tradition turning boys into men, custodians of civilised white men's values in the heart of darkest Africa. Now standing and looking as subservient as we could, the boys were separated into those from 'English' universities and those who had studied at the prestigious Afrikaans institutions, Stellenbosch, Free State, Pretoria and the like.

'Graduate Intake' it was called. I thought I detected in the voices of the non-commissioned officers a lapse in intensity, perhaps a hint of humaneness when addressing the Afrikaans boys, who were almost 'invited' to select a barracks, find a bed, shower, unpack, and generally take things easy until further notice.

I recalled fleetingly, how Mum had insisted that I and later my sister, despite having Afrikaner heritage on Dad's side of the family, would receive an

'English' education, Mum being oblivious to the gravity of the situation I would find myself in on this day when Sergeant Major Jones, who no doubt had had some time to stew, glibly halted proceedings on his arrival, and invited the 'English' boys to join him for a little discussion. 'Christian national values' was the subject of his talk, as he embarked on a fresh demonstrative tirade following a substantial show of hands revealing those who had not brought bibles with them to the army.

This was followed by what was commonly known as an 'opfok' session, directly translated as 'up-fuck', as in PT designed to destroy body and morale, or perhaps to provide a small measure of satisfaction, a flexing of ego for men such as Jones and his crew. This still before the sun had risen. So ended my first hour in the camp in Oudtshoorn, jewel in the crown of the South African Army, Infantry School, where we would all be moulded into 1st Lieutenants, infantry officers, by December, to be posted as platoon and company commanders to various infantry units around the country to prepare our charges for war internally or in South West Africa and Angola.

Sticking together, my mates and I were able to bunk down in adjacent beds in the same barracks, where someone had thoughtfully left the windows ajar to cool the place, or so I thought. Just as the crickets surrendered their domination of the night air to the golden outline of sunshine over the Outeniqua mountains in the distant east, I gazed out of the window as the light intensified. The warmth of the morning quickly enveloped the place as the din of the daytime shift of cicadas kicked off, desperately trying to outdo their nocturnal rivals.

The 'English' boys mostly seemed to end up in the same barracks on the edge of the parade ground, the parade ground made of dust—red, powdery relentless dust—which deftly made its way into every conceivable crack and corner at the slightest hint of a southerly breeze. We had not yet learned that in this semi-desert environment, mini tornadoes happened every other day resulting in bedding, clothing and everything else needing to be shaken out or scrubbed, courtesy of that red, powdery parade ground on the doorstep of our barracks. Closing windows became mandatory. So, either the heat would get you, or the dust. In those particular barracks, the choice was yours.

Iron bedsteads—a latticework of black metal slats—buckled from the weight of many a soldier who had contributed to their form. These 'beds' were complimented by thin foam mattresses with 'pissvels'[12]—black pin-striped, stained, yellowing canvass covers apparently designed to protect the 'mattresses'.

"I'm guessing that these have not had the 'big tick' from the orthopaedic foundation," I commented to my mates who were not finding me particularly amusing at that moment. For the first time that morning, we had thought about a smoke, whereupon we each chose a bed, sat down and lit up. But we weren't even halfway through our recreational cigarette, when one of those rasping, nasty monsters invaded our barracks, demanding that we stand up and put out our cigarettes. There were no ashtrays to be seen, whereupon the cigarettes were put to flight out of the window, which apparently amused Korporaal van Wyk.

Indeed, it amused him so much that he made us go and collect them and keep them in our pockets. We were then met with push ups, and when done were instructed to recite our force numbers (every conscript was assigned a unique force number).

This of course, we couldn't do, so the punishment was more push ups. He gave us five minutes to memorise our force numbers, and he would, he said, be back. Scratching for any and all documentation I might have brought, relieved, I found my force number, and memorised 78432564BG, a number I have never forgotten. That first day was devoted to paperwork, more paperwork, collecting bedding and kit, and a lot of being fucked around until bedtime, by which time we agreed that it felt as though we had been in the army for weeks, not just one day.

At 5.00 am on Friday, the fun recommenced at which time we were informed that: *"jou meisie gaan binnekort sweet in die arms van 'n ander man… word gewoond daaraan!"[13]* I was no prude, but that lewd message, delivered with childish gusto I really thought was uncalled for. To amplify matters, despite being exhausted the night before, I had not slept at all well, the bed had proved most uncomfortable, and I had been awakened many times in the night firstly by the unbearable heat, and finally by what felt like an army of ants entering every orifice of my body in their desperate quest to find moisture or liquid. Eyes, ears, nose, mouth, and throat it seemed, were all fair game for these parched little creatures of the desert night. My tired mind played cruel tricks on me, until

---

[12] 1 Piss skins/covers.

[13] Your girlfriend will soon be sweating in the arms of another man… get used to the idea!

consciousness revealed the reality of things. Close to panic, coughing and spluttering, I rushed to the showers to rid myself of this invasion. Throwing on a brown, button up overall which felt like prison garb, we were literally chased to the mess for breakfast, which consisted of cold baked beans, rock hard toast, crispy stuff which sort of tasted like bacon, all swimming in a watery powdered egg-like substance, to be washed down by tepid 'moer coffee', coffee carefully drunk so as to avoid the bitter-tasting coffee grounds lurking at the bottom of the tin mug.

Day two was, we were told, to be devoted to medicals, collection of weapons, and haircuts. It felt to me though that the day was actually devoted to more of the same, getting fucked around at the whim of the corporals, who thought it highly amusing to make us 'climb' into and out of the barracks, over and over, and over ad nauseum. The 'medical' resulted in my medical classification being G3K2, as a result of me ticking a 'yes' answer to 'have you had backpain', which I had suffered on a few rare occasions as a teenager, possibly as a result of sport. I was hurried to the local civilian hospital for X-Rays which revealed a spinal condition that the doctor called Spondylolisthesis, a condition I had been unaware of, and had never heard of. The classification exempted me from any activity which might be harmful to my back or spine, so I embraced my new found friend 'Spondylolisthesis' with open arms and graciously accepted the Medical Classification ID card which would accompany me for the remainder of my 'military career'. Later examinations and scans back in 'civvy' street revealed that there was, in fact, nothing wrong with my back or spine. It seemed that I and I alone would be sole judge of activities which might be detrimental, in order to avoid hurting my upper or lower back. *Perhaps the army might not be so bad after all,* I thought.

Haircuts hadn't simply been haircuts, but heads were shorn completely. This I could live with, given the heat. What did strike me, though, was that the shorn look rendered everyone identical, and finding your mates quickly, became almost impossible. I detected that individuals were starting to withdraw. Where there had been personalities, these had been replaced by a need for anonymity, fear visible in the eyes of most. For example, there was a depressing silence in the mornings. Guys would get out of bed, not talking, putting finishing touches to their beds and equipment readying for that dreaded inspection, then they'd be forced to sit on a 'trommel'[14] at the foot of the bed. 'Stiltetyd' they called it, 'silent time' to read the bible. I would sit, pretending to read the Gideon bible, distributed to those who hadn't brought bibles.

Although it was a particularly depressing time of day, I did welcome a brief few minutes when we could be assured of not being fucked around. One of our mates, Keith, flagrantly would not read a bible, but chose instead to read the *Rand Daily Mail* newspaper, sent to him by his girlfriend in Johannesburg. Now that particular newspaper had been the vocal mouthpiece of the small community of largely white English-speaking opponents of apartheid, and indeed it was highly critical of the government and the South African condition. Keith was, as far as I was concerned, one of the bravest people I knew. I mean, who under these circumstances would dare to brazenly issue to Sa' Majoor Jones a challenge in the form of a declaration of his atheistic, anti-apartheid beliefs when confronted about a lack of compliance around stiltetyd and the devotion to the reading of the bible? It became abundantly clear, and very quickly, that the army would not tolerate this display, and one day Keith was no more, his bed and cupboard cleared when we returned after the day's activities.

Hair shorn, uniforms issued, equipment and steely cold South African manufactured Israeli-designed Galil assault rifles, named R4s (these did indeed resemble Soviet and Chinese AK47s), were signed out to every new man in the camp, along with other equipment including a chest rig (battle jacket)—a type of 'vest' with compartments to hold additional clips or magazines for the rifle— a spare water bottle, and grenades etc. Let the games begin.

---

[14] 1 A green tin container, about the size of a small credenza, in which weapons etc could be locked.

2. Illegitimi Non-Carborundum[15]

"Cognitive dissonance refers to a situation involving conflicting attitudes, beliefs or behaviours. This produces a feeling of mental discomfort leading to an alteration in one of the attitudes, beliefs or behaviours to reduce the discomfort and restore balance."

"Cognitive dissonance was first investigated by Leon Festinger, arising out of a participant observation study of a cult which believed that the Earth was going to be destroyed by a flood, and what happened to its members—particularly the really committed ones who had given up their homes and jobs to work for the cult—when the flood did not happen. While fringe members were more inclined to recognise that they had made fools of themselves and to 'put it down to experience', committed members were more likely to re-interpret the evidence to show that they were right all along (the Earth was not destroyed because of the faithfulness of the cult members). Both alternatives have their good points and bad points. The rub is that, making a decision cuts off the possibility that you can enjoy the advantages of the unchosen alternative, yet it assures you that you must accept the disadvantages of the chosen alternative. People have several ways to reduce dissonance that is aroused by making a decision (Festinger, 1964). One thing they can do is to change the behaviour. As noted earlier, this is often very difficult, so people frequently employ a variety of mental manoeuvres. A common way to reduce dissonance is to increase the attractiveness of the chosen alternative and to decrease the attractiveness of the rejected alternative. This is referred to as 'spreading apart the alternatives'."[16]

---

[15] Do not let the bastards grind you down. Faux Latin phrase.

[16] McLeod, S. A. (2018, February 05). *Cognitive dissonance*. Simply Psychology. *https://www.simplypsychology.org/cognitive-dissonance.html*

The hushed silence was disturbed only by what would become in time, the all too familiar sounds, of a man shuffling slightly on his 'trommel', an occasional muzzled cough echoing through the complex, and the now quiet, gentle yet unmistakable thud of boots with high density rubber soles slowly making their way up and down the walkway in the middle of the barracks. This would be 'Korporaal van Wyk', sometimes overseen by 'Luitenant Du Toit' or Sa Majoor Jones. 'Stiltetyd', a time for introspection, a compartmentalised ritual, compressed into the routine, providing stout young men a brief daily opportunity to connect with their creator, a whetting of the appetite perhaps prior to the main event which would come on Sunday at Church Parade. Or perhaps it was a subtle message from those in power that 'all of this' was done in the name of God, hence 'His' blessings would be bestowed on all who fought the 'good fight'.

For me, this daily ritual represented, in no small measure, the duplicity of the institution, which was so easily rubbing off onto its devotees, albeit many of whom although not so at first, evolved into the unquestioning role of disciple, whether they were English or Afrikaans. During the first few days of this enforced custom, I had rather welcomed the brief respite from being fucked around. Sadly, it was during these times in later days and weeks that I detested the silence, haunted by nothing but my own thoughts, ever darker as the days wore on. I had been a keen student of the bible as a young child, and imagined that I knew more about both old and new testaments, than many people. Attempts at contextualising spirituality in this place of anger, incarceration and aggression failed dismally. Questions of a highly practical nature accompanied my now almost sombre state of mind. "Why 10 Commandments?"—this seemed like too neat a public relations exercise. Why not nine or 14? And what about: "Thou shalt not kill?" Generally speaking, or so it seemed, God himself disregarded the severity of this one, claiming fine-print perhaps—Thou shalt not kill, unless the South African Army determines otherwise.

We were running, as usual, in a squad, three rows deep, 10 or 11 men in length, the unison of the boot heels thudding down on the asphalt, making it easy to keep in step, providing a rhythmic background, as a man somewhere in the middle of the 'peleton' was always chosen to lead the group in song. We would sing about infantry soldiers' legs being made of gold while the parabats'[17] legs were made of lead. Songs would be quite melodious, despite referring to how

---

[17] Parachute Battalion soldiers.

one wanted desperately to go to Angola to kill that Sam Nujoma, the dissident leader of SWAPO—SWAPO being a 'terrorist' organisation operating out of Angola attempting to overthrow the South West African Administration. These 'running' squads could be heard and would be a common sight all over the camp, sometimes outside of the camp, on their way perhaps to the shooting range or the bush for an opfok away from prying eyes. The ritual was somewhat reminiscent of the scene in movies, of which there had been an abundance in recent times, depicting green recruits, 'toughing it out' in Fort Jackson, South Carolina or Fort Leonard Wood, Missouri, their fear of and hatred for the legendary Drill Sergeant preparing them for the hell which would be Vietnam. Each soldier would undergo a metamorphosis and the message would emerge clearly that through the punishing drills in the cold and rain at night, as well as the camaraderie bolstered by helping the overweight, bespectacled kid to find grit and unearth his confidence on the obstacle course, true character would evolve. And the Sergeant's demeanour would eventually betray a glimmer of affection for his charges, convincing all that it had been nothing but 'tough love' from the get go, a vital ingredient of the lessons learned if these boys were going to have any chance at survival in the commie-infested jungles of South East Asia.

It was a Monday morning, and our platoon had been co-opted. Sa Majoor Jones was chuckling quietly that we were on our way to the 'kroeg', bar or pub. The bar was situated within a grandstand overlooking the rugby field, across a road from the main parade ground. We had learned quickly that the favourite sons of Infantry School were the mighty rugby players. It was these gladiators who entertained and brought glory every Saturday afternoon and, of course, being university graduates, they were no doubt older, bigger, faster and stronger than many of their opposition players from camps around the country, who had the previous year been mere schoolboy rugby players. Not only did the team enjoy superiority on the field, but were treated like gods, being in a separate platoon, rugby practice each day taking precedence over military duties or training. These men, the chosen ones who would have mingled freely with the officers and NCOs over drinks after a good win on a sunny Saturday afternoon. Entering the place, we were bowled over by the awful stench of old beer, body odour and stale cigarettes, all trapped within the place for almost two days. We had cleaned up the 'kroeg' which had been strewn with empty and half-filled bottles, tins and glasses, dirty dishes from the accompanying meals, ashtrays overflowing and sticky floors, tables and counters. Back into our 'singing peleton', we began a run to the far side of the camp, when Jan Roux, to my right-hand side, collapsed in a heap, apparently in a state of semi consciousness. I stopped immediately, and having had some training in first-aid and a fair amount of exposure as a boarding school house-master during my student days, recognised the writhing and other signs of what I suspected to be grand mal seizure. The corporal, clearly taken aback, and some of the others tried to pull me away. One or two who had obviously seen this before told the rest to leave me, since my main concern was that Jan's twitching could cause him to bang his head on the asphalt road. In the absence of anything soft like a pillow or items of clothing, I tried as best I could to position my right hand between his head and the surface of the road as a cushion. His writhing stopped, and I gently placed him in the 'prone position', checking that his airways were unobstructed, some concerns circulating that sufferers sometimes swallow their tongues. I had never been sure if this was true or not, so I made certain anyway.

Jan, a fairly slight man from Bellville in the Cape, spoke Afrikaans with a 'brei', a hangover rolling of the 'r' from the French Huguenots. He had been in the bed next to mine for some weeks since we had been allocated into barracks following our medical classifications. He and I had chatted comfortably, and he soon revealed a lovely sense of humour. He always spoke to me in English, obviously comfortable in either language. Through Jan, I met some other mates of his who hailed from or had studied in the Boland or at Stellenbosch. Afrikaners yes indeed, but somehow not the same as those I had encountered before. I would sometimes drink beer with them at night before prepping for inspection, enjoying their company, while being accepted into their circle without question or suspicion. These were people whose gentle urbaneness seemed to govern their verbal behaviour, making them instantly likeable. They spoke their language in a different dialect, and general speech took on a whole new meaning, every utterance designed to entertain and amuse in a poetic, almost lyrical, manner. Whether it was by design or default, Jan seemed reluctant to delve into discussions of great consequence, preferring to keep the banter light, injecting at all times some humour into whatever situation he might find himself, including our 'post-mortem' of that morning's events. The more I urged him to see the doctors, the more he swore me to secrecy, stressing that he needed to be seen to be healthy enough to complete the officers' course, returning to his people and his girlfriend at the end of the year, two stars adorning the epaulettes on his shoulders. Not completing the course for any reason at all was simply not an option for him, as he convinced me of the shame he and his family would experience as a consequence of failure, perceived or real.

At the time I recall an awareness slapping me in the face—I hadn't given my family's opinion on this matter even the slightest consideration, convinced, in fact, that my family had not so much as succumbed to even a brief moment of pensive thought as to my feelings and views on the subject. Enlightened families were sending their sons to Britain, the USA, or Australia, providing an opportunity to escape this barbarism posing as National Service. I felt that if more families had sent sons abroad, the military would be deprived of manpower and cannon fodder, possibly forcing the government to face their demons and embrace the ambiguous realities of the country. Then again, I was young and idealistic, or was that perhaps wet behind the ears and naïve? Aside from stiltetyd and getting fucked around, weekdays consisted of daily inspection, 'political' awareness lectures a.k.a. white supremacist propaganda posing as motivation! Bushcraft, map reading, weapons training, shooting, marching or drilling ad nauseum on the parade ground, daily PT and obstacle courses, all constituted the curriculum for 'Basics', or Basic Training.

I recall thinking at the time that with the exception of the brainwashing sessions, the rondfok, the drilling, and the puerile nature of the daily inspections, I might have immersed myself in the training and really enjoyed it. The reality, of course, was that the overarching rationale for the existence and survival of the South African Defence Force lay buried deep behind the subliminal messages beamed out to the conscripts, over and over, spaced repetition eventually capturing souls, the other choices simply no longer a feasible option, in much the same way that a cult would force a choice to gain loyalty. The military, applying some science to their approach, did not differ vastly from the way a cult might spread its sugar-coated toxins, in a push to ensure that the masses were ultimately 'of one mind'. The mental and emotional metamorphosis of many of my 'comrades' was disturbingly clear and obvious, as I witnessed before my very eyes the 'winning of hearts and minds', a mantra underpinning the very foundation of military heritage. My heart and mind resisted fiercely—to my detriment some would surmise—but deep within me, not only did I suspect, but I knew without fear of contradiction that I was right and that the government of the country, and their military organ were misguided. My thoughts turned to drastic measures, tempting me to declare that I had, after much deliberation, arrived at the realisation that I was, in fact, a conscientious objector, and should be immediately handed over to the authorities. A spiral took hold of my mind, reminding me that religious objectors might be viewed through a more sympathetic lens, since religion was something these people could relate to. A conscientious objector on the other hand resisting on moral grounds, would be thought of as the enemy, particularly in my case, since I'd had every opportunity in the world to 'align my views' with those of the government and its army. There was no question that 'those who aren't with us are against us' held very true in this arena which rejected intellect, logic and robust debate. I had really created for myself a difficult situation. Jan and I were mates, occupying adjacent beds, enjoying a few beers and some laughs in the evenings, but our motivating forces could not have been further apart.

3. The 'Lie' of the Land

"That's what it was like being black during apartheid. No matter how hard you worked, or how much money you earned, you couldn't own land, businesses, or homes. You couldn't buy your kids a safer suburb to grow up in or buy them a better education. Every generation started back at zero. Being white was like being the only one with a save function. Everyone was working through the game, but only white people got to accumulate an advantage. I want to make this crystal clear: saying that white people enjoy a privilege is not saying that their lives are easy or that they haven't worked hard. White people are not immune to the human condition, they suffer loss and hardship like everyone else. So then what is it? What is white privilege? For me, it's simply a preference for whiteness that saturates our society. I guess if you are white, it's sometimes hard to see the privilege because you're in it and it's all you've ever known. It's like asking a fish to notice water."[18]

Peals of laughter could be heard emanating from inside No 423 Highland Rd, as I stood on the red polished floor of the stoep, ringing the doorbell... but to no avail. One could never be sure if the doorbell was out of order, or if there just so much fun being had inside the house, that the ringing couldn't be heard. Anxiously, I rang again, fearing that I would miss the fun and antics. Again... no response. In desperation, I decided to knock loudly on the door, which was two thirds timber, the top third of the old door containing an arched, beautifully framed, patterned frosty glass, crafted as so many of the old homes' doors were, with lead lined diamond shaped panes. One never knew which was more acceptable, knocking on the timber door, or the glass bit. For me ordinarily, knocking on the glass seemed disrespectful and should only be contemplated in an emergency, so on that day it was upon the glass which I knocked furiously,

---

[18] *Johannesburg, South Africa*—Extract from a speech given to pupils of Jeppe High School for Boys in Johannesburg by deputy principal Kevin Leathem, June 2018.

mine, not an imagined emergency, since there was no doubt that that I was missing out on the fun.

In and around the golden face-brick house, diagonally opposite ours, there was, it seemed, almost always something going on. David, answered my knock, and hurried me into the house, in the middle of which was a carpeted passage, and to my astonishment, I was met by a very large lobster, or as we called them 'crayfish', moving rather more quickly than I had imagined 'crays' could walk on dry land. It seemed that it would chase and nip whoever was nearest, resulting in howls of laughter from all spectators. Now we lived some 600 km from the ocean, so yes, being entertained by a live cray most certainly was quite novel.

My friend and classmate, David, had an older brother Sean who had just a few minutes prior, walked into the house on a pass from the SA Navy in Simonstown in the Cape Province, where he was a conscript. He had brought the creature with him, no doubt to prepare with garlic and lemon butter to be enjoyed with a chilled refreshing white wine. Apparently, he was extremely 'lucky' to have been allocated to what was perceived to be the most 'enlightened' branch of the armed forces. Of all the 'older' siblings on Highland Road, Sean would have probably been the oldest, and had gone off to the navy when I was about 12. He would be followed by older brothers from families in our road, as sure as night followed day.

We would always be intrigued when these boys appeared at home for weekend passes, in no great hurry to change into civilian clothing. Upon arrival, they would seek out siblings and their mates, gaining the full attention of the neighbourhood schoolboys who would clamour around listening in awe to the tales of adventure and stories of these shiny new war heroes, dressed either in their glamorous formal uniforms, 'step-outs', or their battle fatigues known as 'browns'. We would hang onto every word emanating from these now sage and suddenly 'grown up' erstwhile playmates. The tales would range from hilarious incidents often emphasising how stupid the 'Dutchmen' were, to stories of heroism, many of which, I now suspect, were somewhat exaggerated. We would be enthralled, and as time went by, most of the neighbourhood gang would be shipped off to places like Bourke's Luck, Valhalla, Upington, Middelberg, Heidelberg or Potchefstroom. I later discovered that many of these training camp sites were adjacent to small towns, their locations chosen to provide some relief to ailing town council coffers. This would be achieved through generating demand, leading to bolstered industry and thus job creation.

In the 1960s and 1970s, our situation had been somewhat unique, in that about 20 homes, pretty much adjacent to or across the road from each other, housed some 30 children of similar ages, of which only four (my sister being one of them) were girls. The names hinting at the origins of these 2nd, 3rd and 4th generation immigrants from various parts of Europe. Names such as Starkey, de Silva, Thomas, Amiridaki, Malan, Mankie, Steyn, Cason, Greiner and Crawford, described the diversity of the origins of these families. The accent shared by these kids, however, was homogenous and fundamentally English—urban South African. A new offshoot of the English language had in fact evolved, littered with Afrikaans adjectives and expletives, including some words which referred directly to the literal meaning of the word despite their absence from the Oxford English Dictionary. A 'lightie' being a young boy, due to his light weight? To be beaten up was to be 'donnered', from the Afrikaans for thunder—donder. Had you taken something from a mate you'd 'diefed' it, from the Afrikaans for thief—dief. Don't 'tune me grief', meant stop being disagreeable, the tone conveying the level of irritation and how close you were to being 'dondered' or 'moered'—beaten, or how close the user was to 'stripping his moer' (losing his temper), as in Afrikaans—stripping of the thread of a nut (as opposed to bolt). If you were talking nonsense, you were said to be talking Kak (shit). The word 'fuck' used liberally for emphasis, worked quite well, and when something was good it was said to be 'tit' or if it were really good it was 'fucking tit'. A girl was a chick, dads were 'toppies', and mums were the 'old queens'. An alcoholic beverage was a 'dop,' a cigarette a 'skyf' and a hangover a 'babalaas'. Come over to my place became 'pull in to my possie', possibly because the old queen was out, and you'd 'diefed' or 'zikked' (stolen) a 'skyf' from the toppie's pack of Rothmans or Texans.

School holidays at the end of Highland Road, were great. Highland Road ended running a 'T—junction' into Sovereign Street, beyond which lay many square kilometres of open 'veld'—bush, dry and sparse in the winter, green and dense in the summer. A typical day would include: bicycle races (before BMX), war games, tree climbing with ropes and tackle, clay fights in an old quarry (clothes were discarded after these, since I had been told not to venture to the quarry), long walks up the 'mountain' separating Cyrildene and Linksfield, stopping on the way to make a fire to cook some 'boerewors' over a fire—farmer sausage, on a stick—before pressing on to Gillooly's Farm for a swim in the Jukskei River.

This walk would take up practically the entire day, but left one in a pleasing state of exhaustion. Back yard cricket, soccer and rugby was responsible for the financial success of the local glazier, and some very sore bums. Other favourite activities included shooting of bottles with Daisy or BB pellet guns in the old service lanes—a hangover from the days before underground sewerage, also handy for 'fruit picking expeditions'. Kensington gardens yielded delicious grapes, plums, peaches, mulberries, pears, passion fruit, figs and pomegranates, which we ate until we sometimes felt ill.

Most people allowed kids to continue uninterrupted to 'pinch' fruit, turning a blind eye, in the knowledge that there was usually such an abundance, that waste was inevitable. Some, however, did not take so kindly to this mischief, resorting to chasing us down the lanes or calling the police. These people would often have their 'roofs rocked', a hail of rocks from countless kids after dark landing on the galvanised iron roof. When one is in the early stages of slumber, I imagine this would be quite disturbing.

We'd also take bus rides to the city to see a movie starring Sean Connery or the new James Bond, Roger Moore. There was so much laughter in the Bud Spencer and Terrence Hill movies that it brought tears to our eyes. *Planet of the Apes* stirred our curiosity, and I took up spitting after seeing Clint Eastwood as the *Outlaw Josey Wales*. The way he spat was so cool! All these adventures added up to great school holidays for the boys, but were for some reason a tad harrowing for all the parents who could be heard to heave a collective sigh of relief when each new term dawned and the 'gang' were once again off the streets for 10 weeks or so. Something which struck me back then and still intrigues me today, is the fact that 26 naughty little 'shits' with sewer mouths, would never show disrespect to adults and girls by way of cursing in their presence. These kids, without exception, became the epitome of fine manners when interacting with the parents, friends of parents, or any other adults for that matter. Urban, white English-speaking families were the norm, black kids were nowhere to be seen, and black adults worked in our homes and gardens, while we, the white kids enjoyed the most carefree of childhoods, blissfully unaware of our privileged existence or the plight of black South Africans.

Each year a new generation of boys would return home for weekend passes wearing the blue uniforms of the air-force or navy, some, army browns but wearing the maroon berets of the medics or the purple berets of the elite parachute battalion. Most, however, would simply appear in the standard army browns and the green berets of the infantry. Mostly, it seemed, the families of all these boys were in favour of their sons' allegiance to the South African Defence Force, and subsequent acceptance and submission to conscription. Now and then a hushed scandal would spread through the neighbourhood like wildfire, as we would hear of a family whose son would not wear the uniform, on the grounds they were not South African citizens, rather they were 'resident' in SA and held foreign passports, or worse, they were conscientious objectors. As a general rule, these lads were said by most parents, my own parents included, in quiet conversation, to be cowardly, living off the cream of the land without being willing to defend the country which had given these kids so much. As children, it was always ingrained in all my friends and me that military national service was not to be questioned, but to be undertaken with pride. Parents, grandparents, schoolteachers, ministers at church, and indeed any and all authority figures in our lives not only encouraged this patriotic fervour, but also many men, my father included, felt huge disappointment that they had not been given the opportunity to play their parts as young men themselves.

Edging ever closer to the inevitable day when it would be my turn, as a student at Jeppe High School for Boys, the reality and inevitability of conscription became embedded in my mind, and in fact in the minds of all the boys, as every matriculant simply accepted as a rite of passage, reporting diligently as per instructions on his call up papers. For some, conscription was deferred due to tertiary study. Every man's fate was now in the hands of a 'higher' authority. But the stories of the servicemen and then of course, the veterans over the years, had so whetted our appetites that two years in the military was perceived as a marvellous adventure at a critical juncture in our lives, in which we would prove our mettle and be hailed by our families and friends as heroes. Notwithstanding, girls love a man in uniform, so there was the added bonus of a romantic element. I was fit, strong, young and determined… yes, I would have the time of my life. Mum and Dad convinced me to complete my teaching studies before undertaking the military adventure, on the grounds that graduates almost automatically qualified for acceptance into Officers' School, emerging as full lieutenants. This I thought a really good idea, because in addition, qualified teachers received full teacher salaries while completing national service, officers enjoying enormous privilege.

4. Inspection, Circumspection and Introspection

Ek het stip na hom gekyk. Meteens is ek deur 'n vreemde gewaarwording beetgepak. Of dit sy nederige drag of sy magnetiese persoonlikheid was wat my geboei het, weet ek nog steeds nie, maar dit was vir my kompleet of 'n hipnotiese krag my bemeester het. Ek het geen marsmusiek meer gehoor nie en meganies gemarsjeer. Soos 'n outomaat het ek die res van die bevele By die aanskouing van Adolf Hitler het die Duits-Ierse bloed onstuimig deur my Afrikanerhart gebruis en ek het in my eie moedertaal die bevel gegee. Mis-kien het ek probeer om die Führer te beïndruk. Ek wou aan hom in die taal van genl. De Wet vertel dat hier voor hom nasate van 'n heroï'ese volk verby-marsjeer. Ek het toe reeds geweet dat Adolf Hitler 'n besonder hoe dunk van genl. De Wet en die Boerevolk in die algemeen gehad het.

Robey Leibbrandt vertel alles in 'Geen Genade'. Bienedell Publishers, Pretoria, July 1966.

"My eyes locked on him. In an instant, I was over-awed and overcome by a strange sensation. Whether it was his humble attire or his magnetic personality which entranced me, I still cannot be sure, but I had been overpowered by a hypnotic force. I no longer heard the music, as I now marched mechanically. I shouted the rest of the marching orders. The sight of Adolf Hitler caused the Irish-German blood to course through my veins, my Afrikaner heart roared as I gave the final orders in my own mother language. Maybe I was trying to impress the Fuhrer. In the language of General De Wet, I wanted to convey to him that right here before him, a march past of a heroic people. At that point, I was aware that Adolf Hitler held General De Wet and the Afrikaner people in general, in high regard."

(Robey Leibbrandt leads the South African Olympic team at the opening ceremony, 1936 Berlin Summer Olympics).[19]

In identical brown uniforms they would stand before me as the bile overpowered my inner man, no doubt a combination of running back and forth in the relentless heat which somehow was oblivious to the fact this was still early morning, our bellies having just been filled with the slop which seemed to pass for breakfast. Civilised folk knew only too well that full tummies and exercise were far from compatible, and of course, now, the dreaded morning 'inspeksie'—inspection. Day after day, they would look one up and down to determine if your person was indeed clean, face shaved, and brown 'prison overall' ironed, (not sure how this made us better soldiers given that mere minutes after said inspection overalls would be sweaty, creased and filthy from yet some more opfok PT because our 'inspeksie' had been 'kak'—shit).

There they would stand, four grown men; a corporal who was about 20 years old, a lieutenant, who was perhaps 23, both conscripted national servicemen, and the PF (Permanent Force career soldiers), the Sa' Majoor and the Major, both men apparently in their mid to late 30s, yet seemingly much older. It struck me as odd or petty that at 7.00 am in the middle of a forsaken desert, adult men had nothing better to occupy their minds or their time, than by taking every opportunity to belittle or degrade perfectly innocent young men who had been up half the night. And not just that night, but every night, cleaning, and polishing floors, windows, weapons, cupboards, toilets, showers, and also ironing clothing. Then there was the bed. We had to turn a buckled bed with a mattress covered in canvas into something akin to a perfectly square giant matchbox. This would take several hours constructing, using starch, ironing and finally front teeth to perfect every edge of the blanketed bed. The only way to pass a bed inspection was to make it once, perfectly, and thereafter sleep on the hard unforgiving cement floor.

There were inane comments and insults—a daily diet of derision—as the G3 platoon weathered life in the barracks adjacent to the dusty parade ground. Many a morning we would stand at the ready, next to our beds awaiting the arrival of the inspection party, only to discover a fine layer of red dust having invaded the barracks, settling on every conceivable surface following our return from

---

[19] Robey Leibbrandt tells all in 'Without Mercy'. Bienedell Publishers, Pretoria, July 1966.

breakfast and 'rondfok', getting fucked around, affording the inhabitants at best, a few minutes, at worst a few seconds to try to remedy the situation, with dust everywhere, on the floor, beds, trommels, window ledges, and of course the beds, those beds.

So, the G3K2 medical ID which had initially been my 'get out of jail' card was turning out to be a millstone on many a morning as inspection turned our lives into a hell, daily accusations from the 'brass' that we were 'vuilgatte', 'dirty arses', since more often than not, despite our nocturnal sacrifices, our barracks was seldom clean at inspection time. The corporals were unable to conceal their glee when they dished out daily opfok sessions to our platoon, as they knew, and we knew that they knew, that the barracks was fated to be spotlessly clean only until a wind swept across that parade ground which was about the size of two rugby fields. And the wind did blow. Every day without exception the wind blew, as sure as night followed day. This was the platoon which had it easy, medical conditions and all. So, this was their way of teaching us a lesson for being 'gypogatte'. My estimation of the NCOs and officers dwindled directly proportionally to the frequency and intensity of the unnecessary fuck around such as this, to which we were subjected each day. Within a few short days, I had reached a point in which I had no respect for these people at all. But feeling that I was still mentally tougher than they were, I pressed on.

Now, one of the aforementioned officers, a company commander, presented a non-descript façade, a tanned, uniformed, moustachioed clone. He was physically a bit bigger than average, about as loud as the rest, but there was something... something about him which did not sit easy with me in particular. An enquiring little worm crawling around in my mind simply would not let go, as every day I observed this man, his verbal and non-verbal behaviours, looking for tell-tale signs.

I concluded eventually that he had an idiosyncrasy, which manifested itself in his apparent infatuation with everything military, from the discipline and weaponry, to the very fibres of his uniform which infused into the fibre of his DNA, his rank which being represented by a 5 pointed Cape Castle proudly perched atop each shoulder, and providing him with a warm glow of satisfaction when he dressed each morning, of this I was certain. That, and I did notice a slightly bulbous nose.

Given that tomorrow was 'sacred' Sunday, which meant no inspection, I could indulge myself on this second Saturday night. So here I sat on the ground, headphones firmly in place and my Walkman issuing the unmistakable strains of guitar as acrobatic hands conquered the fretboard and Mark Knopfler's genius reminding me how Juliette delighted in the return of her 'love', "Hey now... my boyfriend's back!" I was being transported back home and to better times.

With a giant purple-wrapped slab of Cadburys, a 2L bottle of Coke, a packet of Chesterfields, and well selected music, I was all set to patiently spend the prerequisite hours in the queue waiting to call home on one of six, blue 'tickey box' phones. Eyes closed; I could transport myself to other worlds. The queue would shift a few feet forward about every 10 minutes or so. All that was required was a little forward shuffle, as Dire Straights' *Alchemy* eventually gave way to Foreigner's iconic *Foreigner 4*, and then on to Alphaville's *Forever Young.*

The solitude, accompanied by fine, familiar music would hearten me, memories of a life-time would flood the crevasses of the unsuspecting mind. Guiding my thoughts to a time long ago, warmth and emotion crept in, vividly. I was returned to my childhood as I recalled how the humidity had been overbearing as the camouflaged army of insects outside continued to 'zing' unabated on those waves of unrelenting heat.

News crackled from the radiogram, the erudite reader giving the latest on events from Saigon, the Mekong Delta and more about Pol Pot from the news desks of South East Asia. The swoosh of the airliner overhead as Peter Stuyvesant's passport to pleasure was followed by John, Paul, George and Ringo: "It's been a hard day's night."

I was asked if I was a Beatle or a Rolling Stone as I closed the lounge curtains in a vain attempt to keep the tortuous midday African summer at bay. The room darkened, a lad of 6, as I had done so many times before, sat at Oupa's feet, listening eagerly to tales of days gone by. I had heard many of these stories countless times, but never tired of them as Oupa and I settled to savour juicy green grapes, gently exploding one at a time in the mouth, and at other times if he was feeling a little rebellious, a tub of ice-cream on a particularly hot day shared with furtive glances toward the door, followed by gurgling giggles.

Oupa (Grandfather) Petrus Jacobus Steyn was born in Jagersfontein, a hardy child of the former Boer Republic of the Free State in the newly minted Union of South Africa, during a frosty cold winter of 1914. His mere survival as an infant defined him as teak tough, in a hostile world in which new-borns perishing was distressing, but not unusual. As had happened in nearby Kimberley, a settlement had sprung from the ground as quickly as a new sapling takes root following a downpour, diamonds were discovered in a Kimberlite pipe, attracting hordes of hard men, 'would be' miners from all corners of the globe.

So, the story would usually commence, tales of his adventures, his boxing days, skirmishes with old foes and of course his travels. When Oupa became lost in stories of old, the aquamarine sparkle in his eyes, embedded now in furrowed, sun-crinkled sockets with leathery lids, matching the sparkle of those diamonds dug so painstakingly from their hiding places of thousands of years, looking… fixing into a distant gaze at some random, far-off horizon. Eyes which had learned to look into those of another in order to extract that which lay concealed in that soul, and if that soul were dark, it would be seen to squirm, unable to escape scrutiny, so perceptive and demanding were the windows to Oupa's soul.

Rudely, I was jolted back into the present, "***Maak fokken gou Engelsman***"[20] I was instructed by a chorus of 'Dutchmen'[21] in the queue behind me. As the teary-eyed large Afrikaner in front of me reluctantly returned the telephone to its cradle, I gathered up my paraphernalia to get to the phone. Picking up the instrument, now hot from hours of use, I dialled 011 616 2985. The telephone creaked and crackled as it dialled, deliberately stretching its reach across hundreds of kilometres in a matter of a few seconds, each digit, a few seconds of silence, a ringing 2… 3… 4… 5 rings as I heard the instrument being lifted, then 'Gooie naand' (Good evening) greeted the familiar voice.

"Hello Oupa," I responded, a lump forming in my throat as he spoke, unable to mask the joy in his voice, switching immediately to English. A lot of the usual chatter ensued, as this was the first my family had heard from me since I had left Johannesburg some two weeks earlier. "Oupa," I enquired, "I remember as a small child, you talking about a fellow by the name of Leibbrandt whom you'd known from your days as a boxer?"

"Ja, of course," he responded. "Robey Leibbrandt. I knew him well, a bloody good light-heavyweight, fought above his weight division to become South African Heavyweight Champion. He went to the Olympics in Berlin 1936. Ja, he was so impressed with Hitler that he went back to Germany to be trained, and he came back to assassinate Prime Minister Jan Smuts. They caught him you know, and he was going to hang for treason, but the death sentence was commuted to a

---

[20] Fucking hurry up Englishman!

[21] Our derogatory term for Afrikaners

41

life sentence, by Jannie Smuts himself, and the Nats let him out in '48... Why do ask my boy?"

"Did Leibbrandt have children, Oupa?"

"Ja, a few. Why?"

"Well,' I said, 'We have a Major Leibbrandt here, and I can't say I think much of him."

"Ja," retorted Oupa, "Robey was in the police and the railway police, and he loved uniforms almost as much as he loved himself, and when he told people how much he loved the Nazis and he wore that little Adolf Hitler moustache, I didn't think much of him either."

As it turned out, our Major Leibbrandt was, in fact, Major Izan (Nazi spelled backward) Leibbrandt, son of the Nazi sympathiser Robey Leibrandt, he of integrity, yet so easily seduced by the Nazi propaganda machine. This piece of information I kept very much to myself, not being entirely sure how such news would be received or what sort of treatment the purveyor of such stories might be subjected to. With the passing of the days, the pieces started to fit more and more, and it seemed the backdrop and, in fact, the entire construct of this army was engulfed in duplicity.

Never having been in an army before, I wondered if all military institutions operated on this basis. In this case, a very shaky foundation loosely constructed around a Calvinist Christian mould of sorts (when it suited), the building blocks being presented and burnished were those of national pride, bravery and unquestioning, unwavering loyalty. My interpretation of bravery really revolved around a strength of character in challenging a status quo which was unquestionably evil and misguided, being overseen by narrow minded, men of intransigence; men who feared anything or anyone from whom might emanate even the tiniest hint of a challenge born of intelligence or intellect.

The default response to anything which hinted at academic consideration, or a moral challenge was to bully and ridicule as erudite highbrow rantings, turning the group on the one who had fleetingly had the temerity to assume that he might know better than the institution which was the mighty South African Defence Force and its Permanent Force disciples. Biblical sheep springing to mind more and more as the days wore on. They hated me for speaking English, and they hated the fact that I could refuse orders due to a medical condition, and they made no bones about their resentment. I hated what they stood for, how on their

God's Earth, could they hope to garner from me anything resembling tolerance, let alone the required unquestioning, unwavering loyalty.

One Monday morning, lectures were prefaced by a video clip clearly showing a bloodthirsty mob of black people 'necklacing' one of their own. While the word 'necklacing' seems inane enough, the words sinister and barbaric would better describe how a mob of people in a state of mass hysteria would force a car tyre over the shoulders of the victim, 'pinning' the arms, while the victim would be doused with petrol and set alight.

And all this accompanied by ululation, jeering and whistling, drowning out the screams of the poor unfortunate victim while he or she experienced the most gruesome end in a pall of smoke-filled frenzy. Such punishment would serve as warning to other would be 'sell-outs' to the whites, or Amaburu. The video, and many others like it were to be seen thereafter almost on a daily basis, via 'lectures' or on screens in the mess hall and barracks. So it was that many erstwhile 'Kaffirboeties' (derogatory term for a 'brothers of the black man') systematically began to yield to the daily indoctrination designed to inculcate fear, derision and deep hatred of black people—the enemy, and puppets of the communist masters in Moscow. Sergeant Major Jones, a regular on the lecture circuit, after the beginnings of a debate reared its head in a classroom, would turn and write impatiently on a chalk board: "ANC + PAC + CP + HNP + NP + PFP = KAK,"[22] quickly extinguishing the debate with "*Manne dis bloot eenvoudig, ons skiet kaffirs daar bo in die noorde!*"[23]

I imagined this wouldn't have been an opportune moment to enquire of the good Sa' Majoor whether he might be familiar with the works of Alan Paton, Andre Brink, or Nadine Gordimer, all good white folk who had through their writings devoted some time and energy to revealing and exploring the underbelly of the South African condition. Similarly, perhaps he had read some illumination from writers who were not South African at all, Ngugi Wa Thiong'o or Chinua Achebe, revealing a little about the effects of colonisation on the constructs of their African societies? The enormous emphasis placed on their 'stiltetyd' and church attendance led one to suspect that these men might have received all the intellectual and moral nourishment they required from the Old Testament of their bibles, or so it seemed.

---

[22] CP-Conservative Party, HNP-Herstigte Nationale Party (Reconstituted National Party), NP-National Party, PFP- Progressive Federal Party = KAK (SHIT).

[23] It's really simple men, we shoot kaffirs up in the north

With each passing day, I grew to hate these people more and more, a people convinced that the might of the gun could stave off the inevitable. A Boer concentration constituting less than 10% of the population of the country had, through the control of the economy, media, educational institutions and the military, kept the black man, now comprising about 90% of the population, under the jackboot of apartheid for too many decades, but with many white people enjoying a standard of living unsurpassed anywhere on the globe. This was a situation both immoral and untenable in the extreme, given the widespread scale of impoverishment of the vast majority of black South Africans.

5. Decisions, Obstacles, Obstacles and Decisions

The apartheid government had a policy of compulsory conscription for young white men who were expected to perform military service at regular intervals, starting with an extended training which began in the year immediately following the one in which they left school or as soon as they turned 16, whichever came last. Many were granted deferment, for example, to attend university and complete an undergraduate degree first, but very few young men were exempted from conscription for any reason other than being medically unfit or for a race classification error. Valid reasons included conscientious objection based on religious beliefs, but these exceptions were tightened in 1974. Increasingly stringent laws were passed increasing periods of service, broadening the base of eligible white men who could be called up, and providing stringent sentences for those men who objected.

Objections to military service were generally based on the role of the military and security forces in enforcing the policy of apartheid, as well as opposition to ongoing South African military commitments in South West Africa (Namibia) and Angola.

Those who refused military service were subject to contempt from the minority white community, and left with the choice of either going underground (internal exile), fleeing the republic (external exile), or imprisonment of up to double the length of the allotted military service.[24]

It had been during the third or possibly fourth week that I arrived at a firm decision. I had felt myself slipping deeper and deeper into a state of misery, a dark dank pit, enveloping my soul, exerting a physical, numbing pressure on my

---

[24] Apartheid government's policy on military conscription 2020
Wikipedia

mind each morning, and only showing signs of easing after lunch time when the end of the day began to beckon. As the days progressed, this helplessness worsened, I suspected, as a result of my lack of control over my own existence. I imagined that I might indeed have been better off in prison as a conscientious objector, where at least my very fibre would not have been at the mercy of political bullshit propaganda on a daily basis, spewed by fanatical racist ersatz Christians.

There had been rumours of suicides in the camp, for which if there was any factual basis, we would never know, since the apparatus would no doubt colour such tragedy as misadventure. I wrote a carefully worded letter to the Company Commander and the Commanding Officer of the Infantry School, Colonel Schultz, in which I itemised several reasons why I should not be there, detailing my abhorrence of apartheid, my commitment to liberal and atheistic doctrine, and my state of mind, leaving no doubt that I was less than confident that I might not consider suicide (this part of course was not at all true). Surely, my suitability as an infantry officer would not only be called into question, I believed that I had given them sufficient ammunition to expel me without question or delay.

A week went by, and there had been no response. Now, either the letters had not been delivered by our Platoon Commander, or perhaps the readers' poor grasp of the English language had hampered their understanding of the gravity of the situation. Some two weeks later I repeated the exercise, my correspondence not even being acknowledged let alone eliciting a response. Cynicism toyed with my mind like a salivating alley cat with a terrified mouse.

They were going to let me spend a full year enduring their bullshit, and at the moment critique would expel me as an unsuitable candidate for the passing out parade, no shiny stars to be pinned onto my epaulettes. Perhaps, and probably the more likely scenario, was that their unshakeable faith in their brainwashing system had them convinced that the likes of me would be swayed to their way of thinking. I thought back to my friend Keith, who had been expelled a few days into the nightmare, and kept thinking how my approach had missed the mark. Sometimes, solutions present themselves disguised as, dare one say, 'obstacles'.

Nights were filled with a plethora of smells of floor polish, Kiwi brown shoe polish, Robin starch, and detergents, 'Doom' insecticide, all intermingling, the hubbub of voices speaking two different languages, some not so easy to understand dialects of both English and Afrikaans and easily 12 or more different songs blaring, from Sakkie-Sakkie Boeremusiek to ABBA, or Queen to ACDC.

The smell that lingered the most in my olfactory memory for many, many years was that of Preen. It was difficult to describe. It was an almost sweet, extremely clean overpowering, not unpleasant odour, dispensed from a pink spray bottle filled with a pre-wash spot-removing liquid, which would rid one's rifle of grease, dust and gunpowder residue with one simple spray, and then a rinse when one took a shower. This operation needed to be conducted surreptitiously, since it was illegal, I suspected for no other reason than… It was illegal.

The heat of the Karoo would dry that rifle in an instant after its shower, saving one 30–45 minutes of meticulous cleaning in all nooks and crannies of the rifle's components each evening. Thus, there was never any danger of rust. Besides, these rifles were designed for outdoor combat. What if it rained? Most Dutchmen were too 'paraat'**1** to get their rifles wet, and loved to rat on those who 'Preened' rifles.

Days were filled with drilling, PT, lectures, shooting, and, of course, getting fucked around. Now the sensitive reader may well take umbrage to the constant expletive referral to us being 'fucked around', but please be assured, that is exactly what it was, even officialdom alluded to '*rondfok*', Afrikaans for… "getting fucked around!" Day in, day out, there was very little variation in our scheduled activities, none of which I enjoyed, largely since the heat made anything outdoors unpleasant, and anything indoors was either boring as hell or felt like neo-Nazi white supremacist propaganda.

I recalled reading extensively about the survival of prisoners in Japanese POW camps, and people staying alive in the concentration camps in Europe during World War Two, the common denominator being that these people had found a reason to live, a reason to go on. Those without a reason, it seemed, were doomed to perish. My reason to go on presented itself when we were informed of the date for our first pass, some 3 weeks hence. The elation I experienced was indescribable, for the first time since that fateful morning when we'd arrived, I felt human again—no—I felt superhuman!

My mood changed, my gait changed, I was Fred Astaire, I was singing, I didn't need rain. Corporals, Lieutenants, Sergeant Majors… no one could get under my skin. One day I sensed the distinct smell of a heavenly creature as I entered the room. Aside from the floral scent, she was very attractive and extremely friendly, although what struck me more than anything was how gentle she appeared. Immersed in a world of red dust, heat, overalls, uniforms, sweaty bodies, guns and ammunition, sleep deprivation and crass language, everything smelled of khaki or canvass.

I had forgotten about these creatures who were so soft and vulnerable, easy on the eye. Her picture-perfect pixie face, immaculately groomed honey blonde hair, lots of it, made me want to step closer and deeply breathe in the bouquet of freshly cut flowers. Not an angel sent from heaven, but a mobile travel agent. She had been allowed the use of an office in the Western Cape Command administration centre to assist servicemen needing to purchase airline tickets to fly home.

Our pass would commence on a Friday morning, and we would need to be back in camp by Monday 1800h. Given that 'home' for me was some 1,100km away, a bus or train ride made no sense, so a quick 95-minute flight it would be, from the airport at George, a nearby town.

Time of course dragged and dragged until that day could no longer elude us. "I want to break free... I want break free..." crooned Freddy Mercury as we awoke to the strains of Queen, my eyes opening that morning to the reality of going home on that very day. Home, and the sweet taste of all things comforting and familiar. No Afrikaans for three whole days, home cooked meals, sleep as much as I like—all contributed to a weekend which was over all too quickly. I had decided to drive back to Oudtshoorn on Monday, since having a car at the barracks was all part of the grand plan to transfer elsewhere.

A 13-hour drive ended with a reality check—collecting kit and weapons, preparing for that dreaded morning inspection, having to do the bed, cupboards and barracks all over again from scratch, a long night lay ahead. I once again made a decision that I would do whatever it took to get out of this mess, and without knowing it at the time, it was going to take *some doing*.

A week or two later, my wishes came true. The Colonel wanted to interview me, and everyone else for that matter. My moment arrived, when I was marched into a large panelled boardroom smelling of wood, leather and polish, housing the 'Keuraad'—'Selection Committee'—headed by the Colonel, and attended by some four or five other senior officers resplendent in their formal regalia, shiny buttons, medals and badges glistening all over the place.

Seeing these men, a cursory thought entered my mind about men playing at soldiers like little boys who never grew up, fomenting a war that had no place in a moral, modern world. This was not quite what I had in mind, a bit like a deer in the headlights. I boldly stood at attention before being told to sit in front of this predatory assembly of South African infantry's finest. Col. Schultz led proceedings, opening in Afrikaans with some general questions, which I answered in English, hoping to annoy him.

I went into detail about my lack of suitability as a trainee officer, given my political views. I stressed my dislike for the place and the people, and concluded with an attempt to persuade all present that Oudtshoorn would be better off without the likes of me, and I should be far more useful to the army working in an office somewhere other than Oudtshoorn. Never in my life until then had the wind been taken out of my sails as occurred that day.

Everyone to a man on that Keuraad smiled, the Colonel warmly assuring me that the Infantry School was not meant to be a fun place, and given how neatly my uniform and boots were turned out, my strength of character and conviction, as well as my ability to skilfully articulate my thoughts into words, 'put my mind at ease' insisting that I was the very epitome of the type of officer they sought in the infantry, needing only some minor adjustments in my world views. He was of the opinion I would become a very good military leader. Dismissed with their very best wishes for my progress for the remainder of the 12-month course, I saluted and was marched out by a corporal as escort, thinking nothing, other than "Fucking hell!"

It was from that moment when my mind and soul became enveloped in something very dark. What it was I couldn't be sure, but what I was sure of was that it constituted an overwhelming feeling of despair. It would burden me, uninvited whenever it seemed I was at my most vulnerable, resulting in lethargy, loss of appetite and no desire to talk to others, socialise or drink beer in the evenings. Unbeknownst to me at the time, this invisible fiend had an official name… 'depression'.

I had learned to cup my forehead into my palm and curled fingers, so as to create the impression of being deep in thought. In reality, I would be sitting bolt upright, fast asleep. Many Afrikaner and English boys did the same, and very often were caught out, a punishment of sorts being administered for not paying attention during the 'lesing', lecture or lesson. So deprived were we of proper sleep, that we were easily able to sleep sitting up, merely needing to close the eyes for literally a second or two before being overwhelmed by slumber. Sleep, thus, came very easily, sitting on the pew in the very back row of the Anglican Church in Oudtshoorn each Sunday.

While Sundays were a little easier to cope with, following a breakfast of a rusk and mug of moer koffee, we were required to dress up and be marched in a squad by a corporal to the church of our preference. I chose the Anglican Church, for no other reason than I could be assured that there would be no Afrikaans spoken for 60 minutes. The minister was never fooled, and smiled as the sermon ended and about 25 sheepish, groggy servicemen shook his hand on the way out to meet the impatiently waiting corporal, pacing like a caged carnivore.

He would politely suggest that we 'klim in 'n squad', 'climb into a squad' while in earshot of the civilian church congregation, and once we were a block or so down the road, the nature of his true rasping character would reveal itself again. Once back in the camp, we would have a short break and then be back to preparation for Monday morning 'inspeksie'.

Saturday mornings were generally reserved for 'chicken parade', which entailed hundreds of us spreading out literally across the breadth of the camp, a meter or so apart, and then edging forward, eyes scouring the ground for anything which could be thought of as litter. Bottle tops, cigarette ends, pull-rings from soda cans, matches, or anything that if seen afterwards would ignite the ire of the Sa' Majoor. Also, on Saturday mornings might be 'fun activities' 'bondel sport', which the Dutchmen found highly entertaining, the English boys—not so much.

Three-legged racing, fireman's lift racing, tug 'o war, bok-bok (a game involving one leaping and throwing oneself on top of others) etc, none of which I enjoyed. I had always been a keen, competitive sportsman, and held the belief that if you were to play sport, do it properly. Be trained, practice often and compete against the best. This just struck me as a waste of time, overseen by people who were unfit to do so, all participants running the risk of serious injury. Once these activities were over, we were well and truly free to do as we pleased (without leaving the camp of course) until church parade on Sunday morning.

I found myself clinging, arms and legs clasped and locked around a wooden beam suspended about four metres above the ground. I was halfway through an obstacle course, which according to the lieutenant in charge required lateral thought to solve puzzles in order to progress to the end. It was a Saturday morning, and I wanted to get through these obstacles quickly, for no other reason than to attain my freedom for the week once we were finished. In teams, we were required to calculate ways to improvise creating bridges to cross an area without feet touching the ground.

Using equipment like old truck tyres, logs, ropes and buckets we planned and discussed possible solutions. We had been at it for quite some time, out in the heat of the sun, dressed in our long sleeved 'prison overalls', boots and hats. Army protocol demanded that we wear a webbing belt (a wide canvas belt around the waist) with a one litre plastic water bottle housed in a large moulded stainless steel 'cup' called a fire-bucket, all contained inside a canvass 'skin' attached to the belt.

The bottle filled at all times with water, would reside on the hip, but my activity had caused the bottle to slide into a position now directly up against my lower vertebrae. Fatigued muscles from hours of hanging, climbing and stretching, combined with sweaty hands, resulted in me slipping from that beam, landing on the ground some four metres below. I fell directly to the ground, landing on my back, the fall exacerbated by the very rigid plastic water bottle.

A nasty, painful fall indeed, and the dramatic manner in which my pelvis extended forward on impact with the bottle and the ground had the officers in charge in a panic that I had fractured my spine or pelvis, or worse still... both. I lay motionless, unable to move, the first thought through my mind a question. I wondered: *How long would this keep me out of preparing for inspections?*

The officer in charge of the soiree reacted quickly. A loud 'clipped' set of instructions over a two-way radio demanded a vehicle and medics to collect me, and for the duty doctor and nurses at the camp sick bay to prepare themselves for my arrival. My mishap spelled the end of the day's activities as my platoon was dismissed, and the officers in charge stood around gawking at me, some showing genuine concern, others seemingly indifferent. I arrived at the sick bay just as lunch was being distributed, the doctor asking me if I was hungry, which I was not.

After a cursory examination, and an inspection of my medical file, his face was unable to conceal the obvious concern going through his mind. He told me that he was reluctant to make any assumptions until he had seen the results of an X-ray, which of course could only be done on Monday morning at the Oudtshoorn Civilian General Hospital. In the meantime, however, he felt it best to prescribe a cocktail of drugs to alleviate pain, relax the muscles and essentially put me to sleep after the nurses had administered a 'bed bath'.

This regimen was maintained, dosage and efficacy timed to coincide with waking for breakfasts and dinners, as I slept through until Monday morning. Morphine is a wondrous thing, obliterating the pain, while putting my mind at ease, since I had not been able to move any part of my body at all since the fall. Naturally, I was terrified.

While the nurse held it up against the light, the doctor and I squinted at the large film. Nothing, either good nor bad, was easily visible, largely due to the lack of fine detail on the somewhat hazy X-ray. A slight grimace on his face, and a few shakes of the head led me to believe that the doctor was far from satisfied. Turning to me, he asked: **"Dink jy dat jy 'n motorreis na Kaapstad kan oorleef?"**[25]

I pondered this momentarily, considering I'd spent the day alternating sleeping and sitting up, I thought that I could, but then I asked him how long the drive was, to which the entire ward, in unison sang out "Five hours!"

It seemed that I was the only one who had never driven from Oudtshoorn to Cape Town. Due to the mountainous terrain, the five-hour option seemed better than the train ride which apparently took some 24 hours. It was explained that the No. 2 Military Hospital in Cape Town was really modern and well equipped, boasting machines which did MRI scans, which I'd never heard of. He went on to say that the scan would detect the slightest element of damage to or around the spine and spinal cord, if it did indeed exist.

Singing the praises of the facility, he urged me to go since he said that they were far better equipped to diagnose and to treat injury, with specialists, surgeons and specialist physiotherapists, these being non-existent at the Infantry School. No second invitation was required, and it was settled. Later in the day, confirmation arrived that I would be driven by car to Cape Town on Wednesday morning.

---

[25] "Do you think that you could survive a car ride to Cape Town?"

6. Holidaying in Cape Town

Cape Town, it has been said, is the most beautiful city in the world. For those lucky enough to find themselves on the 'right' side of the mountain, this is true. 'Bad luck', pure and simple, would see many born without white skin on the wrong side of the majestic Table Mountain. For most of them, Cape Town is a living hell, where unemployment, crime, poverty, drug abuse, rape and gangs proliferate. [26]

Sipping on warm cocoa with a shot of rum was quite pleasant. Wolfgang, a thirty-something long-haired, bearded 'Suid Wester' (South West African) terrorised people in the passages, being pushed in his wheelchair, up and down at breakneck speeds, he all the while grinning and shouting: "Vinniger, vinniger!"[27] He was the unofficial 'leader' of our orthopaedic ward. It was he who instructed someone to go around the ward just before bedtime carefully tipping rum into every mug of cocoa, after he and one or two others returned from the balcony outside the ward for their nightly 'zol'.[28] Wolfgang had been in the hospital for some years, almost it seemed, a permanent resident, having damaged his spinal cord literally days before his national service was ending.

Wolfgang had been a navy diver, one of the most dangerous jobs in the military; he and some mates had been relaxing at an unfamiliar beach, when Wolfgang misjudged the depth of some water, diving into the sea he had struck his head on a submerged rock, he was unconscious from the collision. To his friends sitting some way down the beach, their mate's floating body triggered the alarm… it appeared that Wolfgang had drowned.

So, of course the emergency response from them was to pull him out of the water, snap his head back in order to clear the airways, when in fact they had

---

[26] The writer

[27] Faster, faster!

[28] Cannabis cigarette.

unwittingly exacerbated the damage to his spinal cord, leaving Wolfgang paralysed from the neck down, except for very limited movement of his left arm and hand. Others in the ward related horrific stories of triggering Soviet anti-personnel landmines in Angola, or spines being damaged as a result of vehicles being ambushed or blown up, a parachutist who had survived despite being riddled with bullets from an AK 47 just before landing, the place was a veritable house of horrors, and yet morale seldom seemed to ebb.

Mornings at No. 2 Military Hospital in Wynberg began with a bed-bath, breakfast, and then I was wheeled to physiotherapy. A number of Polish female physicians and physiotherapists had escaped the Eastern Bloc and somehow ended up in South Africa working for the South African Defence Force. Klara's baby blue eyes looked into mine the first time we met, and I was in love. Her voice a tad gravelly, so sexy. This petite blonde creature with the strongest of hands, would massage a silky substance into my lower back, one hour every day.

I would sleep, she would finish and leave me to sleep for a few minutes, then gently she would whisper into my ear: "C'mon soldier, your orderly is waiting to take you to your ward." Back in the ward, I would snuggle into the bed and sleep fitfully until lunchtime, wake up, eat and read books from the mobile library for the rest of the afternoon. This was the army I could grow to know and love. But wait... there's more.

I learned early in the game that on Friday afternoons, those who could walk unaided were permitted a weekend pass. Although the pain in my lower spinal area was immense and MRI scans had shown muscular swelling, I knew that in a very short space of time, I should display at least enough improvement to allow me to walk on my own. Mission accomplished, and the second Friday afternoon in hospital saw me walking gingerly down the long hill from the hospital to Wynberg Station to take a train to Cape Town.

I was dressed in army uniform, boots, beret, and full regalia. It struck me that I should stop in at one of the myriad shops near the station where I bought a pair of jeans, civvy shoes, 4 pairs of socks and two colourful sweaters. Now I was set for my weekend. I had recalled years before thinking that Woodstock Holiday Inn had looked pretty cool from the motorway, so after boarding the train, I watched out of the window like a hawk for the Woodstock Station.

After checking in to the hotel, I luxuriated in a large bubbly spa bath, listening to the TV blaring in the adjacent bedroom. It was a magazine programme previewing the *Killing Fields*, the commentator describing the milieu against the backdrop of beautiful, haunting pipe flute music. A journalist, trapped in Cambodia during tyrant Pol Pot's bloody reign, was exposed to the horrors of the situation.

I switched off mentally, my mind demanding respite from anything potentially unpleasant. A room service order of steak, chips and a Castle Lager was so good that I ordered the same again. Having cleansed my body of anything which could possibly remind me of armies or hospitals, I ate my fill, and in high spirits headed down to the hotel bar where a jazz trio strutted their stuff while I enjoyed a few drinks and a cigar—yes sir, this was the life.

The next morning after a late breakfast I headed by train to the city centre, where after walking around for a while I found a 'Spur' steak restaurant, a Cape franchise where I sat and ate my fill. Watching the crowds on the street below, it occurred to me that army food had made me miss good food. A weekend spent on my own, eating, drinking and sleeping in, left me in a blissful state of calm, comfortable in the knowledge that I could do it all again the next weekend.

So it was that I spent a really good six weeks in Cape Town, weekdays filled with massage and rest, weekends consisting of leisurely meals, movies, pubs and yet more rest. The wonderful Klara had become an essential component of my life, the focus of all I could look forward to each and every week day, with her gentle caresses, comforting, soothing hands, and lots of conversation. I would get lost in stories of her childhood in Gdansk, a small port city on the Baltic Sea.

She had been one of eight children, her father working as a labourer in the shipyard. She talked of growing up under the boot of communism, her parents before her enduring a brutal occupation by the Nazis. At the shipyard, her father had known Lech Walesa, a dissident who opposed communism.

A remarkable leader, achieving that which was thought impossible when in the heart of Soviet communist rule he established, not without monumental opposition, the first trade union in Poland, later graduating from trade unionist to founding and leading 'Solidarity' activities which would land him in prison for his beliefs. We were unaware at the time, that he would establish the foundation in years to come for a free Poland. Walesa becoming the president of the country.

Klara visibly travelled back in time, as her bright blue eyes sparkled when she extolled the beauty of her home town with its magnificent structures—some dating back to medieval times—and a rich history when the area was governed by Teutonic knights. The beautiful city displaying a water frontage to rival

Amsterdam, Paris or Prague, populated by a wonderful people whose 'chutzpah' kept them bubbly, demanding that their collective morale would not be undermined by external Soviet or internal communist influence.

A palpable sadness was evident when she talked of the hardships her people and family had endured, and the sacrifices required so that she could receive a tertiary education, and then the heart-wrenching decision to leave her kin and all that she knew, to travel to a foreign land of which she knew very little.

Klara, as part of her university course, had chosen to study and become proficient in English. She now found herself in a working environment which was predominantly Afrikaans, disappointing she admitted, since she was able to converse with very few of her patients, me of course, fast becoming *her favourite*, as I would reciprocate with childhood tales of my own, which paled into insignificance when compared with the richness of her sagas.

Klara and I would chat incessantly, laughing sometimes until the tears would cascade down our cheeks, me clutching my sore back, begging her to stop, often wondering what those outside her rooms were thinking. While in my own mind I might have considered myself Klara's favourite patient, I also calculated that this 26 or 27 year old, highly intelligent, vivacious blond bombshell sporting the sexiest of accents, wearing the rank of Lieutenant on her epaulettes, had little need of a 22 year old private with a bad back trying to escape an infantry camp in the desert because of what might have been construed as a few 'morality concerns'.

Distance between me and the Infantry School, as well as some weeks, had all contributed to me wondering if I hadn't been overly sensitive, over-reacting to people and events back in the camp, a hint of self-doubt. When Klara admitted that she had kept me in hospital for a little longer than she really should have, I was most grateful to her, since my condition had improved remarkably, and she provided a letter for me to hand to my commanding officer, in which she left no room for doubt that I was to be removed from physical military training of any description, going on to say that if the army was unwilling to discharge me from military service entirely, I was to be utilised in a sedentary capacity working in an office of sorts, with access to ongoing physiotherapy should the need arise.

So, after what felt like a 6 week sojourn, which had been quite cathartic both physically and emotionally, I found myself in a carriage, pulled by an old steam train slowly chugging out of the Wynberg train station mid-morning. Sharing a compartment with Herman, a fellow serviceman, also discharged from the hospital on his way back to Oudtshoorn, I discovered that this Afrikaner was an affable chap, somewhat introverted, a fellow school teacher who reluctantly admitted that he was 'shit scared' of returning to the hell which was Infantry School.

I couldn't bring myself to admit to him that in my pocket was the key to my freedom, courtesy of the lovely Klara. I had become once again my old self, happy, thoughtful, gregarious, fearless… yes, armed with my 'letter' I was untouchable, so of course, I was light of heart and yes, fearless indeed. Enjoying meals in the dining carriage, beers, sampling the Cape's finest Cabernet Sauvignon, enjoying the company of my new friend, who despite his Afrikaner roots, displayed an extremely liberal outlook, we were in agreement that this was turning out to be one of the most scenic journeys each of us could recall.

Traversing the majestic jagged mountains of the Langeberg, magnificent in their starkness, interspersed with the greenest of wineries and fruit cultivating valleys, home to generations of French religious refugees, and Dutch families having fled English rule, we sat staring in awe from the window of the dining car, or our compartment. Striking eastward, the line then hugged the coastline of the Indian Ocean through historical villages, where Portuguese explorers had set foot on the land and erected monuments in the 15th century.

They would give thanks to their creator for safe passage across thousands of miles of treacherous ocean at a time when superstitious folk reported sailors facing unspeakable demise, sea monsters awaiting frail ships in order to quell their bloodlust. Through Mossel Bay, Hartenbos then on to George finally turning to go inland, the old steam train took a deep breath preparing to puff it's way on the final leg of the journey over the mountain barrier into the little town in a dustbowl, encapsulated by the black mountains to the north, the 'Swartberg', and to the south east, the Outeniqua mountains, named by the Khoisan people, who it is reported, had occupied the area for some 260,000 years.

A little flutter in my stomach as the train puffed slowly into the Oudtshoorn station, memories of that place flooding my mind. Twenty-four hours had passed in the blink of an eye. This time, however, no rows of monsters, but one lone figure, his maroon beret betraying the fact that he was not an infantryman, but a medical orderly, lounging on a shaded wooden bench on the platform, puffing unenthusiastically on a cigarette, in no hurry to go anywhere. As usual, it was a scorching hot day, the cicadas screeching in protest, a few passengers hurriedly making their way off the platform, the little station deserted within moments.

He spotted us, a gentle wave of the hand. It seemed he wanted to finish his cigarette, since walking and smoking was taboo in the army. Standing in the shade I lit up a cigarette of my own, immediately cementing the bond between us, as is often the case when smokers meet for the first time. Herman, visibly agitated, joining us as we savoured a leisurely cigarette in silence, standing in the cool shade, contemplating the inevitability of our re-entry into the eye of the shit storm.

7. Moving Along Swiftly

"Institutionalisation is a process intended to regulate societal behaviour (i.e., supra-individual behaviour) within organisations or entire societies. Institutionalisation is thus a human activity that installs, adapts, and changes rules and procedures in both social and political spheres."

Wolfgang Keman Political Science researcher and author. Encyclopedia Brittanica.

The cicadas, having sung their final chorus several weeks before, left the desert air eerily still, interrupted only now and then by distant, rasping orders, instructions and the rhythmic thud, thud, thud—the meeting of asphalt and squads of high density rubber boot soles. Suddenly, there was an uninvited, but oh so welcome, assault on the silence—the unmistakable richness of the voice of Billy Ocean demanding: 'Wanna be your loverboy!' as I turned on the high-powered Pioneer in-car stereo, the volume knob having been pre-set to maximum. I drove from that parade ground on what promised to be a sunny, windless day, windows wide open. We cruised, slowly, deliberately.

The sweet sound of beautiful music made by a black man with dreadlocks saturating every crevasse of that bastion of white supremacy, with just a tiny hint of mockery—this was heavenly. That parade ground whose dust had made life unbearable on the left, on the right, the unsightly red bricked administration offices where I had seen my first woman in months, that gorgeous creature who had sold me my ticket to freedom in the skies. In the rear-view mirror, the HQ office 'huts', Alpha, Bravo, Charlie, Delta, Echo, Foxtrot, Golf and Hotel Companies.

The boys on chicken parade on the rugby field now on our left hand side, alerted by the music, stopping, looked on like a Mississippi prison chain-gang as we drove by. Corporals drilling squads of 'marchers' along the road looked on disapprovingly. The Military Police manning the main gate boom spilled out of their guard hut to jump out in front of us, demanding that we stop. Their overnight patrols had noted the parked car, and "what business did you have parking on the hallowed parade ground?"

With a huge dose of indifference, we both handed our transfer documents for them to see, my passenger Jurgen, grinning, unable to contain his delight, as I'd not seen him before. Our parking transgression becoming completely devoid of substance and meaning in an instant, as their attention was diverted by the scrutiny, unnecessarily, to the transfer documents, as though the MPs somehow still held some sort of power over us. We smiled, sat back and enjoyed the music as all who were damned to be in this place were forced to listen and observe us as we fled the coop.

Promising myself that I would never again smell that parade ground dust, our hearts joined our voices as we sang over Billy when we heard that boom come down behind us—next stop Johannesburg for four lovely days. The car meandered through the sleepy streets of Oudtshoorn early on that Saturday morning. The only ones awake were to be found in the army camp, my trusty Nissan seeking out the only road to Dysseldorp, De Rust… just as the sun burst over the mountainous horizon and the little town started to surface, and we began our dash to freedom.

Jurgen had been a frightened, jumpy creature when I was ushered into the offices of the company commander to hand over my letter from Klara and explain the story of my long absence. Sitting meekly at his desk, his demeanour betraying fear, his eyes darting about, he shuffled papers trying his best to appear engaged in his work as the Major emerged from his office. The CO made no effort to conceal his disdain while his eyes scanned the document before him, the indifference on my face concealing so much more than disdain.

The context of the situation I would contemplate on numerous occasions for many years to come. My generation had provided thousands upon thousands of fighting men—nay—boys for this army, most of whom had been naïve, somewhat ignorant perhaps, but generally well intentioned, if misguided.

Some would be thrown into frightening enemy firefight contacts in far off places, some exposed to horrific situations, emerging physically scarred or suffering the invisible post-traumatic stress, some returning home in coffins. Six weeks in a military hospital had illuminated for me the gory, visible results of war, providing further confirmation of the status of conscripts as pawns in a much bigger game, the scale of which I was yet to learn.

Some of these young men would emerge as heroes in the eyes of their comrades and superiors, and would be recognised as such, having medals pinned to their chests accompanied by a stirring rendition of the national anthem played by a military brass brand, the 'oranje, blanje, blou'[29] proudly, serenely, fluttering in the sky. There is no question that many of these men displayed conduct and bravery which can only be described as exemplary. Patriotic fervour I could fully understand, and at times I had almost—almost—felt aggrieved that I could not bring myself to grasp in both hands, this patriotism, and submit without question, like everyone else, well nearly everyone else.

Something inside me, and I could never be sure precisely what it was, would simply not allow me to concede to that defence of apartheid which I knew to be immoral and loathsome, and which had evolved into draconian. Brave soldiers, I thought, deserved better leadership and straight shooting, honest politicians; I guess this is a contradiction in terms. At Liberty Life Management School in later life, I learned the difference between oversight and leadership. Oversight of a team despatched to chop down trees, creating a path through a jungle would entail a supervisor seeing to it that saws were kept sharpened, tree fellers well rested, fed and hydrated, and, of course, ensuring that deadlines are met.

The **leader** would be the one carrying only a ladder, climbing up high from time to time, he would be the first and only to be able to announce "Hey fellas, wrong jungle!" As a young man I sensed this without being able to 'label' what I was experiencing. Instinctively I was aware that the government of South Africa micromanaged everything, obsessed with oversight and supervision, dramatically amplified in the military context. The fact that the country's polity was completely at odds with the vast majority of its people should surely have been glaringly obvious to even the most casual observer.

Sadly, this was not the case, the National Party government having honed its skills in so many facets of South African life, as master propagandists—most white South Africans desensitised over generations—to the extent that they found anything anti-government totally objectionable, to be ridiculed and dismissed out of hand as socialist or communist disinformation, or worse still, treacherous or treasonous. Stoking the fire of fear through repetitious misinformation became a major arrow in the quiver of the 'Nats'.

---

[29] Orange, white and blue national flag.

For me, the political leadership of South Africa had systematically led the country into a racist, Calvinist 'wrong jungle', aided, abetted and defended by an unquestioning military machine, my conscious and sub-conscious relegating any and all activities in this place to a huge bin labelled "waste of time, human life and taxpayers' money" I was at the time totally oblivious to the large, sinister hand hovering above, moving the pieces, controlling the game.

Jurgen and I became close allies very quickly after I had been removed from training and given a desk job in the company HQ offices until the powers figured out what to do with me. Jurgen had been in a similar state of limbo for several weeks, and was becoming more and more despondent as each morning we entered the cramped, musty offices, the overpowering stench of years of stale cigarettes and smoke having permeated the entire place.

We would sit obediently at our desks awaiting menial chores, being screamed at if we were too slow to react. "Fuck you!" I would answer in my mind as I meekly listened while the Major, Captain or one of their lieutenants chose to admonish or scold us as one would a troublesome mongrel in the street.

Two beers were the 'legal' limit per evening, when handing over ration tickets to the dispensing barman. Purchasing of surplus tickets from teetotallers was neither difficult nor unusual, as Jurgen and I would sit at night, anaesthetising our souls well beyond our 'legal two'. We would come to savour this time as cathartic, really enjoying each other's company, him a 'cerebral being', having completed an honours degree at probably the most 'liberal' of the Afrikaans universities, Rand Afrikaans University.

Our major commonality was the abhorrence of the racist laws which governed the country weaving their way into the fabric of South African society. Jurgen would enlighten me with the stories of Kafka and we would discuss the pros and cons of Noam Chomsky's views on Indo-China and Middle Eastern politics, much to the chagrin of those in earshot. Every waking minute in the HQ offices, our ears attuned to the ringing of the phone which would hopefully convey news of our imminent transfer, we waited on tenterhooks, not knowing when, or to where our fates would lead us.

So, the weeks dragged on, as we evoked more and more the contempt of our contemporaries in the barracks. We were looked down upon and dismissed as 'gypogatte', some of our erstwhile 'mates' resorting to 'accidentally' bumping into us in the passage ways, in the hope, I felt, to curry favour with the NCO's, by igniting a situation leading to a fight. I wasn't biting, and would move along swiftly as I felt the growing resentment toward me by the rest of the platoon.

Out of the blue, on a Thursday morning the phone rang, and within moments both Jurgen and I were elated to learn that he would be transferred to an office in Pretoria, and I would be sent to Military Intelligence School in Diskobolos in Kimberley, about 500km from Johannesburg. We were both required to report on Wednesday of the following week. Friday was spent returning to stores, weapons, kit, bedding etc, and completing what seemed like more paperwork than when we had arrived.

By lunchtime, we were done, and bags packed, we presented ourselves at HQ offices to hand over paperwork and be dismissed. We hadn't been the only ones to be transferred that day, and we were instructed to collect tickets for the train, due to leave that afternoon for Cape Town. We were then required to transfer to a train to Kimberley, along with about 10 others from different platoons. I explained to the lieutenant on duty that I had a car and would not require a ticket, and suggested that Jurgen, who also lived in Johannesburg could drive with me.

He agreed. However, he stated categorically that he would not sign off our release until the next morning, as a matter of avoiding potential liability to the army should we drive through the night without sleep and come to a sticky end.

"But Lieutenant," I implored, "We've handed in our mattresses, sheets, blankets, pillows and sleeping bags. Where will we sleep?"

"Not my problem," he retorted, bearing in mind that the stores would close at 4.00 on Friday, only to re-open on Monday morning, so even if we had kept our bedding, we would not have been able to clear out with appropriate documents signed off. He shrugged when I pointed this out to him. *Fucking army, run by fucking idiots,* I thought to myself, not for the first time.

I had a fight on my hands to get my car out of the pound on Friday afternoon, knowing that the duty officer would be nowhere to be seen early on Saturday morning. No civilian cars were permitted inside the base which presented a challenge—where to park? Only in the army of course. *Fuck this,* I thought, *I've had enough of this shit.*

I parked my car on the edge of the parade ground, knowing that I could see it from the barracks, and furthermore, should the Regimental Sergeant Major have anything to say about his sacred parade ground, I was sufficiently irked to challenge him. I also happened to have heard that he enjoyed a few on a Friday night and would be nowhere to be seen on Saturday morning, so I was willing to take my chances.

A few beers of our own on Friday night aided our sleep on the hard floor using kit bags as pillows, and great coats as blankets. We were, however, delighted when first light showed itself the next morning. We were able to get up, brush teeth, and pack and carry our gear contained in a 'balsak'[30] to the restless chariot awaiting us on the parade ground.

Dropping Jurgen off at his mother's home in Crosby, a modest suburb in working class Johannesburg near to the Rand Afrikaans University, I wished him well, and sadly never saw him again.

---

[30] 1 Literally—scrotum or ballbag, actually a large canvass, tube-shaped kit bag to be slung over the shoulder.

8. Kimberley

"... I'm going back to Kimberley to gamble my last game" was the song that my mind couldn't escape, as I recalled hearing on many occasions, the LP record of the movie Kimberley Jim, starring gospel and country singer Jim Reeves, a firm favourite of my Ouma and Oupa, often playing on the old Pioneer turntable when I was a child.

The road wound through old diamond diggings; over dry, dusty semi-desert like landscape in places, and then through little towns Bloemhof, Warrenton and Wolmaranstad, where I would in months to come contribute considerable revenue to the local authorities, courtesy of speeding fines, sometimes two in the space of minutes (one on the way into town, followed by another as I would leave town). I was convinced that the speed restriction signs were strategically positioned so as not to be noticed when the motorist was required to slow from 120km to 60km, or a 60km zone appearing for all the world like a safe, open motorway.

'Kimberley might be an interesting place to spend some time,' I thought to myself, having at one time been a thriving diamond mining town, and a city under siege during the Anglo Boer War. So, my mind meandered on that long, not particularly pretty drive.

The cheeseburger was tasty, huge, then the slightly greasy chips drenched in tomato sauce, and finally the thick chocolate milkshake were slowly, consciously devoured, since this was to be my last 'civvy' meal before throwing myself to the mercy of the army once again, having had four wonderful, carefree days at home. In my pocket, two most prized possessions, my new medical classification card G3K3, now just a few little digits away from full exemption—G5—and, of course, my letter from the lovely Klara. Slowly, reluctantly I stood, paid for my meal, and asked for directions to SAINTS—South African Intelligence School. 'SAINTS' seemed to have a nice ring to it, as I mulled over the concept of 'military intelligence'.

I pictured myself with a camera at the international airport, surreptitiously awaiting the arrival of a Soviet spy, my directive to ID him and provide photos of him meeting with his 'asset'. Thoughts wandered this way and that as I drove from Kimberley CBD across flat, barren countryside. The day was quite overcast, and when I thought about it, quite chilly, with the onset of autumn. Following the road signs to 'Diskobolos', I passed the Kimberley Airport, which if one were to blink at the wrong moment, you would miss it altogether.

Approaching the non-descript white walls and pillars at the entrance to the place, seeing guards carrying R4 rifles, I glanced around at the diamond wire fencing with rolled razor wire neatly attached on top. Was that to discourage people getting in or out I wondered. A nagging little voice in my head suggested that this was nothing other than an army camp, just like all the others. Parking the car outside the base, I was ushered in, the Regimental Police demanding an explanation as to my presence. I was told to wait in the guard tent while enquiries were made.

As I lay on a random bed, everyone in the camp was suddenly shuffling or running with large silver things resembling tea trays, but with shallow compartments of differing shapes and sizes. It was lunchtime, and I was later to learn that these were called 'varkpanne', in English, 'pig pans', for dishing food onto, in the absence of plates in the mess. Suddenly, the place was deserted, and I quickly fell asleep, having left Johannesburg at about 06h00. The drive had been quite tedious, taking about six hours including stops and a meal, so I slept easily.

I was awakened by some infantrymen from Oudtshoorn, easily recognisable by the green berets and unit flashes on the upper shoulder attached to epaulettes. Returning from lunch they recognised me as one of their own, asking me if I knew what was going on. These were the fellows who had taken the train, and had been awaiting instructions, lounging in the guard tent since the day before, with no word of their fate. It seemed that SAINTS was totally unaware of our existence, no-one knowing from where the signals or phone calls had emanated or indeed, why.

In short, had we gone home and never pitched up in Kimberley, it seemed, no-one would have been any the wiser. I tell this story, not because it is hugely entertaining or enlightening, but to illustrate the ineptness of the military, and later it would become more and more evident to me how this mismanagement would be a common denominator throughout the infrastructure of the South African civil service.

A single gunshot was followed by the 'sssshhh,' like a sky rocket on Guy Fawkes night. It was the light of a flare hanging gently high up in the pitch darkness, invading the icy cold night air, bathing the rows of little tin-roofed houses in a ghostly sepia glow followed by a long stretch of sinister silence. The shadows on the ground grew in length as the flare slowly began to drift down to Mother Earth. The silence of the world suddenly shattered by gunfire, the distinct staccato 'tap tap… tap tap' of R4 assault rifles, unmistakable rasping orders barked out… again… 'tap tap, tap tap'… feet sprinting… urgency… *Those were boots… Ours!* I say quietly to myself.

A dog barks, a corrugated iron gate slams shut. More shouting of orders ripping through the night air: **"Skie'die fokken ding!"**[31]

'Tap tap, tap, tap'… the thudding of more boots, shuffling, muffled voices, difficult to determine the exact source of the commotion. It would have been around 0230h. I had been wiping sleep from my eyes, yawning, shivering in the sub-zero temperature, having just climbed out of a warm sleeping bag, trudging wearily along a dusty road, dutifully pointing my R4 at the ground, making sure I maintained the 20m distance behind the guy in front of me, his eyes scanning to the left, mine reluctantly to the right. I was never really sure what we looking for.

This was 'Township Duty', in which white soldiers sought to 'maintain the peace' in reservations housing exclusively black, largely poor people; deprived of electricity, tarred roads, proper sewerage, lacking adequate facilities in general. Galashewe, a settlement on the outskirts of Kimberley, housed some 80,000 people in tiny cramped homes, and was no different to any other 'satellite' township in South Africa, where the major make-up of the town or city housed white business, industry, residences, schooling, and general infrastructure; black people were permitted to work within these precincts but were required to return each evening to their own 'locations', later known as townships.

Exceptions were permitted in which black employees were required to reside on the premises of their white employers, usually in the residential areas and mines, which made life easier for employers having their staff on call at a

---

[31] 1 "Shoot the fucking thing!"

moment's notice. Fear of criminals, and later no doubt, white soldiers, forced the inhabitants of these townships indoors by the time darkness overcame the world. A smoke filled artificial silence would descend over these pitiful dwellings as night fell, resulting in Township Duty usually being quite uneventful.

This particular occasion revealed the ugly side of the Duty, when all patrols were suddenly ordered to meeting points where instructions were issued for us to pair up, safety latches on rifles to be put onto 'R'—rapid fire—and then to enter every home in search of 'dissidents' who had been spotted and chased. A cordon around a portion of the township would create a dragnet and the ensuing enter and search operation would result in the capture of the so-called terrorists. Doors not opened quickly enough were to be forcibly opened, and we were told: "… if in doubt, shoot first, ask questions later."

A few minutes into the 'raid', I realised that once again I had landed myself in the wrong place at the wrong time, what with the mix of fear and hatred, unmistakable in the eyes of the occupants of those sad, dark little homes. The terror was particularly evident in the doe eyes of the little children, as they eyed our weapons, our trigger fingers at the ready. Some of the kids were unable to hold back the tears. I felt like one of Hitler's storm troopers banging down doors in search of concealed Jewish families in an attic, as armoured vehicles with high powered search lights added to the picture, the distinctive growl of their diesel engines and the dust-storms they created on the sandy roads, completing the intimidation.

The fellow I was 'paired' with couldn't wait to get onto the next house, as though all his Christmases had come at once. By the time we had entered the third or fourth house I felt waves of nausea, as my 'buddy', a simple-minded farm boy from the Orange Free State—'plaasjapies' we called them—gleefully admitted that he was really enjoying himself and hoped someone would resist since he was itching to shoot. The next hour or so melded into a horrific real-life nightmare, as I vowed that this would be the last time I would be put into the position of invading poor peoples' homes.

My intuition upon arrival had indeed been correct, that this was an army camp, much like any other, but considerably more relaxed than the Infantry School in Oudtshoorn. Servicemen seemed to come and go, in and out of the camp at will, after hours and on weekends, and I learned that any half-plausible story would persuade the duty NCO to sign one's pass book, granting the freedom to drive to town for a few hours any night of the week for a movie, drinks or a meal, and since our cars were parked inside the camp this all became really easy.

Now a really good story might be sufficiently persuasive to fashion a weekend pass to Johannesburg. Basic training had just been completed when we arrived, so morning inspections were far less frequent, and cursory at best, freeing up our leisure time. Due to my medical classification, the only 'training' I could withstand was related to 'classroom lectures', so for me, there was only limited shooting of rifles until my back started to 'hurt', no drilling, route marches, or carrying anything of any description. In short, very little 'getting fucked around'. This type of army life I could endure as the only 'leverage' held over me was the enforcement of some guard duty and Township Duty, which up until that night had been tedious yet tolerable. But that which was tolerable had overnight become unacceptable.

I called my father one evening to enquire whether he had ever removed me as a beneficiary from his medical insurance policy. He had been meaning to, but fortunately for me he hadn't, and I asked him not to, just for the moment, and I made a note of the policy details. I explained to him I needed to see a specialist, which he did not question, having been aware of my sojourn at No. 2 Military Hospital. Next, I bribed the company clerk with beer tokens, getting him to photocopy all documentation relating to my medical history.

I penned a letter to an orthopaedic surgeon in Johannesburg, explaining that I was unable to sleep on the army beds, which provided no support or comfort, particularly for someone with my condition, going on to explain that I was in a constant state of discomfort, which to an extent was true. I included, for his perusal, copies of documentation detailing my full medical history, and requested an appointment for a consultation, asking him to assist by writing to company commander, Commandant (Lieutenant Colonel) Sadie, a somewhat unapproachable man.

I provided medical insurance details, as well as contact details for my father, the principal insurance policyholder. I made arrangement for the document to be sent 'registered mail'. My plan was now to tidy this thing up for once and for all, to clear that final hurdle—a review of my medical status with the intention of being reclassified as G5 and full exemption from national service and military duties. All that remained was for me to sit back patiently and wait, convinced that the dominos would start to fall within a day or two.

Needing to make a telephone call to Johannesburg during office hours in order to talk to Dr Katzen, I bribed the same clerk to allow me to use the phone in his office. Two days, three—eventually a week had gone by, I had heard nothing. As the phone call was answered in the orthopaedic surgeon's office, I was greeted by a curt, shrill, woman's voice. "Consulting rooms," she spat out.

"Good morning," I responded politely, "may I speak to Dr, Katzman please?"

The smirk on her face was almost audible as she retorted sarcastically: "The doctor doesn't take calls, and he is Mr Katzen, not Dr Katzen," as though everyone knows that.

Taken aback, I enquired after my correspondence to the doctor, her reply quickly dashing any hopes of my plan progressing, as she jubilantly announced: "Mr Katzman receives hundreds of letters on a daily basis. People advertising, insurance companies demanding reports on patients… the surgeon would not have enough hours in the week to open and read every letter, let alone be able to see patients and conduct surgery," she said, reciting no doubt for the thousandth time.

"Well, can I book an appointment to see the surgeon please?" I asked.

There was another almost audible smirk: "He will see you only following a referral from your GP, and then unless your condition is regarded as dire or is life threatening, there is a 12–14 week waiting list of patients wanting to be seen." So, my brilliant plan had no legs.

I had noticed some guys leaving training and lectures a little earlier than everyone else each day, and a couple of weeks or so into my stay at Diskobolos, I enquired as to their early dismissal. I had noticed that the same group never seemed to report for guard duty or Township Duty, and were absent on the weekends. I was interested to learn that these were soccer and rugby players. Now I had played both sports, rugby at high school, and soccer for a club, and inter-faculty at university. No doubt rugby would be a 'no-no', given my bad back, but soccer—here was a thought.

After lectures one afternoon, I made my way down to the soccer field, and chatting to the 'coach', Lt Bernieri, an English speaking 'Italian' South African, a really nice guy, all military protocol seemingly dispensed with on the football field. He was delighted to have another player, and invited me to practices immediately.

Having no football boots, I asked if he would sign my pass book for the next morning so that I could buy some boots in town. No problem at all and my new buddy 'Angelo' Bernieri was unwittingly responsible for the welcome reclamation of my sanity, confirming that 'his' footballers were not required to do night time duties including guard and township duties. Me 1, Army 0.

Tiny adjustments to my world made life just a little better. I bought some 'instant' porridge, Pronutro, powdered milk; sugar, a bowl and spoon, and breakfast was sorted. No more would I be at the mercy of the 'chefs' and their breakfast slop. Loaves of sliced bread, cheese and ham, margarine all put together, my toasted sarmies sizzling on an inverted iron wedged between two trommels, became lunch each day. SAWI-Suid Afrikaanse Weermag Industrie[32], a general dealer cum tuck shop providing sausage rolls and pies in the evenings. At weekends I was out and about playing football, providing us with the freedom to eat whenever and wherever we chose in town. Voila, no more army food for me.

So, life continued in Kimberley, as we played in a fairly tough regional soccer league. Lt Bernieri proving to be not only a nice guy, but also a very good football coach—some players in our teams being quite exceptional—we became respected opposition. We trained each weekday afternoon, and became accustomed to the sound of a crowd cheering in the stands on a Saturday afternoon, as the winning goal would etch a broad grin on the tanned, moustachioed face of Lt Bernieri, earning us delicious meals, beers galore and introductions to the local girls as we enjoyed many successes at the stadiums of local country clubs, and De Beers and Eskom.

Army life, I thought, was about as good as I could have hoped. Military Intelligence training turned out to be at least a little interesting from time to time, as a small group of us learned the identification, origins and practical use of Soviet, Eastern Bloc and Chinese weaponry. We became proficient users of the Kalashnikov assault rifle, the 'Avtomát Kaláshnikova', commonly known as the AK47, named for its final completion in 1947, and legendary due to the low cost of production, its simplicity, and reliability in harsh conditions.

We learned of the use of bakelite, a type of resin, in Eastern Bloc landmines and weaponry, in lieu of metals, making the instruments of death harder to identify by metal detectors, as well as providing the enormous benefit of not rusting. Raw intelligence gathering and synthesising techniques, observation techniques and skills, and of course, the clincher I shuddered to learn about, the science behind, and techniques perfected in the proliferation of misinformation and propaganda.

---

[32] 1 South African Defence Force Industries.

Following the end of the football season, our intrepid company commander had boldly volunteered all men, about 20, myself included, who had completed 'Counter Intelligence' training, for an imminent transfer to the Operational Area, i.e., the hotspot of South African military operations aiding in the fomenting of the Angolan Civil War. I was surprised, since I had hardly applied myself during the training, less so in the tests and examinations.

I had certainly not been a model student, not by any stretch of the imagination. If anything, I had been quite surprised that I had never been expelled from the course as sub-intelligent, based on my test results, or reprimanded as lazy or disinterested. Sitting in the 'NDP Saal'[33], I went cold as the words of that man sank in, an audible buzz of excitement surrounding me. We were to report to a classroom to have drafted by the law officer, a 'last will and testament', make arrangements to travel home for a seven-day pass. With seven-day some 'travel time' tacked on this would actually total nine days.

We were to return and await instructions. For purposes of security, we would not be furnished with a departure date or destination, and we were to notify families that we would be away for at least six months, during which time they would not hear from us. To suggest that I was not a happy camper would be to redefine euphemism. In a heartbeat the thing had gone horribly awry, and now more than ever before I needed to think clearly, to think on my feet, to manufacture a solution. My redefined goal in the army was to make it through the two years with as little fuss as possible. This development was not in any way aligned with my thinking.

---

[33] 1 Nationale Dienspligtes Saal—National Service-mens' Hall.

9. SWA—South West Africa

In 1915, during the South West Africa campaign of World War I, South Africa captured the German colony. After the war, it was declared a League of Nations Class C Mandate territory under the Treaty of Versailles, with the Union of South Africa responsible for the administration of South West Africa. From 1922, this included Walvis Bay, which, under the South West Africa Affairs Act, was governed as if it were part of the mandated territory. South West Africa remained a League of Nations Mandate until World War II and the collapse of the League of Nations.

The mandate was supposed to become a United Nations Trust Territory when League of Nations Mandates were transferred to the United Nations following World War II. The Prime Minister, Jan Smuts, objected to South West Africa coming under UN control and refused to allow the territory's transition to independence, instead seeking to make it South Africa's fifth province in 1946.

Although this never occurred, in 1949, the South West Africa Affairs Act was amended to give representation in the Parliament of South Africa to whites in South West Africa, which gave them six seats in the House of Assembly and four in the Senate.

This was to the advantage of the National Party, which enjoyed strong support from the predominantly Afrikaner and ethnic German white population in the territory.[9] Between 1950 and 1977, all of South West Africa's parliamentary seats were held by the National Party.[10]

An additional consequence of this was the extension of apartheid laws to the territory.[34]

The base seemed to stretch to the horizon with hundreds of rows of Cuban and Russian manufactured tents, PLAN (Peoples Liberation Army of Namibia) filled

---

[34] Wikipedia. *https://en.wikipedia.org/wiki/South_West_Africa*

with infantrymen in their hundreds, perhaps thousands, certainly a battalion perhaps more, it would be hard to say at a glance. There was an airstrip alongside an apron, upon which stood a predatory fleet of camouflaged Soviet MiG21 fighter aircraft, tents alongside to accommodate the team of crack DDR East German pilots. This was the size of a small town, including a maze of hospital tents, messes, latrine areas, parade grounds, fuel and munitions dumps, and completing the picture, columns of vehicles, waiting patiently, some armoured, some for transportation and then of course tanks, the Soviet T55 and gleaming new T62s, brought in because the old T55s had been no match for the mobility and firepower of the SADF vehicles.

This forward base, and many others like it, were filled with PLAN fighters, the soldiers of SWAPO, South West African Peoples' Organisation; MPLA, Cuban fighters and Soviet officers and advisors. The forces in many bases such as this one, just inside Angola on the border with South West Africa, eagerly awaiting the order to mobilise, ready to cross the border to drive the South African forces from South West African soil, completing phase 1. So vast were these armies that they would overrun the SADF, leapfrogging into the Republic of South Africa unopposed, quickly occupying the capital, Pretoria, driving white people into the sea, establishing an outpost with Nelson Mandela at its head, the ANC constituting a vital provincial branch to satisfy the voracious appetite of the *Kommunisticheskaya partiya Sovetskogo Soyuza* (Communist Party of the Soviet Union), to be overseen by the Politburo in Moscow. Counter Intelligence training had systematically sketched in my mind vivid pictures of such 'enemy' military facilities.

Yet such facilities did not exist. The 'facts' of the South West African and Angolan situation had been terribly misrepresented, the reality being a world away from the propaganda fed to us and the South African public. This, I learned quickly.

Glancing out of the Puma[35], I shouted to our escort, as loudly as I could above the relentless 'chack-chack-chack' of the engine, **"waar is die grens?"**[36], to which he responded by pointing downwards, almost directly below us. We were about to land in a South West African border town, and from the chopper high

---

[35] Military helicopter

[36] Where is the border? (South West Africa/Angola)

above, one could see for miles into Angola, the vista revealing nothing but dry, fairly sparse bush, not very different to the area around Kimberley, or Oudtshoorn for that matter. Certainly there were no tented cities bristling with armaments as we had been led to believe. Speaking in English he added "The rains are late this year. That's why it is so dry."

I asked naively: "Where are the enemy bases we had been told about?" Somewhat bemused, he asked about these 'enemy bases', and I felt quite stupid when he explained that bases on such a scale did not exist.

Corporal van der Merwe had been our escort, and after landing, we learned that he was in fact, to be more of a mentor to us in an intelligence office. He seemed to be a decent guy, very gentle, thoughtful and by all accounts very intelligent, speaking flawless English, albeit with a very heavy Afrikaans accent. Three of us had been sent from Kimberley to learn from three other intelligence office conscripts, their roles in and around the office, prior to hand-over when they would finish national service and return home.

On the first night, we had a beer with Corporal van der Merwe, and I asked many questions. He rejected as utter fiction, large forward bases ready to 'pounce', confirming that most 'bases' were SWAPO temporary fortifications, and were more 'hideouts' deep within Angola, than fully functioning bases, and were certainly incapable of launching full scale attacks across the border without such mobilisations being detected very early in the game.

Morning dawned, as I opened my eyes, scanning the tent in which we were sleeping, 'Spartan' springing to mind, the dusty smell once again almost desert-like. I needed to get out of here—this place would surely push me over the edge. After breakfast, we were ushered into the intelligence office, and introduced to a Captain Botha, and I quickly realised that the strict military protocols were not observed in the operational areas. I learned that most of these CSI (Chief of Staff Intelligence) Permanent Force officers and NCOs were not true military men, but university graduates whose rank was awarded, and progressed following a curriculum of courses in Pretoria.

Mostly Afrikaners, they were cut from a different cloth. None of the barking of orders was present, rank apparently unimportant in their interactions, and they all seemed to have a quiet air of confidence about them. It was at this point that I believe my 'education' re-commenced, as we underwent training each day, and chatted to our instructors in the evenings about the dynamics of the war in Angola. On the surface, the complexity of the war seemed immense, but when a highly intelligent officer spoke with me one evening, he simplified matters to the very lowest common denominator.

The apparent complexity of the dynamic was borne of the number of players in this theatre; SADF, SWATF, UNITA (National Union for the Total Independence of Angola), the American CIA, who had trained and armed UNITA, and in opposition SWAPO, FNLA, MPLA, Cuban soldiers, Soviet instructors and advisors, as well as the ANC. The 'elephant in the room', the simplified version, stripping away the layers, was to conclude that that this was a proxy war. USA and Soviets flexing muscles, without committing boots to the ground, the largesse of Fidel Castro's dramatic display of solidarity with oppressed nations, no doubt designed also to curry favour with Moscow.

South Africa, South West Africa; and the ANC and SWAPO, were little more than useful pawns providing temporary bulwarks in a game involving oil, diamonds and political posturing, the playing board being the globe for the long game, the short game—Sub Saharan Africa. There was one obvious thing which did prick my imagination, as I was warned on more than one occasion, to stay right away from the CSI stores, which was kept under lock and key at all times. No reason or explanation was ever provided, but many months later, my curiosity would be satisfied.

The beer, I noticed was extremely cheap, and with no restrictions on consumption, long chats late into the night ensued. One such evening led to Corporal van der Merwe sharing some of his experiences of his tour of duty. He talked of accompanying an infantry patrol across the river into Angola, on an intelligence gathering expedition, and some days later they walked straight into a Swapo ambush.

The South Africans, held their ground in a firefight. Swapo, realising that this could become a long, protracted affair, contrary to hit and run guerrilla preference, radioed for armoured assistance. The arrival of an armoured vehicle buoyed them for a while, until the South Africans did the unexpected—they went on the attack, killing and injuring a few SWAPO, whereupon the crew of the armoured vehicle abandoned their vehicle and fled on foot. This and similar stories confirming that the SWAPO fighters generally were poorly trained, operating on patriotic fervour, or fear, but not much else.

Prior to departure back in Kimberley, we had once again completed a mountain of paperwork, including various documents indemnifying the SADF from liability in the event of our deaths or injuries. What I also learned quickly, within days, was that my medical classification, within the framework of military law, precluded me from being physically far away from one of the 'big three' hospitals viz: No. 1 Military Hospital, Pretoria; No. 2 Military Hospital, Cape Town; No. 3 Military Hospital, Bloemfontein.

The exact distance from said hospitals seemed to be the subject of debate, some saying 100km, others, 50km. No matter really, since other than approval of security clearances, no-one had so much as glanced at our paperwork—until now. Captain Botha called me in one morning and apologised profusely for the 'fuckup', since Intelligence School had not considered my medical classification prior to transfer. He continued:

"Ons sal reelings tref, en jy sal verplaas word na Afdeling Militere Inligting in Pretoria. Ons kan nie dit waag om jou hier te laat bly nie."[37]

Again, he apologised, and promised that he would arrange a chopper or a vehicle to transport me to Grootfontein, where I would be booked onto a 'Flossie' (Hercules transportation aircraft), which would fly me to Pretoria, a large city, only about 50km from my home in Johannesburg. Hooray.

No need for apology, I thought, as my heart sang with that familiar wave of euphoria first experienced on the drive out of Infantry School, settling, seducing me as my facial expressions attempted to share the disappointment, very evident on the face of the captain.

I was relieved of the few duties I had inherited, and as with everything else in the army, once again it became a clear case of hurry up and wait. The waiting this time was a lot more palatable, given that no-one paid me much attention. I ate the finest quality steaks cooked over an open fire on some evenings, washed down with as much beer as could be managed. I had plenty of time to reflect, brought on by a real sense of well-being, and the more I thought about it, the more I was pleased that I was no longer required to be a part of the machine plotting the downfall of poor, illiterate, rural tribesmen.

These men who had had AK47s shoved into their hands and convinced that they were now freedom fighters in the Namibian War of Independence, the

---

[37] "We'll make arrangements for you to be transferred to Military Intelligence Division in Pretoria. We cannot risk having you remain here."
Afdeling Militere Inligting (Directorate Military Intelligence) under the control of CSI, Chief of Staff Intelligence.

backdrop of which was so far beyond their realm of comprehension, that white South African soldiers could just as easily have been from a different planet.

What I was able to ascertain while sitting around waiting for my ride, was that Captain Botha had assured me that I would be deployed within CSI somewhere in or around Pretoria. In all likelihood, it would be at the AMI headquarters in the Liberty Life Building, Vermeulen Street in the heart of the Pretoria central business district, or one of the satellite offices or facilities. So once again, my days were spent lazing around, napping, reading and not much else.

Evenings were for eating, drinking beer and chatting in the 'bar'. I'd heard a commotion in the early hours of the morning on a few occasions before, normally centred around operations into Angola and normally followed by very little, if any discussion. "Staan op, Staan op!" screeched the monster as he entered our tent. Although he was a 'korporaal', Corporal van der Merwe had proved to be no monster, and his shattering of the peace in our tent was really to assist me.

I'd been vaguely aware of some activity throughout the night, and the good corporal had rushed in to tell me to grab my possessions which had been packed and ready to go for what had felt like some weeks. Operating out of the base was 34 Battalion SWATF[38], many members of which were 'turned' SWAPO soldiers. A 34 Battalion patrol had engaged in a firefight on the Angolan side of the border, and a badly shot up SWAPO cadre was being transported into the camp while a Puma helicopter had been despatched to take him to hospital in Grootfontein, a small town and 'permanent' SADF strategic logistics facility some 200 km away. It was thought this cadre held a senior rank within Swapo, so it seemed important to do everything possible to keep him alive, for 'extraction' of useful information by Intelligence officers in Grootfontein.

The fear in the man's eyes as I looked at his pitiful, bloodied form, was overwhelming, as were the petrified doe eyes of the little children in Galashewe, whom I had dreamed about many times. "Why is he so afraid?" I shouted into the ear of the interpreter, competing with the noisy chack-chack-chack of the powerful turbine engine flicking the blades of the helicopter around at speed, the pilot flying fast and low. Having to repeat myself multiple times, eventually the man, himself a 34 Battalion ex Swapo fighter, smiled as the question became clear to him.

---

[38] South West African Territory Forces.

"He is afraid, because he has never seen a white man so close to him before," he chuckled, two perfect rows of glacier white teeth revealing themselves as he smiled broadly at me. This was my ride, the CSI 'killing two birds with one stone', as I was tasked to 'interrogate' this man in case he died prematurely before MID officers could get to him. I was, through the interpreter, to extract as much information as possible, recording in writing everything that was said. Our man turned out to be a veritable treasure trove of information, confirming that he was indeed a Swapo PLAN officer.

So eager was he to provide information that I questioned that very thing, my interpreter telling me in English, exposing again another toothy grin, that he had explained to our man how I would throw Swapo soldiers from the open doors of the helicopter if they did not cooperate. Did people actually do that? I later learned that the practice of taking a few prisoners up in a chopper, throwing one out at altitude would loosen the tongues of his comrades.

Barbaric behaviour such as this would be carried out by so called normal people in the course of a 'normal' day's work; boys or young men who could have been at school with me, perhaps a neighbour, or worse still—a cousin or family member. The twisting of societal norms when a military machine takes hold of a mind is very real, incredibly frightening, and for those who've not experienced life in a military establishment may be viewed as surreal or even fiction borne of fantasy.

Not a shift, but a twist, since that which was seen as good is now bad, and that behaviour hereto which was bad is now good. A whole new set of brotherhood rules, with an overarching mantra, "these are our principles, and if they no longer produce the desired effect, then don't worry, we do have others!"

10. Brakkie

SADF Non-Commissioned Officers Army Rank, based on British military protocol.

Lance Corporal

Corporal

Sergeant

Staff Sergeant

Warrant Officer 2 (Sergeant Major)

Warrant Officer 1 (Sergeant Major) More senior.

The mould which had been perfected over time for the SADF Sergeant Major (A Warrant Officer or Senior Non-commissioned officer—NCO) would ordinarily reveal the finished product to be a middle aged, portly, hard drinking, red faced, moustachioed, grumpy 'Dutchman'. His voice would have learned to be louder than all others, the barbs contained therein would exert discomfort bordering on a mild pain inflicted upon the ears of the captive victim of his sardonic vitriol.

The range of his vocabulary would certainly have diminished directly proportionately to the number of years he'd been institutionalised, ordinary or normal phraseology making way over time for very little other than cynical, expletive-encrusted epithets with no purpose other than to insult or belittle, and of course, to amuse officers (his superiors) within earshot of the theatrics. The elliptical physical nature of the creatures made it difficult to believe that these men had proved themselves on the battlefield as section leaders.

A reasonably intelligent schoolboy can be transformed into a second lieutenant in a matter of weeks, should that be required. Surviving a few months of action, he might well make a competent platoon or company commander. A civilian with suitable skills can be transformed into a junior staff officer even more quickly with considerable success. All of these things have been achieved historically by various armies in which an urgent need has arisen. An outstanding senior NCO, however, takes years to mould and it is experience that makes him what he is.

Consequently, there can be no short-cuts other than intensive, extended combat experience in the role of section leader, directly responsible for the lives of a dozen or a few dozen men in his care. Perhaps the physical appearance and demeanour of these Sergeant Majors to whom I had been exposed were nothing more than a manifestation of Post-Traumatic Stress Disorder infused with a little 'self-reward' system involving excesses of food and/or alcohol.

The size of the ego attached to these men should also not go without mention. Despite not being officers, they wielded (or were perceived to wield) enormous power, instilling dread and fear into the hearts of troops and junior NCOs alike, and they seemed immune to orders or instructions from officers, all of whom held superior rank.

Disembarking from the Flossie (Hercules C130 aircraft) on the apron of the runway at Waterkloof Air Force Base, my heart skipped several beats as the sight of a Sergeant Major greeted me. Not only was this a Sergeant Major, but the insignia indicating his rank (The coat of arms of South Africa appearing on each sleeve) screaming **Regimental** Sergeant Major—RSM—the coat of arms insignias embedded in a bright red background, RSM's to be feared more than anyone else including God and Satan.

My peripheral vision quickly confirming that I was the last man standing on the tarmac as he stood, unflinching, steely blue eyes fixed upon my person, a lithe figure, leathery, battle-hardened, and icy cold. This was no rotund, stereotypical, theatrical smart-mouth Sa' Majoor, but a sleek fighting machine with a badly scarred face, just in case there was any doubt in the mind of the observer.

As I approached him, I was, in an instant, a 'roof' back at the Infantry School in Oudtshoorn, shaken, uncertain, and once again overcome with fear, as the figure awaiting my arrival was without question, the 'real Mcoy'. Marching smartly while carrying, as best I could, my luggage and paraphernalia, I put down on the ground my 'balsak' kit bags and a few other items occupying my hands, I presented myself, driving the heel of my right boot into the asphalt as I came stiffly to attention. '**RSM**' I stated loudly, confidently, as my arms stiffened and my chest puffed, as I 'strecked' (acknowledge with stiffened arms at one's side and chest puffed) the RSM, who not being an 'officer', was not worthy of being saluted.

The disbelief and surprise on my face would surely have amused him, as I responded to his gentle, almost timid greeting, 'Ontspan Steyn'[39], as he implored me to dispense with the military formalities as he reached out to shake my hand, stepping forward in a motion to relieve me of some of my cumbersome luggage. One surprise after the other, as relief overcame me and I was driven to the SAMS[40] barracks by my own personal driver, RSM 'Brakkie', a nickname meaning 'street dog or mongrel', displayed a somewhat disfigured face. DMI had no barracks facility to house troops or personnel, so the DMI Guards were housed at the SAMS barracks in Voortekkerhoogte, a military village on the outskirts of Pretoria.

Driving along in Brakkie's army issue sandy coloured **pickup,** that awful mantle of foreboding which had instantaneously enveloped my soul on the apron at the airport, gently let go as the familiarity of the bustle of busy roads in the capital city and the unmistakable smell of exhaust fumes entered my nose which had been exposed to nothing but the pure air of the bush in northern South West Africa for some weeks. I embraced the familiarity of these urban evils as the realisation struck me that I was home to stay.

Adding to my newfound tranquillity was the relaxed atmosphere as Brakkie enquired conversationally about my own background, family and military experiences thus far. It was he who explained that I was to be seconded to the DMI Guards, during which time I would be interviewed, undergo Psychological and Psychometric evaluation, while being assessed for a placement within DMI, aptitude and suitability being valued sometimes above military rank.

Brakkie was older, certainly well into his 50s or perhaps even 60, one could never tell with hardened military men who seemed to age rather quickly. He spoke in very gentle tones, always in Afrikaans, leading me to suspect that he

---

[39] 'Relax Steyn'

[40] South African Medical Services

was unable or unwilling to speak English, not unusual, as I was learning. The conversation certainly seemed cordial, two affable strangers forced together by circumstance, yet somehow quite comfortable sharing experiences, he talked of how he had been a career soldier and had later been seconded to the Ciskei Defence Force as Sergeant Major of the Ciskei Army.

This, I found intriguing since I had not been aware that Ciskei has a defence force or army, as he gleefully shared his vast knowledge, explaining the detail of how all 'Homelands' had defence forces.

In my mind, the 'Homelands' had always been artificially constructed theoretical nation states synthesised by ethnic groupings, a country for the Zulu, another for the North BaSotho, South BaSotho, Xhosa, Tswana, Venda, Tsonga, Shangaan, Swazi and Ndbele nation states. Each homeland housed its own parliament, judiciary, police force, military and entire civil infrastructure, so theoretically, each was a self-contained, self-governing sovereign state. The drive to the barracks took some time, as the vehicle fought its way through the Pretoria peak hour traffic, as we listened to traffic reports and news broadcasts on the radio, all in Afrikaans of course.

Arriving at SAMS, Brakkie personally gave me the guided tour of the place, firstly showing me to the barracks where I deposited my gear. I couldn't help but notice the casual air pervading the place as men greeted the RSM, respectfully, but in a relaxed manner. I began to recognise some of the men as those with whom I had trained in Diskobolos at Intelligence School. Brakkie showed me the mess, the bar, tennis courts, explaining that we were welcome to take a short walk into the village of Voortrekkerhoogte, where there would be a supermarket, café, some takeaway food stores, and a petrol station, which made me suddenly realise that I needed my car, and more of a comfort, we were only about 30–40 minutes away from my home, traffic dependent.

After dinner, some of my old mates persuaded me to join them in the bar for a few beers, which turned out to be more than just a few, and I certainly had a good laugh, as I realised just how relaxed these fellows were, having no military ambitions at all, now content with their lot while they marked time until the conscription period would be completed. Those who didn't live too far away were able to spend every third day and night at home, and were subjected to very little 'rondfok'. Taking a good, objective look around, I knew in an instant that there were certainly much worse places to be in the SADF.

Pretoria: the seat of Government in the Old Transvaal during the Anglo Boer War, and the administrative capital of Apartheid South Africa. It is situated in the northern province of what is known today as Gauteng.

11. The Final Destination, an Office Job on 'Civvy Street'

The darkness of the night combined with the frosty air causing my skin to 'creep' momentarily as I was struck by a fleeting awareness of that rare, absolute blanket of silence, 'amplified' perhaps because this was suburbia in the heart of the country's capital city, Pretoria. No insects, no breezes causing trees or shrubs to stir, no rustling of dry leaves, no rumbling of traffic in the distance, nothing. It was shortly after 02h00, late in the winter, when it seemed that the icy air bit into your very bones.

Despite wrapping from head to toe, exposing only eyes through the window of the balaclava, and hands in order to attend to the fine motor coordination actions required when operating and firing an assault rifle, the cold invaded little by little. This was guard duty, and my 2-hour beat was simple, the safekeeping of the occupant of one of the luxury rondavels.[41]

The little building being round, meant that I was walking literally in circles. No detail had been provided around the subject of our protection, but, seeing him ambling through the gardens upon our arrival in the late afternoon, I recognised immediately the unmistakable large, heavy, bearded presence of a black man whose photos we had studied during counter intelligence training. A not quite middle-aged man who exuded an infectious grin, exposing what appeared to be more gleaming white teeth than were contained in the mouth of any other man.

There was no doubt in my mind that this was Jonas Savimbi, flamboyant, enigmatic leader of UNITA (National Union for the Total Independence of Angola), a guerrilla army opposed to the post-colonial political status quo in Angola. He was enigmatic, because in classic Orwellian type, he had at some

---

[41] Very traditional, African, round cottage or hut, usually with a thatched straw roof. Many hotels and game lodges housed guests in upmarket luxury versions.

point been a member of his arch enemy organisations the MPLA as well as FNLA (National Liberation Front of Angola). Who was this chameleon who had accepted aid and assistance at different times from the USA, South Africa, USSR, and Communist China?

At that moment in 1985, he wore the mantle of 'anti-communist', and was 'in bed' with Pretoria's racist government, engaged in strategic talks while being hosted by the South African Military Intelligence at the 'Kop', a suburban convention/training facility with 5-star hotel quality accommodation, for CSI staff conventions, covert or sensitive meetings, or for those involved in training for operations or in training to progress through the ranks. While I listened through the window which stood slightly ajar, to the thunderous snoring of this rotund man, I had thought that he had probably very rarely slept in accommodation such as this, having for many years, been a bush dwelling guerrilla leader.

It occurred to me that I could change the course of history possibly ending the Angolan Civil War, and overnight, become the darling of MPLA and their close allies the ANC. Fleetingly, I wondered that night if this had not perhaps been my destiny. I contemplated the actual act of moving the safety catch on my rifle from S-safe to A-automatic. Threading my rifle through the window while pushing aside the curtain, having all the time in the world to adjust my eyes to the dark in the cottage, I would smell the distinct wild African dry grass thatching and creosote beams which was the rustic roof, while lining up the target, aiming and pressing the trigger.

My mind seemed removed from my person as it engaged in some mental arithmetic, trying to calculate how long it would take 35 rounds housed in the rifle magazine to be expelled if the rifle could fire at 500 rounds per minute. I figured that 35 was roughly two thirds of 50, so if the rifle fired at 50 rounds per minute it would take two thirds of a minute, about 40 seconds. Extrapolating, I estimated that 35 rounds would take a mere four seconds. It would be very quick indeed.

Then I timed four seconds quietly under my breath; one Mississippi, two Mississippi, three Mississippi, four Mississippi. A long time indeed, particularly on a deathly quiet, icy night, when Jonas Savimbi would have enough time to awaken and be fully conscious of what was happening to him, alerting twenty or more guards, armed intelligence men and in fact, intelligence women, to find out about the commotion and arresting yours truly.

Of course, I'd known I did not have it in me to kill another human, but the exercise made my mind forget the cold, the two-hour watch passing quickly as I meticulously planned the assassination. Savimbi saw his end in battle in 2002, killed by his erstwhile comrades and long-standing enemy, the MPLA. Considered today to be one of the most effective guerrillas of all time, he was at the head of UNITA, fighting in the Angolan bush for almost 40 years.

I had been seconded to the 'Guards' and I would be guarding people or buildings in the so-called prestigious *'AMI Wag'*—Afdeling Militere Inligting Wag, 'Directorate Military Intelligence Guards'. Progress at a snail's pace in the army of course was deemed 'progress' nonetheless, and yet again it was hurry up and wait. Being in the 'Guards' was not all terrible, given that on a rotational system one was on duty for 24 hours while standing 'beat', for 24 hours on leave, those living within easy reach, free to go home, and then 24-hour standby in the camp in readiness for the 'shit to hit the fan', playing tennis, sleeping, drinking beer, swimming, or taking a short walk to the shops in Voortrekkerhoogte.

These, of course, were the things people do in readiness for civil war—or while on holiday. Standby was such a 'loose' arrangement that within no time at all I had calculated that to round up a full platoon in such a large camp, some indeed perhaps having spilled into the village, could conceivably take an hour or more, since no one had really thought to install a siren or some such-like warning system to bring the troops together for an emergency response.

I certainly was not going to be the one to make such suggestions in light of the fact that I lived about 40 minutes away by car, and a friendly comrade, armed with some coin could easily phone me at home while on 'standby' giving me ample time to return for the war. Other fellow servicemen who were not so fortunate to live nearby found the whole experience quite monotonous, some displaying entrepreneurial skills, selling the one commodity which they had in abundance—time.

For a fee, they would slot into a roster, and do duty for whoever was willing to pay. So, for the writer, my three-day cycle evolved quickly into three days off, cycle after cycle after cycle, popping in to the base from time to time to make payments, further arrangements and generally to show my face.

It was a warm, early spring afternoon when the telephone shrieked. I leapt from the couch, a very stern voice on the line causing that awful feeling, accompanied by the free fall of all your organs into the pit of your stomach. It was our CO, Lieutenant Homan. He spoke quietly, deliberately and without any traces of anger or frustration. I had been at home for a number of days, some legally, mostly not. This was definitely a guard duty day, a day on which I should have been turned out in my uniform, weapon in hand, protecting a 'strategic' DMI site.

No mention was made of any of this, only what seemed a somewhat apologetic request for me to return without delay to the base in Pretoria. The 'banana yellow' 1500cc Nissan Langley had never been driven at the very edge of its capabilities, certainly not as it was driven on that day. Both car and mind sped almost out of control, all my indiscretions had been 'rumbled', I was to be arrested immediately, sleeping in a detention barracks at the pleasure of the provost and Military Police, then within days, marched before a 'Court Martial', a raft of charges ranging from AWOL, gross dereliction of duty, aiding and abetting terrorism, and of course, the 'jackpot winning number'—desertion, the resultant punishment for which is death by firing squad. The anguish my family would endure, their son and brother causing indelible disgrace and shame to wash over them for generations to come.

Lieutenant Homan paced the sidewalk outside our barracks as he awaited my return. My car roared up to the barracks. I jumped out and ran over to him still dressed in my civilian clothing. He barely hesitated as he motioned for me to accompany him quickly to his waiting car, a white army issue Datsun Stanza, which he referred to as the 'Porsche', always exaggerating the final syllable as he would talk affectionately of his *'Porshay'*. There was none of the light-hearted banter on that day, only the earnest, deliberate haste of the man as he ushered me with my 'kit' into the car.

Lieutenant Jan Homan, our new commanding officer, was a little younger than I, and in so many ways we occupied opposite ends of a scale. The son of WO1 Homan, the Sergeant Major of the South African Army, the most senior Warrant Officer in the South African Army, his father was responsible for the discipline of the entire army. Here was an ostensibly Afrikaner boy with an English name, raised in a household whose father was conceivably the strictest disciplinarian in the country, militaristic to core, a professional soldier, clearly having swallowed the Nationalist racist party line without a hint of objection or question.

His son, by all accounts had followed suite, and at the ripe old age of 20 was a committed Permanent Force officer, running around barking instructions to young kids who frankly, couldn't care less, since these were the rejects of Intelligence School, manning the so called 'prestigious' *AMI Wag*.

Strangely enough, the good lieutenant and I got along rather well, him possibly recognising that I was a little older, and perhaps in the old-fashioned Afrikaner tradition he afforded me a measure of respect. He was certainly not unpleasant or unintelligent, and I felt that he sometimes sought my friendship. I was unsure of the reason why, but we would chat at length deviating this way and that, debating issues, with me maintaining the necessary decorum, not always revealing to him my truest, deepest feelings.

Seated beside him, in my 'civvies' in his car driving hastily to who knew where, I felt a deep uneasiness coming over me. I soon realised that we were taking a route to the Pretoria CBD, and he started to speak. Lieutenant Homan's speech had always crackled with supreme confidence, often light-hearted, frequently containing a trace of sarcasm. None of those characteristics were present on that fateful day as he finally let it out: "Your friend 'Estment' has hanged himself in the Cinderella Prison in Boksburg."

"How?" I asked, sadness and anger combining to cause me to want to scream at this man now.

"I'm not sure of the detail," he responded meekly.

"You know that I blame the army for this!" I spewed, his reaction one of silent contemplation. Craig Estment, just a decent fellow from a modest background, had indeed been a good friend, the two of us having met at Intelligence School in Kimberley. It had been early days for me, when I noticed one Saturday night, Craig, whom I barely knew at the time, was sitting on his bed diagonally opposite mine, the dark rings around his eyes betraying his normal jovial disposition, as he remained motionless for a long while like a person with something weighing heavily on the heart. I jumped off my bed, the top bunk, and asked him what was up.

Bleary-eyed he looked at me like a helpless little bird that was injured and frightened. "It's my dad," he said.

"They think he's very ill. I've just got off the phone with a neighbour saying he was picked up by an ambulance and no-one seems to know which hospital he's in." Craig had approached the duty officer, to be told that he could see the welfare officer on Monday morning.

"Bullshit," I seethed, instructing Craig to come with me as we sought out the RSM Blignaudt, whose house was actually in the middle of the camp. Craig was horrified as we approached the door.

"We can't talk to the RSM," he retorted, by now a quivering mass of nerves. Boldly I knocked on the door which was quickly opened by the particularly portly Sa' Majoor. I apologised for the intrusion, then confidently introduced my friend who needed to travel to Johannesburg without delay, as his father was critically ill, and the other fact was that Craig had no mother or siblings, with his dad living alone.

"Sonder twyfel!"[42] boomed the NCO. *"Gaan haal vir my jou pasboek, jy kan onmiddelik ontrek."*[43] The look of astonishment on Craig's face was priceless, as we thanked the Sa' Majoor, and ran back to the barracks to get the magic ticket in the form of a pass book. I handed my keys to Craig, and instructed him to take my car, since he did not own a car. Despite recovering from that particular episode, Craig's dad's health declined steadily, and he'd been given a transfer to the guards in Pretoria to be closer to home. We immediately rekindled our friendship when I arrived in Pretoria, Craig arranging a bed for me alongside his in the barracks.

I had brought a portable TV and we would lie on our beds and watch *Mike Hammer*, *Magnum PI*, and a host of other favourites in the evenings. When the weather was foul, I would drive Craig to Johannesburg for our 'day off' since the motorway would be a nightmare on stormy days for motorcyclists. I met his girlfriend, a student at the university, a very gentle, introverted soul, much like Craig.

With the rapid deterioration of his dad's health, Craig had repeatedly driven home from Pretoria at breakneck speeds on his 500cc Honda to his ailing father when he'd collapsed or was unable to get up from the bed. Numerous requests to be transferred to a unit in Johannesburg where he could sleep at home, providing assistance and support for his dying father, seemed to go unnoticed. Craig hadn't had the financial means, or one suspects, the presence of mind to pay others to stand in for him on duty days, which, although highly illegal, to a large degree would have solved his problem. On several occasions, Craig had gone home and simply not turned up for guard duty. AWOL, Absent Without Official Leave, was written onto the roster, and sadly, more than once, following arrest, Craig had done some time in the detention barracks, where I had visited, taking him shampoo, shaving cream, biscuits and some other 'nice to haves', hopefully, easing his burden, even slightly.

---

[42] "Without a doubt!"

[43] "Go and fetch your pass book (for signature) you can leave immediately."

Either Lt Homan was aware of my little scam, turning a blind eye, or he simply did not know. I could not say which, as he apologised for calling me at home on my 'day off', explaining that we were on our way to the Provost Officer at DMI, who would 'debrief' me following the unfortunate death of my friend. The debriefing concluded quickly enough, the Provost Officer, a National Serviceman Lieutenant, law graduate, asking questions of me, making notes and then thanking me for my time. Lt Homan drove me back in silence to the base in Voortrekkerhoogte, making no mention of my absence from the camp for days on end, so I concluded that he had no inkling of the number of times I had been AWOL of late.

A mixed bag, I was in the clear, but my poor friend was dead, having hanged himself, I suspected due to the torment of being faced with yet another spell behind bars, this time, potentially several months, while his father edged ever closer to his final days. The time spent behind bars would be tacked onto the 24 months of national service, I was sure, leading to a complete breakdown of Craig's mental and emotional state. The severity of the event led me to be a little circumspect for the next few days, slotting back into a normal, legal routine. I had pushed the envelope, and decided that Lady Luck could not smile on me forever.

12. Let the Truth Reveal Itself

'Military intelligence' while it is often joked, is a contradiction in terms, has attracted as many definitions as there were and continue to exist today, the number of intelligence agencies in South Africa and indeed in most countries around the world. Army, air-force, navy, police, tax revenue office, secret police, special forces, as well as government departments, all involve themselves in intelligence gathering, intelligence synthesis, espionage, counter-espionage and proudly, secretively, boast 'dirty tricks' departments under various guises. It is in this vast sea of currents and undercurrents that the waters are muddied, lines distinguishing friend from foe blurred, facts concealed, fiction offered up with bowed heads and outstretched arms on golden platters foisted upon the naïve and unsuspecting as gospel truth.

The air in the corridors was a little stuffy. There was a low background murmur of voices intermingling with quiet music and different radio stations emanating from different offices, in the somewhat Spartan but reasonably modern maze on the 8th floor. The ambience belied the fact that this was in fact a military establishment. Many people both old and young were going about their business in civilian clothing. Very few were in military attire which ranged from army, air force and naval uniforms to the uniforms of old fellows called Pioneers. I was no longer in the 'Army' per se. I was, and had been since my short time in South West Africa, in the 'Directorate Military Intelligence', a gleaming, apparently sanitised arm of the military, but in reality, a dark evil beast, into whose belly I was about to be thrust, this being my 'home' for the next 14 months.

I was an administrative placement at DMI, my position being contingent upon a security clearance: 'Secret' grade. Applications, interviews and psychological evaluations all satisfactorily completed, I was shown to my own office and duties were explained, the perfect way for a pacifist conscript to quietly see out my two years. The work, although quite mundane, involved documentation revealing details of people's lives, ranging mostly from insipid to bland, almost formulaic in the vapid descriptions of their very lives.

Born in "… place and date… attended school… avid churchgoer, plays sport, loves reading and movies… is very ambitious and really wants to make a difference in his country, 'volk en vaderland' (people and fatherland). The occasional welcome appearance of a file containing the details of a colourful personality, making for a brighter day, but in reality, these were few and far between."

Johannesburg and Pretoria are separated by a motorway allowing fast moving traffic, encouraging many to commute to work in one while living in the other. And so, it was with me, commuting to Military Intelligence HQ in Vermeulen Street in Pretoria, Monday to Friday. Enterprising as always, I'd arranged to be transported by a Toyota Hi-Ace 10-seater minibus, courtesy of the DMI vehicle pool, serviced, maintained, insured and fuelled at the expense of the taxpayer.

I had bought a modest house in Sunny Ridge, a typical leafy, working class suburb on the outskirts of Johannesburg, made possible through a government mortgage subsidy scheme for school teachers, and in fact, almost all white employees of the state. The vehicle, although a blessing, was granted to me to ferry seven or eight Permanent Force DMI personnel in the mornings, from a collection point in Birchleigh, Kempton Park, a satellite town of Johannesburg, more or less on my route, dropping them off again in the late afternoon.

Now, some of these were military officers, others, civilians with special talents or skills, all dressed in civilian attire, some very 'chatty' on the drive, more so when it was learned that I was the proud holder of a 'Secret' grade security military clearance. As time went by, tongues loosened a little, so I was 'accepted' into the 'Intelligence Community', and sponge-like, I began to soak up information.

Gradually, I was trusted more and more in the secretive halls of power which meant more freedom to wander around the maze of offices which was the DMI and on the 8th floor, Counter-Intelligence, ostensibly the cerebellum of the mighty South African military machine, the largest and strongest on the continent. The ever-increasing trust which I enjoyed led to additional work which, as time went by, became more sensitive. Files containing sensitive information started to cross my desk each week, the contents of which were meant to be perused for context only, for purposes of collation.

Being a bit more enquiring, I was unable to 'peruse only', my voracious appetite for information getting the better of me more and more every day, as I gradually came to the inescapable realisation that this was one fucked up army, at the helm of which were some deeply disturbed individuals. Somewhat reminiscent of Shakespeare's often referenced 'appearance and reality', this time constituted for me a symbolic end of innocence, ushering in the early stages of a newfound cynicism, and a critical awareness of the duplicity interwoven into the very fabric of society, country, and indeed the entire continent.

This was 1985, and sworn enemies Iraq and Israel, were both surreptitious beneficiaries of largesse, courtesy of the South African industrial military machine. South Africa and Israel had co-operated closely on the development of nuclear and conventional weapons for a number of decades. While at the same time, Saddam Hussein's military had negotiated the purchase of G5 canons from Armscor, the South African manufacturer of military materiel. South African soldiers had been deployed for the training of Iraqi military personnel subsequent to the purchase, not to mention the provision of ongoing supply of munitions to Hussein.

I was in total disbelief as I read, over and over, until it sank in, the intricate details of how the CIA had furnished the South African authorities with the intelligence leading to the 'moment critique', when the trap was sprung, and Nelson Mandela and his 'accomplices' were finally netted.

This, when for two decades, American media had unequivocally been supportive of Mandela, condemning South Africa and leading international pressure to dismantle the apartheid machine, in so doing to release Mandela and his men from their Robben Island prison to take their place as political representatives of the majority of South Africans. And so, it continued, that which started as a trickle was now a tidal wave, nourished each day by new information, truths which seemed stranger than any shadowy fiction which might have been constructed by Joseph Conrad in his *Heart of Darkness* or intrigue woven by Ian Fleming.

Assassinations were planned, and many were carried out at Vlakplaas, a farm purchased for the purposes of 'eliminating undesirables', or planning elimination, including it was suggested, the assassination of Olaf Palme, Swedish Prime Minister, a possible reward for his liberal thought, rejection of the legitimacy of the South African apartheid government and support, both vocal and financial of the ANC. This place of evil, baptised 'Vlakplaas', in English,

'Shallow Farm', a seemingly nonsensical name, even somewhat innocuous, was camouflaged and concealed from the gaze of inquisitive onlookers who had no business prying into important matters, imperative to the safety and security of 'ons land'—our country.

Dirty tricks, I would learn, extended way beyond military matters. Some 1500 privately-owned companies were systematically established to operate on the periphery of the military machine, funded and established to keep the machine rolling, including Armscor and its allied companies, Atlas Aircraft, Kentron et al. In many instances, these hundreds of peripheral companies not only profited from the sale of goods to Armscor, but also from investments Armscor made in their businesses, thereby subsidising the development of weapons and materiel that could be sold for profit on the international stage.

Pariah status meant that the country had, to all intents and purposes become economically isolated, with embargoes and sanctions being the order of the day, rendering these international arms deals illegal. I learned that the dark hand hovering above, orchestrating almost all matters was a mysterious organisation called the *Afrikaner Broederbond* (Afrikaner Band of Brothers), ensuring prized contracts of varying shapes and sizes were awarded to its disciples.

Driven now by a siege mentality, the *'Bond'* as it was innocuously termed had been formed by Afrikaner men in 1918 to alleviate poverty among the white Afrikaner communities, reeling as a consequence of the 2nd Anglo-Boer War, World War I, the Spanish Flu, a high rate of illiteracy and unemployment, with Calvinist Christianity and Nationalism at its heart.

By the 1970s and 1980s, the organisation had successfully entrenched its existence and it's secretive character, but morphed into something much, much more, now more akin to and unashamedly like the Freemasons, or indeed a mafia, all the while providing from its ranks, leaders in all fields, no longer intertwined in society, but inexorably controlling the country including the economy, the military, education, judiciary, police, infrastructure, and political machinations to the point whereby every prime minister since 1948 had graduated from the ranks of the bond. The Broederbond had redefined collaboration, collusion, and in fact corruption.

13. Two Cities

National socialism, wrote Emile Lederer in 1937 in the Annals of the American Academy of Political and Social Science, is an economic system based on a totalitarian concept of the state to which everything—economics included—must conform, under coercion if necessary. [44]The ANC should be credited for its successes, racial justice and democratic fairness in general, although, in my view the organisation has overplayed its hand in the equity stakes on the equal employment opportunity front.

The consequence of which has seen the emergence of cronyism in the form of 'jobs for mates'. On balance, the ANC has fallen short as an efficient government, and shining a light on the failure is construed by party apparatchiks as racism or unpatriotic behaviour.[45]

"The truth is that the apartheid government was just as crony-capitalist and corrupt as the government of today. The economic policies of the ANC and the apartheid state's National Party government are almost identical, and have a lot in common with national socialism. National socialism, wrote Emile Lederer in 1937, in the Annals of the American Academy of Political and Social Science, is an economic system based on a totalitarian concept of the state to which everything—economics included—must conform, under coercion if necessary."

"Half of the white population had protected jobs in the public sector, complete with dinky little government-subsidised houses. Many of the rest would get rich working for the Broederbond-controlled big business cartel. In

---

[44] Emile Lederer in 1937 in the Annals of the American Academy of Political and Social Science.

[45] The writer

the face of the glaring racial injustice. What was less frequently noted was that the prosperity-generating private sector was in fact tiny.[46]

White people living on the South African 'highveld' (A plateau some 1,800m above sea level) would boast that the climate is amongst the best in the world, matched by a quality of life which attracted thousands upon thousands of young white immigrants from Europe seeking their fortunes. Hillbrow in Johannesburg becoming a destination of choice through the 1960s and 1970s, resulting in the area at one time tagged 'the most densely populated square mile on the planet'. Houses and townhouses long being a thing of the past, high-rise apartments reaching into the sky, both old and modern, blotted out the sun until the urban jungle could be illuminated from directly above only for a brief couple of hours late morning 'til mid-afternoon.

Dusk would herald the sea of lights on the streets, the bright illuminated signs advertising the multitude of cafés, bars, and nightclubs enticing locals to let their hair down and enjoy, laughter on the streets, the hooter of a Vespa, absolute hustle and bustle, as chic folk made their way to a disco, restaurant or bar. Drawn by the lifestyle and an abundance of job opportunities, these young folk, mostly British, Greek, Italian, Portuguese and German would change the complexion of the area slowly but surely.

They would bring with them fashion, hairstyles and a nocturnal lifestyle, culinary and hospitality influences which would see an eruption of establishments with exotic European flavours: Café Zurich, Mi Vami, The Goblet, Hotel Moulin Rouge, Peppermint Park, The Continental Restaurant, Barbarrelo's, Munchner Haus, Undergound at the Chelsea, and many more would enjoy enormous success thanks to armies of loyal patrons who welcomed a glitzy, modern European way of life, teenagers and young adults flocking from the 'tame' suburbs to immerse themselves in life amongst the bright lights on the hill after dark, where festivities would continue until the small hours. Johannesburg would never be the same again, as the influences spilled over to adjacent Rocky St in Yeoville, Rosebank, Braamfontein and indeed, the Johannesburg city centre.

By virtue of their Caucasian attributes and features, these immigrants were an automatic 'shoe in', enjoying a huge welcome upon arrival in South Africa,

---

[46] Ivo Vegter, Daily Maverick, 21 August 2012.

the government delighted to be increasing the white population by 'acquisition', immediately bestowing upon them the benefits of the privileged (white) class which, no doubt many would relish. Sadly, along with their newfound appreciation of a remarkable quality of life, many would adopt the uninhibited, overt habit of the racism of locals, sadly some with more than a small measure of enthusiasm.

One tried to imagine the thoughts running through the mind of a middle-aged black man overhearing an unfamiliar language spoken by a 20-something white man, newly arrived and adorned with all the rights, when he himself was unable to rent an apartment in the area, visit a local restaurant for a meal, or even in a case of extreme need be shooed away from a public toilet bearing the status 'Whites Only'!

Such was the anomaly of this, the most duplicitous of lands. Many of these immigrants would start families, putting down roots and prospering, some becoming very successful, some to become wealthy, most retaining dual citizenship. Some would simply enjoy the ride until it seemed imminent that the house of cards was beginning to teeter, at which time they would simply bid their new friends a fond farewell, returning home, or moving on to the next adventure.

The cities of Johannesburg and Pretoria both nestle into the 'highveld', statistics revealing little to no winter rainfall, the general area being not particularly attractive nor unattractive, dominated by dry and dusty 'veld' (pronounced felt), open fields and 'koppies'[47] dotted by trees, and very few waterways, in many of which the water trickles desperately, some beds being dry for much of the year. The stark landscape is accompanied by stunning blue, often cloudless, skies, very little to no wind, boasting midday temperatures in the summer of 32–36 degrees, while often in excess of 23 degrees Celsius during the winter months, contrasting the icy cold nights and mornings at sunrise.

It was on such a day that my little portable radio crackled as it strained to pluck the 1.00pm news on Radio 702 from the multitude of stations competing for attention on MW—medium wave. At my lunch break, I had made a cup of instant coffee with powdered milk on the 'coffee tray' on my side credenza. Sandwiches were unwrapped as I gazed through the large window in my office. Absorbing the entire northern vista, a particularly clear day, I was able to identify

---

[47] Little hills/rocky outcrops

the Pretoria Zoo, the white working-class suburbs Capital Park, Wonderboom and Pretoria North in the distance.

The scene, although it was 'built-up' white suburbia, suggested gently undulating hills and undramatic, much like the rest of Pretoria. The weather, of course, was also undramatic. It was simply a beautiful day, much like the day before, and in all likelihood the day before that. Were one to scan the horizon of neighbouring Johannesburg, no major differences would be visible in the nature of the landscape or weather. It was unremarkable, undramatic, perhaps the envy of those living in the cloudy, often wet, cold, grey industrial areas in Europe or the UK. Undramatic of course, since that is how things had been orchestrated by the government for decades.

Drama did indeed exist in abundance, a seething hades, as tunnels and humans snaked and writhed in the pitch-black furnace underground beneath Johannesburg, in some instances up to almost four km beneath the earth's surface, more than two km below sea level, men toiled. White men, and black men, the white men being the bosses and supervisors, the black men providing the muscle for the backbreaking labour.

A beast of a sweatshop, a hell hole hotter than a sauna, the reef of gleaming gold ore as it burrowed it's way deeper and deeper toward the core of the earth enticing the mine owners and miners ever downwards. Promises of mishap and danger as the mining shafts and stopes edged further down into the beast's belly, was what the miners had to look forward to every day. At day's end, white supervisors and shift bosses would shower, dress, pop into the pub at the mine 'rec' for a beer and a chat with their colleagues before making their way home to their families, occupying highly subsidised mine houses, replete with all one would expect in a suburban home—an adequate number of rooms and amenities with a garden and conveniently of course, very close to work.

Low monthly expenses and being well paid meant disposable income for life's little luxuries like nice cars, boats, caravans and, of course, the South African institution—Christmas holidays at the seaside for two or three weeks each year, a real treat, since the mining belt was some 600km or more from the ocean. Life for a black miner, however, promised a very different existence. Relative to their white colleagues, these men were paid a pittance, and the end of the day would mean a walk to the compound, housing men only (wives and children not being permitted to live with the miners), the worst of the dormitories housing their inhabitants on concrete bunks, upon which men ate meals and slept, sometimes double, sometimes triple bunks with thin foam mattresses.

Later they were renamed hostels, with living conditions improved to a standard similar to an army barracks with a mess. There were communal showers and toilets, and constant noise as shift changes would have seen men active at all times of day and night, showering, chatting, moving around en masse. It was a maelstrom really, often a tinderbox, sometimes alcohol induced, sometimes ignited by tribal differences and centuries old hatred. Occasional brutal violence, accompanied by injury, even death, led to heavy handed responses from mine security or the South African police.

Annual leave time would see these mostly migrant miners returning to their distant homes, often rural, to see wives and children. It was not unusual to hear of rural families who had seen the men after a few annual visits home, never returning, and never hearing from them again, as the city of Johannesburg or, Jozi as it was known, would swallow them up, some ending up with new families, some turning to crime, some ending up dead or in prison.

The advent of migrant labour had been the kickstart for 'Absent Parent Syndrome', a condition which spread and embedded itself into black South African families, an invisible cancer, cruelly metastasising systemic dysfunction in black communities and societies across the nation. This led to dysfunctional families, dysfunctional societies, and as a sad, sad consequence, generations of dysfunctional individuals, capitalists unwittingly germinating a keen audience for Marx's 'emancipatory potential of the proletariat'.

These thoughts flooded through my mind, as I recalled visiting a mine as a high school student, dressing up in overalls, boots and a helmet with a light to show the way through the dark tunnels. Simulating a day in the life of a mine official, the tour group resurfaced, everyone showered, made their way to the 'rec' for the largest, juiciest steak I had ever seen.

Appetite satisfied, a talk followed to outline the benefits and prospects of joining the mine upon leaving school. The title of 'Learner Official', an apartment in the grounds of the residential part of the mine, a generous starting salary and annual leave, as well as initial exemption from military service, were all on the table for those white boys who'd been invited to the shindig. I shuddered, and snapped back into the present.

14. The Kid from the Country

"I wanted to help. Right. I meant it very sincerely. But I wanted to do it on my terms. And I am white, and they are black. I thought it was still possible to reach beyond our whiteness and blackness. I thought that to reach out and touch hands across the gulf would be sufficient in itself. But I grasped so little, really: as if good intentions from my side could solve it all. It was presumptuous of me. In an ordinary world, in a natural one, I might have succeeded. But not in this deranged, divided age. I can do all I can for Gordon or scores of others who have come to me; I can imagine myself in their shoes, I can project myself into their suffering. But I cannot, ever, live their lives for them. So, what else could come of it but failure?" [48]

My lunchtime memories and day-dreaming had been prompted by a file which lay opened on my desk, ready for completion. The photo of the security clearance candidate nonchalantly staring up at the ceiling was that of one Johannes Nkosi Nkwenkweze, a young Xhosa man born in a rural hamlet in the Eastern Cape Province, a little younger than me. Obviously, a bright child, he had been one of the fortunate ones chosen to attend a Christian Mission School, receiving glowing reports for his academic progress and by the age of 14, it seemed that university and unusually, a bright future, had beckoned for this fortunate child plucked from obscurity.

It was at about this time that his father who had long since disappeared somewhere in Johannesburg, stopped sending money home each month, as should have been expected. When payment became less and less frequent, his mother decided that the only course of action available to her was to travel to one of the big cities to take up employment with a white family as a maid or

---

[48] Andre Brink, lecturer and one of South Africa's most distinguished writers, both in English and Afrikaans, his gritty works exposing the apartheid machine for what it was through countless gripping novels.

nanny, sending funds home each week while she deprived herself of some of even the very basics in life.

She would however, take some comfort in the knowledge that her son Nkosi would be assured of a future having trained to be a lawyer, an accountant or perhaps a doctor, and it would be he who would halt the crippling spiral of poverty, taking care of his mother and siblings in a large modern home, where they would want for nothing, generations of hand to mouth subsistence farming and struggles fading into distant memory.

She had been away for some three years, returning for a long weekend every now and then throughout the year, and then two or three weeks over December when her white employers went to the seaside for their annual holidays. On her last visit, she had grown a little thin, even slightly frail, and when confronted she brushed it away as too much hard work, and the fact that missing her children weighed heavily on her heart.

One year she failed to appear for the holidays, sending word that her employers had elected not to go on holiday that year, but would allow her to take leave at a later stage in the year to make up for it. It was a few months later that news of his mother filtered back, and she was, it was said, very ill, soon to return home, and further, hushed voices suggested that the largely matriarchal society which was the nucleus of the small hamlet, might turn their thoughts to preparations for a funeral, and all the associated rituals.

As with many such things in life, a funeral for the Xhosa people involves rites which take time and money; money which would go some way to exhausting savings which would have at least seen the young man through his first year or two of study at a university. Now, the family would be left with very little in savings, and no source of income at all.

Family and neighbours in the little settlement were shocked beyond belief at the sight of the woman alighting from the dusty white minibus taxi, aided by a walking stick; her clothing covering most of her body, concealing seeping sores wrapped in bandages, a long dress hanging from her skeletal frame like a starved rag doll, she shuffled slowly like an octogenarian belying her 36 years. She spoke quietly in low tones, trying in fact to avoid speaking, as her children sat quietly in their hut at night.

The flickering candlelight accentuated what seemed to be large black moles covering her face, which, like many Xhosa, was not a dark-skinned face at all, but now seemed to be of another world. None of this made any sense at all, since when she left for the city, she had been an upright, buxom woman who would not shy away from or complain about working from sunrise until bed time, washing laundry by hand, cleaning house, cooking, tending to livestock, seeing to her children, assisting with neighbours' babies, helping the elderly in village.

Seldom taking a day off for herself, her existence consisted of toil, seven days a week, snatching moments here and there each day to chat, laugh and sing with the other women while they worked. [49]

Other women while they worked. What had ailed his mother, she never did say, and no-one asked. The women in the village talked quietly of this condition having been heard of recently in neighbouring hamlets, the common denominator being that the afflicted, both men and women, had become sick in the big cities. The accompanying notes compiled by his interrogators, stressed that Nkosi had been highly emotional when he relayed the story of his mother's last days.

In the days following the funeral, the village elders and matriarchs would spend more and more time with Nkosi, going to great lengths to ensure that he understood the gravity of the situation regarding finances and his schooling. Rural Africa had never had a need for orphanages, since it is unwritten in tribal lore that people take care of their own, every village woman being a surrogate mother to all children.

In the absence of their biological mother, the young ones would be cared for, but the financing of further schooling for Nkosi was simply a bridge too far, and he would need to return to the village to share in the workload and responsibility, any dreams of further education now eluding his grasp. With a heavy heart, he conceded that there was no other way forward.

In the days following, he settled into the dull routine which had defined life in the village for as long as anyone could remember, each day much like the previous day, and doubtless the coming day, day in, day out, week after week. Within a short time, the broadened horizons and incursions into abstract thinking which had come with education started to re-ignite the flame of desire in Nkosi's heart, having been reduced to smouldering embers with the death of his mother.

---

[49] 2017 estimates seem to concur that at the time there had been some 2,800,000 AIDS in South Africa, about 16% of children in the country, constituting 60% countrywide, the earliest known cases of HIV AIDS recorded in 1982.
https://borgenproject.org/10-facts-about-orpWolfgang-in-south-africa/

A restlessness set in as Nkosi started to question the old tribal ways borne of custom, supported only by superstition in a vain attempt to defy logic, reason and rational thought. Dogma perpetuating superstitions and devotion to the spirits of their ancestors, the elders struggled with Nkosi's dismissal of the traditional ways, seemingly disrespectful as it seemed an unstoppable force was on a collision course with an immovable object, so incompatible was the African way with western education, aspiration and ambition. Frustration and guilt, a natural by-product of such circumstantial ambivalence, and many hours of introspection drawing the 17-year-old to conclude that he needed to leave the place of his birth. He needed to leave soon, and he needed to go far away... as far away as possible.

Nkosi had heard from some that the money in mining, particularly for those willing to work underground, wasn't bad, and of course, there was the free accommodation to consider, and so with an overpowering sense of obligation, felt he owed it to his deceased mother and his younger siblings to leave his home in order to provide for the children, since the village would struggle to feed these mouths. He sought out those who had been to the big cities before and tried to find out as much as he could, so as not to appear a 'mampara' or 'ignorant country boy' upon arrival.

He was told that he should have an Afrikaans name, to make it easier for the white 'baas' (boss) to pronounce and remember. So, 'Johannes' would become his urban alias. Having drawn most of the remaining savings from the family bank account to travel to Johannesburg, he was able to secure work on a gold mine relatively easily, since he had almost completed his high schooling, and had school reports and letters of recommendation to prove it, and a literate 'kaffir' was quite unusual and potentially useful.

Although somewhat daunting at first, he settled into the role, quickly realising that the entire situation smacked of double standards, a situation he simply could not abide. He pleaded with the trade union shop stewards to become more actively involved in mass action for a better deal for the black miner, but was dismissed as a 'foolish country boy', which strengthened his resolve to intensify his resistant stance. Soon branded by mine management as a troublemaker, his attitude and behaviour becoming ever more militant.

After several encounters with mine security and the police, he found himself under arrest facing the wrath of a magistrate for breach of 'riot and insurrection' laws. Having had his 18th birthday, he was eligible for prison, where he was struck by the horrible treatment of black prisoners by white warders, treatment akin to the treatment of farm animals back home or worse.

Receiving letters being something of a rarity, he excitedly opened mail one morning to read of his dismissal from his job at the mine, which left him somewhat ambivalent, since his younger brothers and sisters would receive no more money each week. However, every fibre in his body screamed that he could not work under the conditions he had experienced.

Having grown up in rural Transkei, Nkosi recalled seeing very few white people, and these would only be people driving in their gleaming cars, passing through the countryside, some of them apparently very rich farmers from neighbouring South Africa. His village being considered part of Transkei, termed a homeland, Nkosi and his people were not considered South Africans, but natives of Transkei. He did recall thinking how unusual the white girls and women looked with their long, straight, flowing hair, never quite deciding if they were attractive or not, particularly the ones with the 'white hair'.

He had never had occasion to talk to a white person before, but now in prison, and after his experience in the mine he could say without doubt that whites were simply not nice people, perhaps even evil. It was abundantly clear that they harboured disdain for black people and made no attempt to hide the fact. He had heard of the ANC, but had not known anything about them other than one of the leaders was a black man named Nelson Mandela, from a nearby village in the Transkei it was said, who had been arrested, and was something of a saviour of black people, possibly more important than Jesus Christ, which was interesting, since he was definitely a white man.

Nkosi knew this as he had seen statues and pictures of Jesus Christ in the classrooms and chapel at mission school. It was in prison, that he started to learn about the ANC. Apparently, it was an organisation run by black people, whose aim it was to drive the white people out of South Africa by any means necessary, thus alleviating poverty, provide equal education for rich or poor, with jobs and homes for everyone.

This was an incredible organisation. His ears pricked up, and he wanted to know more. He was introduced to some ANC elders, who realised that here was a bright lad with a quick mind, suggesting that he might consider leaving the country to join the ANC and possibly be eligible for further training or education in one of a number of countries abroad which were sympathetic to the ANC cause.

Now this kind of detail, I noted, was seldom contained in these files, but the unusual nature of this applicant had warranted a full transcript of recorded interviews. His six-month prison sentence concluded, Nkosi had been whisked across the border into Botswana, and then to Angola for military training with Umkhonto we Sizwe (known as MK, The Spear of the Nation, military wing of the ANC).

It was here that his hatred of injustice reared its head again, when he dared speak up, publicly denouncing the behaviour of camp commanders who chose women at will, allowing no choice, fundamentally raping them, as well as showing ethnic favouritism and living the high life using ANC donor funds. For being too outspoken, he was sent to the notorious Camp Quatro, a place of punishment, and to all intents a prison camp, those in charge having been trained by the KGB. What followed was a period of brutality, emotional pain, hardship and torture at the hands of sadistic overseers.

When he had been 'retrained', he was returned to his training camp, training completed, he then went on to a transit camp in Botswana and after a long, frustrating period of waiting around, he could no longer bear the uncertainty, boredom and ill-tempered behaviour of his comrades, he mounted a daring escape, setting out to return to South Africa which he calculated was not too far away. Calling on all the survival techniques and crafts he had learned during his months of basic military training, he made his way towards the South African border, going to great lengths to cover his tracks.

Travelling under cover of darkness, he stole food, avoided people, and rested while in hiding in the bush during the day. One evening he decided to take a risk. Concealing himself on the back of a flatbed truck covered by a tarpaulin, he deftly hitched a ride without the knowledge of the driver who transported him a good distance, speeding his progress, and easing his mind that he was not being followed.

Regular reference to a compass and maps gave him comfort that they were travelling in the right direction. The truck then slowed, often changing gears and stopping from time to time. This alerted him to the fact that they had arrived in the industrial southern suburbs of Gaborone, the capital city of Botswana, very close to the border with South Africa. In the small hours of the morning, he quietly slithered unnoticed from the truck at a red traffic light, glad to be able to move around again, providing relief for his aching muscles. *Keep moving*, he thought, while he had cover of darkness.

He was unaware of the fact, that he had reached South African soil well before sunrise, but what he *was* well aware of was the fact that he had been aided by generous amounts of dumb luck. It was not long after he crossed the 'barrierless' border into South Africa, that this luck ran out and he was tracked down by a South African Army border patrol soon after sunrise, and following a brief chase, apprehended.

It was only when he came face to face with his hunters, that he realised they were white soldiers, reminding him that he was indeed in South Africa. He had stolen clothing along the way, discarding his MK camouflage combat fatigues, but, unable to find suitable footwear, had kept his boots with the distinctive tread of Soviet manufactured military foot-ware. Allowing his guard to slip just a little, sleep deprivation leaving him a little careless, his tracks had been noticed by an infantry patrol, and they gave chase, calling on a vehicle to head off their prey.

Having experienced treatment at the hands of white employers in the mines and white jailers in prison, his stomach heaved in anticipation of the treatment he was about to receive at the hands of white South African soldiers, his thoughts rushing to stories relayed about the gruesome treatment of legends of the struggle like Steve Biko, Griffiths and Victoria Mxenge, names he had heard in prison, all brutally murdered by the security apparatus. He felt a numbness overcoming his exhausted body and mind.

Soon realising that their newly-captured terrorist was a little different, displaying an extraordinary vocabulary and command of the English language, the intrigue probably got the better of his captors, and viewing him as prized spoils, he was treated accordingly, invited to shower, provided with a fresh T-shirt, and following a welcome sandwich and cup of coffee, he was escorted into the company administrative tent to be questioned by Captain Pringle, company commander of a citizen force unit, all members on leave from their usual jobs. Pringle, was a primary school teacher on leave from his teaching duties, completing an obligatory 'border stint' known in military parlance as a 90 day 'camp', looking forward to boarding a military aircraft home and back to work within the week.

He seemed quite relaxed in his approach to things which was quite typical of 'campers', a far cry from the brittle attitude of career soldiers. "You're amaXhosa, hey?" A smiling Pringle asked confidently in Nkosi's home language of Xhosa, knowing the answer before he'd asked. Nkosi was unable to contain his surprise. How would this 'Umlungu'[50] possibly know that he was amaXhosa, since he'd heard that all black people look the same in their eyes. This was the first Umlungu he'd come across who could speak his language flawlessly, having clearly mastered the different clicks representing consonants.

He couldn't help but feel a tinge of admiration, his heightened sense of anguish dissipating momentarily. 'Ewe Mnumzana' (Yes Sir), he responded timidly, nervously. "What is your name boy, and what on earth is a Xhosa boy doing here, more than a thousand kilometres from home?" he enquired, his interest piqued. It was in that instance that the realisation became clear to him that any story he tried to invent would be transparent and obvious bullshit, possibly turning the amiable disposition of his captor into one of unbridled anger, resulting in harsh treatment or even, as had happened to a defiant Biko, unbearable torture and death.

Nkosi had been on the run for so long, he'd lost track of the days, and sleep deprived, he thought he felt waves of fatigue induced hallucinations as the interrogation, although conducted in a more or less civil manner, continued late into the night. His entire life story relayed truthfully in detail to Pringle, he was to repeat again to an intelligence officer flown in by helicopter the next day. This time, his voice being recorded on a small machine, much like those he'd seen advertised in magazines when he was a boy at the mission school.

Nkosi later learned that Pringle had grown up on a farm, it would seem not too far from his own village. The name 'Pringle' might suggest to a genealogist that the captain's forebears were from England, on a boat carrying one of the many waves of 1820 settlers, who had largely been poor families, promised land and some financial assistance in order to construct farming communities across the frontier where British soldiers had been locked in battle with Xhosa tribes. His family would probably have farmed the area since their arrival.

Conversation revealed that Pringle had been great friends with the children of the farmworkers, gaining an understanding of their ways, and indeed a real mastery of the Xhosa language from the time he learned to speak. He was definitely aware of the difference in appearance of Xhosa and other black people in South Africa, so it seems that Nkosi's luck had held, even determining who his captor would be.

---

[50] White man, often used as a derogatory term.

Appearance and reality would become the overriding theme in the young life of Johannes Nkosi Nkwenkwezi. The reality, as he would learn, was a place far darker than the young man could have imagined as he innocently awaited his fate at the hands of men whose hearts were not only devoid of sympathy or the ability to embrace even a hint of empathy, but could also be said to be infused with evil, having become 'black', which is the antithesis of innocence manifest in a new born baby.

15. Askari

"Consent is meaningless if refusal is not an option."[51]

'Fear and insecurity', undercutting 'the formation of collective struggle.' This 'fear of punishment, of being killed, tortured or reduced to the mere level of survival [becomes] the government's weapon of choice.'[52]

I continued to absorb the contents of this, the most unusual of files, reading that Nkosi after a series of interrogations, casual discussions and psychological evaluation, was deemed to be a perfect candidate for 'turning'; persuading him to work for the South African Defence Forces or police. These turned ANC combatants were known as 'Askari'. This turning was based on his intelligence, but more importantly his knowledge of ANC structures, and of course, his disillusionment with the leadership in the ANC training camps, not to mention the resentment which treatment at Camp Quatro would have ignited.

A generous salary in the offing would ensure that he could once again provide financial support to his younger siblings, who had not heard from him since before he had been released from prison, some 14 months earlier. Psychologists' notes suggesting that his experiences had evoked in him very real emotional upheaval, anger at his father for abandoning him, anger at his mum for dying too soon, vacillating between a hatred for whites, a hatred for leaders in the camps, unspeakable guilt for not taking care of his siblings, all stacked against his own personal ambitions for a better life for himself.

The file of Johannes Nkosi Nkwenkweze was sent to counter intelligence for investigation for claims and verification of declarations, documents separated by people like me. They were to be removed from the file and distributed to the appropriate offices, the ensuing work carried out by highly trained and

---

[51] Saidiya Hartman (born 1960/1961) is an American writer and academic.

[52] Henry Armand Giroux, an American and Canadian scholar and cultural critic.

experienced 'field workers' who found ways to casually contrive and manipulate opportunities to make contact with former teachers, clergy, friends, family, employers, etc without arousing suspicion.

They would also check facts with registration offices to confirm dates of birth, names etc and indeed, any other information required by the COIN-ops (counter intelligence operatives). The information would be returned later to HQ with recommendations. Decisions finalised, offers made and accepted, the files would be collated, microfilmed, information and microfiche catalogued, original files stored for posterity in a cavernous safe, the custodian of which was an old Afrikaans civilian woman, Mevrou Lategan (Mrs Lategan) reverently, affectionately, referred to by all and sundry as Tannie (Auntie) who had worked for DMI it seemed for 100 years. The appropriate security clearance would then be issued... or not.

It was when Nkwenkweze's outstanding documentation made its way back to the 8th floor at DMI, eventually, the dossier complete, that I read Nkosi had been found to be totally truthful in all discussions—all details he had claimed, had been verified. Repeated bouts of interrogation, some heavy-handed accusations that he was, in fact, a spy for the ANC and the communists in Angola, as well as the frequent suggestion that the DMI had no need for 'live' ANC captives, led Nkosi to a state of deep depression, which was deliberately exacerbated by his captors whose demeanour ranged from indifference to hostile displays of derision, and at times extreme aggression.

Combined with frequent reference to his siblings and their suffering which would reduce him to tears, the strategy of the DMI operatives had apparently worked, and worked well. Notes made no reference at all to treatment which might be construed as torture of any description. Later, we learned that these captured MK combatants were exposed to the most barbaric torture imaginable, immediately dispensable once they had provided any information which might be seen to be of value.

What became of them thereafter was of no consequence to their captors, unless if they could be turned. Those who could not or would not be turned would be eliminated (killed), or condemned to a worse fate—being released into the world at large where they would be regarded with contempt and suspicion by their own who would assume, and rightly so, that they had spilled their guts, betraying their comrades. Here they would potentially be dealt with in a manner as brutal, or potentially more so than at the hands of the apartheid machinery.

Completely broken; devoid of any resistance, Nkosi agreed to assume an alias, undergo intelligence training, and avail himself to any task or mission required of him by any of the intelligence agencies in South Africa. His security clearance was issued, and it was agreed that his siblings would receive funding as part of his salary arrangement, the source of the funds remaining anonymous, a benevolent fictious relative would be created.

On release from incarceration, initially it seemed he would be absorbed into 'Counterinsurgency' C10, a police unit housed at Colonel Eugene de Kock's[53] notorious Vlakplaas,[54] and he was issued with a stern warning that his true identity was never to be revealed, he was not to make contact with family or people he knew, and the final warning, that if he ever betrayed his position, new comrades or handlers, he would be hunted down and hanged for treason, his siblings forfeiting their funding, indeed the entire village would be made to suffer. Nkosi had become **'Askari'[55]**.

As intriguing as it might have been, Nkosi's story constituted only a miniscule, yet integral act in a far bigger drama, as I would discover when I learned more about business in South Africa, the Broederbond way. The bedrock of the South African economy, of course, for over a century had been, and continued to be, extractivism, the most enduring economic model in Africa.

The removal of minerals from the ground, for sale on the world markets, platinum, gold, diamonds, uranium and of course coal for local power station consumption, has largely been the 'raison d'etre' for the good, the bad and the

---

[53] Eugene de Kock. A veteran of the Rhodesian bush war, he became known for his successes in hunting down and killing his enemies in the border region bush, using the Casspir armoured vehicle (manufactured in South Africa) while in charge of the infamous Koevoet, a police fighting unit. De Kock was known for his ruthless disregard of human life, and was sentenced to a life term in prison after the ANC came to power. His father had been a well-respected magistrate while occupying a senior position in the Broederbond.

[54] Vlakplaas. De Kock was transferred in 1982 to take over the reins of Vlakplaas, where the elimination of opponents of apartheid, was planned, plotted, and on occasion executed. Potential Askaris were processed here, and many became central to the hit squads operating under orders from Vlakplaas.

[55] A turned 'terrorist' in the South African context. An unenviable position to be in, since he/she was dispensable to the SADF, and hated by his/her own people if unmasked.
An askari (from Somali, Swahili and Arabic عسكري, ''askarī', meaning 'soldier', or 'military')

grotesque; birth, evolution and current state of the nation. At the centre of it all was one family, the Oppenheimers, whose forebear, Sir Ernest, aged 22 had arrived in Kimberley, South Africa in 1902, shortly after the Anglo Boer War, to act as a buyer for his employer, a London-based diamond brokerage. No doubt a particularly bright boy, the story of Ernest and his progeny describes the most remarkable of journeys, detailing how, after becoming the mayor of Kimberley, he started a gold mining company with funds from Britain and the United States, aptly named Anglo American.

It was this company, among others which was to become a legendary financial powerhouse, in essence a British-owned company. Controlled initially by the family, it would in years to come own several mines; diamonds, platinum, copper, coal, the mainstay of which would, of course, be gold mines. Immeasurable quantities of gold lay concealed beneath the surface of the earth, streaks of yellow embedded in layers (reefs) of quartz or 'ore', discovered originally at the surface in modern day Johannesburg. Snaking its way underground to unknown depths, for hundreds of kilometres the 'ore', is mined at great expense, increasing as the depth increases.

Given that the grade of ore in South African gold mines is relatively low, as measured in grams of gold per tonne of rock, in order to be profitable, mining costs need to be kept low in order for the mine to remain profitable for shareholders. Cheap labour in many of these mines is consequently, absolutely vital, thin profit margins always under threat from gold price volatility on world markets.

Oppenheimer's Anglo American, acquired De Beers, the erstwhile Governor of the Cape Colony and British Imperialist, Cecil John Rhodes, having been co-founder. Oppenheimer, assuming the role of self-appointed custodian of a worldwide diamond trade through his London Central Selling Organisation (CSO), he commandeered absolute control of the sale of the gem, including the prices and volumes. Wresting control of the beaches and sea bed on the Coast in South West Africa, it was ensured that De Beers would have unfettered access to, and indeed control of the area to hoover up the deposits of alluvial diamonds, perhaps millions of years old, employing its own army of armed security, policing the area to keep unwanted intruders well away.

Token annual consideration of a few hundred pounds paid to the administrators of the country which at the time was a South African Protectorate as decreed by the League of Nations, post-World War 2, the diamond rich area all but became the property of De Beers. Later through retail and ingenious marketing, De Beers embellished the myth of the extraordinary value of diamonds, which spread like a raging blaze across the globe. Inferior diamonds not discarded, but termed 'industrial diamonds' would be reserved for sale to manufacturers of drilling and cutting tools.

The 'good' or clear and flawless variety boasting sheer beauty as the indestructible nature of a diamond was harnessed, it became a symbol of enduring love and commitment, the now expensive 'stone' finding its way into 'engagement' rings and 'eternity' rings. The larger and more expensive, the more your man loves you... it seemed, as this sparkling, crafted carbon mineral immersed itself into worldwide folklore, seducing minds and hearts, fast becoming the darling of the catchphrase 'Diamonds are a girl's best friend' as sung by Carol Channing in the musical, *Gentlemen prefer Blondes* in 1949, a later version made famous by Marilyn Monroe.

'Diamonds are Forever' sang Shirley Bassey, a memorable track from Ian Fleming's James Bond movie of 1971. So entrenched has the fallacy of the value of a diamond become in too many materialistic societies, that for most, marriage cannot be contemplated until the prospective groom can afford to buy a diamond engagement ring, be it with cash or on credit. A family at the foot of Africa had added in no small measure to their wealth through farce and cunning, a truly remarkable story.

Every new generation of Oppenheimers would return to England for their education, primary through to tertiary, ensuring that the family and their businesses remained quintessentially 'English'. Adding to the wealth of the Anglo-American Corporation had been successful forays into all manner of industries, at first mining related, deviating in time to almost all spheres of life: commercial property, manufacture, steel, motor vehicle retail, insurance, training—diversification on a grand scale.

Historically, Southern African mines were 'English' owned, and an organisation, almost a club, the ostensibly 'English' Chamber of Mines was established to ensure that mines were able to sell all the gold that they produced, control the pricing and ensure standardisation of wages for workers, amongst other things. In short, in today's parlance—collusion. At one point people such as JF Klopper, the leader of the Broederbond, and Nico Diedrichs, the minister of finance, later to become the leader of the Broederbond, and some of their Afrikaner Nationalist associates, became darlings of the Chamber of Mines when the creation of an 'Afrikaner' mining group, Genkor, was accepted as a pay-off for government not nationalising the 'English' mines.

Genkor would go on to rival Anglo American, having interests in mining, banking, insurance, media, and tobacco amongst others. Media was, of course, a vital component of the apartheid engine, controlling almost in its entirety, press, radio and television, keeping white South Africans, if not 'dumbed down', certainly in the dark most of the time.

'Cherry picking' news and footage to further the Afrikaner cause, most folk chose to wallow in the ignorance which had been propagated in the papers, on TV, indeed starting at schools both English and Afrikaans, Christian National Education having been enshrined into curricula across the country. Those newspapers not manipulated by the Broederbond, were silenced by censorship, threats and closure.

The role which Nkosi Nkwenkweze would play remained a mystery to me, until his file containing updated information was ready for storage. It had been in 1982 that an essentially black trade union, National Union of Mineworkers had been established by one Cyril Ramaphosa.[56]

Boasting a membership in excess of 300,000 members, it had become a force to be reckoned with. Strong leadership, a large member base, and grievances, real or manufactured, had culminated in a militancy seldom before witnessed in the country. 'Chilling', would describe the scene when these men gathered en masse to protest against their white masters, 'toyi-toying'[57], almost a war dance while on the move, the ground shuddering as hundreds, sometimes thousands of heels of miners' boots thudded in unison on the tarmac, the collective voices chanting suggested it best to stay right out of their way as many of them adorned in red T-shirts emblazoned with communist hammer and sickle, brandished spears, traditional animal hide shields and knopkerries (a stick with a knob at the top, traditionally used as a weapon by the indigenous peoples of South Africa).

The union, known as NUMSA, had morphed into something more than just a trade union. It had become a haven and mouthpiece for the ANC and South

---

[56] Cyril Ramaposa, President of the Republic of South Africa at the time of writing.

[57] Toyi-toyi was often used for intimidating the South African police and security forces during anti-apartheid demonstrations. The toyi-toyi was also used with chants such as the African National Congress's 'Amandla' ('power') and 'Awethu' ('ours') or the Pan African Congress's 'One Settler, One Bullet'.

African Communist Party, and also a political force to be reckoned with, less and less afraid of mine security or the police.

Having undergone intensive coaching and grooming, Nkosi would once again be deployed as a mineworker with the intention of infiltrating NUMSA. His brief, to get as close to the leadership of the trade union as possible, as quickly as possible. Yes indeed, on reflection he was the perfect candidate, several photos of the Askari revealing a handsome face exuding a youthful innocence and even mischievous enthusiasm. I looked into the eyes staring up from the pages with a feeling of uneasy foreboding, wondering how life might have been very different for this young man had he been born white, and indeed as I had often pondered before, if I had been born black in this country where might destiny have taken me?

I felt that while I had never been ignorant of, or blinded to, the plight of most young black people in Southern Africa, this 'encounter' with the unfortunate Johannes Nkosi Nkwenkwezi struck a painful chord with me, significantly crystalising in my mind, the hopelessness and helplessness of the life journeys for most young black people in Southern Africa.

This would be the last I would see of Nkosi's file, since the role of the offices on the 8th floor was to collate information, disseminate information to fieldworkers, and then to provide storage, safekeeping of, and easy access to documents recording all who's lives had been scrutinised under a microscope and processed for security clearances for all manner of reasons.

16. "All Manner of Reasons," Indeed

Gerrymandering is a practice intended to establish an unfair political advantage for a particular party or group.

Two principal tactics are used in gerrymandering: 'cracking' (i.e., diluting the voting power of the opposing party's supporters across many districts) and 'packing' (concentrating the opposing party's voting power in one district to reduce their voting power in other districts).

In addition to its use achieving desired electoral results for a particular party, gerrymandering may be used to help or hinder a particular demographic, such as a political, ethnic, racial, linguistic, religious, or class group, such as in Northern Ireland where boundaries were constructed to guarantee Protestant Unionist majorities. Gerrymandering can also be used to protect incumbents. Wayne Dawkins describes it as politicians picking their voters instead of voters picking their politicians; Thomas Hofeller the Redistricting Chair of the Republican National Committee, stated: "Redistricting is like an election in reverse. It's a great event. Usually, the voters get to pick the politicians. In redistricting, the politicians get to pick the voters."

In my mind the 'Homelands' had always been artificially constructed theoretical nation states synthesised by ethnic groupings, a country for the Zulu, another for the North BaSotho, South BaSotho, Xhosa, Tswana, Venda, Tsonga, Shangaan, Swazi and Ndbele nation states, all well within the borders of South Africa. Each homeland housed its own parliament, judiciary, police force, military and entire civil infrastructure, so theoretically, each was a self-contained, self-governing sovereign state. Toiling inside the heart of the beast now, I learned more and more about the 'Homelands', the 'raison d'etre', the history, and of course, the dark side of this glittering invention of the Broederbond.

'Glittering' indeed, the entire charade finding itself in the sweet spot of a wonderful Afrikaans saying: "Bo blink... onder stink!" Shiny on the surface, stinky underneath! Supply chain management and tender process was a closed shop, the protective walls of which were seemingly impossible to pierce or penetrate. Even rudimentary observation of government buildings of the various homeland 'countries', would reveal what was unashamedly and obviously a pattern, the vast numbers of very expensive German cars, some arriving and staying, others in and out, the latest Mercedes Benz, Audi and BMW almost swarming about the places.

Certainly, these places were where the 'moola flowed'. White men, black men, Indian men alighted from these vehicles, briefcases the standard accessory, some dressed in suits, some in expensive casual gear, busy, busy, busy! Delivery vehicles, if followed to their places of origin to try to establish a sense of the typical product being shipped, would reveal that these trucks were delivering everything from Coca Cola and biscuits, to high end TVs, sound systems and golf clubs.

By 1990, the Nationalist Party had been in power for some 42 years, and the Homeland or Bantustan system, was rejected in its entirety by the international community as a farce to legitimise the denial of black people's political and other rights within the borders of the theoretical Republic of South Arica, according them, citizenship in their respective homelands.

Had the gerrymandering not been so blatant and destructive, it might have proved amusing since a large majority of second, third and fourth generations of urban dwellers in South Africa had never set foot in the territories earmarked as 'their' homelands, and surveys would reveal that most were unable to point a finger on a map of Southern Africa to identify the areas in question.

Some 'satellite' governments had enjoyed the status of an 'independent state', while others, and most were unsure as to the reasons, were not 'independent', but 'autonomous'. States that were independent were assisted with the creation of a national defence force, which consisted mainly of an army and an air wing. The armies were really infantry and mechanised infantry divisions, with air wings largely for support as well as transportation of supplies and VIPs.

Naturally these defence units needed arms, helicopters, planes, equipment, military materiel, uniforms, vehicles, food, training, banking, insurance, and, and… and! Now, it should come as no surprise that all of these were provided by the South African Defence Force, Armscor, and hundreds, if not thousands of 'privateers' or small businesses, including a tender process infused with more than just a little bit of cronyism. More wealth yet again for the favourite sons of the Bond.

It seemed that there was an unusual number of applications for security clearances crossing our desks, many relating not to escalations in the war in South West Africa, but for those being seconded to the homeland government offices, military, supply chain, and indeed, owners and staff of private companies which had been rubber stamped to sell products of all descriptions to entities within these homelands. If this were to be the measure, then the 'Homeland' system could well be adjudged to be a roaring, unprecedented success, a masterstroke of note.

An insatiable curiosity and much 'digging' through files signed out from the Tannie Lategan's 'kluis'—strongroom—revealed that many of those who had piqued my interest had, in fact, become quite wealthy over a relatively short period of time, revealing links to the Broederbond. Many had owned holiday homes at the prestigious San Lameer[58], a pristine, private seaside resort in the balmy sub-tropical climate of Natal, close to Southbroom.

---

[58] San Lameer

1938—The South African government 'donates' a 200-hectare seaside reserve to Colonel G.H Langeler, businessman and entrepreneur.

1975—SANLAM (Suid Afrikaanse Lewens Assuransie Maatskapy, South African Life Insurance Company, established with government funds in 1918) major shareholder in Genkor ('Afrikaans') Mining Group, purchases the land from Colonel G.H Langeler.

1977—San Lameer is declared a 'Private Township' comprising common areas and 600 individual sections for construction of Mediterranean style villas, followed by the construction of a hotel and conference facilities.

1978—San Lameer is marketed as an exclusive private resort for the more affluent South Africans.

1990—Construction commences of a championship standard, 18-hole golf course and clubhouse'.

1992—Messrs Pierre Steyn, Ronnie Masson and Hendrik Bester of SANLAM are listed as founder members of the golf club

This was to be the forerunner of gated communities incorporating golf estates in South Africa, touted as the place for more affluent South Africans. It was pure coincidence that they should have purchased prized villas in the Afrikaner enclave! Their good fortune had been a consequence of trade in a myriad of products and services with the homelands. Isolating one single, simple commodity. For instance, schools, hospitals, government buildings, a university and any other entities with links to local government would need toilet paper, sold at premium prices to create sufficient margin for those who would 'clip the ticket' along the way.

By 1988, the patchwork compendium which was South Africa was governed by five presidents, nine chief ministers, 14 ministerial councils, nearly 300 Cabinet ministers, more than 1,500 members of various parliamentary or legislative bodies, tens of thousands of local councillors, not to mention numerous white 'advisers', seconded to these governments. All were paid by the state, ensuring wealth and comfort for those in charge, and open season for unscrupulous 'broeders' who were all but guaranteed success in the tender processes when these frail infrastructures required anything from stationery, furniture, or building contractors to vehicles, aircraft and military hardware.

In fact, items and services listed as essential ran into the thousands, elevating 'Procurement' into one of the most lucrative games in town, a universal fact, of course, being that procurement processes lend themselves in no small measure to subjectivity, potentially accompanied by favouritism, or even worse, a cycle leading to habitual unbridled bribery and corruption, in which a legitimate competitor may well be cheaper or offer superior service or the product is excluded by virtue of that very legitimacy. Becoming a self-licking ice cream, little did it matter which side of the transactions one found oneself, cultivating divergent moral codes, one could and would make good money, since this was how the game was played.

This was uncomfortably reminiscent of so many African situations in which regimes, about to implode, experience 'no holds barred' as the inevitability of regime change overwhelms the senses. Ken Owen, *Sunday Times* Editor, with meticulous clarity of vision later suggested: "… the prosperity of the mandarins is teaching South Africans of every race, what matters in this game: it is to get your snout into the trough and grab as much as you can get. For the manoeuvrable man with a flexible conscience, this is the time to get yourself elected to some council or other, or to get astride the floods of money that flow from the fiscus, or simply pick up the contracts that flutter like confetti at a wedding in the name of privatisation."

Further rudimentary investigation revealed that the corrupt tender processes were in fact nothing new, and had been evolving for decades.

The South African parliament and parliamentarians having for decades clutched the reins of control in one hand, and unopposed, the whip in the other, evolved into an upper class of political intelligentsia. There can be no disputing that this was strictly a boys' club, the political wing of the Broederbond perhaps. To the naked eye, these acolytes of the office of the President conducted themselves in a manner beyond reproach, the epitome of respectability. They were to be seen in church every Sunday, accompanied by their picture-perfect wives and pigeon pair offspring, exuberant in their innocence.

They made their homes in the most affluent of areas in Pretoria and Cape Town, enjoying the limelight while displaying just the right measure of piety, these were the pillars of Afrikaner society. Many had been graduates of those magnificent institutions which were universities by the Afrikaner, for the Afrikaner. Many had been senior officers in the police, or military, which of course it seems, resulted in them being highly competent and qualified to accept vital roles in the world of politics. So, it had been for generations, and there was simply no reason to fiddle with the system.

Some scratching at the surface would reveal a paper-thin veneer of respectability, cronyism posing as kinship, dating back more than a hundred years in the old Transvaal. The president of the ZAR—Zuid Afrikaanse Republic, Paul Kruger, frequently announced details of farms, up for grabs due to farmers' government levy payments falling into arrears. Such announcements were only for the ears of those in the 'Volksraad' (Equivalent of the government conference chamber), many of the politicians eventually owning multiple farms, ensuring family wealth for many generations to come. And so, the die was cast.

The Homelands or Bantustans as they came to be known, were by and large, farcical by their very nature, since they were artificially created on a map of Southern Africa, included no cities or large towns to speak of, very little by way of natural resources, and little to no prior infrastructure-promoting enterprise. Their inhabitants were poor to begin with, and remained poor after the gerrymandering.

The upper echelons of their governments and quasi government were enriched through what could be described as institutional corruption, facilitated by the South African government and entrepreneurs who were anointed sons of the Broederbond. The system was dismantled under the new constitution of South Africa, effective on 27 April 1994, when the ANC came to power, the flow of obscene, unknown amounts of funds flowing halted forever.

My mind would wander, picturing an idyllic South Africa, its history having taken a very different course simply as a result of one minor adjustment in 1948. A post World War 2 election in 1948 would see the war time leader Jan Smuts and his United Party winning[59] the general election. Uppermost in his mind was an evolution of a black middle class, the point of departure illustrated by his willingness to accept that urbanisation of black people had come to stay, a notion which the Nationalist Party rejected out of hand.

No amount of legislation or wishing would stem the tide of this phenomenon. Now, do not be fooled into thinking that Smuts was some kind of saviour of the black man—on the contrary, he was as much a racist as the next white Afrikaner, not being opposed in any way to the racial segregation which had come to define the country, but one did sense a pragmatism about the man, born of superior intelligence. It had been said by some of his teachers at university that Jan Smuts was one of the most brilliant law students to ever grace the hallowed halls of Cambridge University.

In my vignette, Smuts, a brilliant visionary placing the interests of the country ahead of Afrikaner Nationalist aspirations, had come to terms with the need to make radical changes to the world as it had come to be known, laying a foundation for the upliftment of the hitherto second-class citizens of South Africa. Billions of rands, instead of being squandered on an expensive, hungry military machine, a futile war, and a diabolical cash hungry homeland debacle, would be utilised instead to educate and incentivise the 'great unwashed' to emulate their white fellow South Africans, having been granted the wherewithal to grab top jobs in the fields of medicine, accounting, law, or become successful businessmen on a world stage, quickly causing a king tide to buoy black society as a whole.

---

[59] Smuts in fact lost the election by a narrow margin, and, it was said that he had neglected to campaign, despite not receiving the majority vote and Smuts gaining 12% more votes, Malan benefited heavily from the Westminster Constituency System. This allowed Malan to form a government by winning lots of small constituencies and gaining 5 more seats than the United Party in a narrow victory for the National Party.

This would, in turn, create a whole new generational avenue of tax revenue. This would flow back into the economy, propelling the development to unrivalled heights, South Africa now competing with the best of the best. A country devoid of corruption would not be funding passive, useless satellite governments, funnelling billions into the pockets of the multitudes of corrupt, greedy and blatantly dishonest.

Our beautiful land, not a desperate, struggling beast unable to shake off the Broederbond-sanctioned parasitism, which ran amok with gay abandon for 40 years or more. My dream had freed up so much money, that South Africa had become not the powerhouse of Africa, but a powerhouse of the world, casting a giant shadow over any and all emerging economies.

I was shaken out of my serial daydream as Bakkies called from the hallway: "Kom Steyn, ons moet ry!" It was about 9.45am on a beautiful clear autumn morning. We made our way to the lifts, down into the bowels of the Liberty Life Building, housing the pool cars, one of which, as happened most days, would take us and our load of files away for most of the day. A leisurely east bound drive along the 'one way', which was Vermeulen Street, we would lower the sun visors as the rays would otherwise blind driver and passenger alike.

Wending our way through the tree-lined white residential suburbs of Arcadia, Sunnyside, Groenkloof and Waterkloof Ridge to our destination at Erasmusklooof. Upon arrival at our destination, we would drive to the main entrance, since our vehicle held a load of heavy files.

"Gaan haal jy die bandiete Bakkies, ek sal by die kar bly."[60] Bandiete, bandits, was the generic term for black men who could be seen working in the gardens of military, government or quasi government facilities. Dressed in distinctive green prison overalls, these were men doing time for less serious crimes. Thought not to be a danger to the public and close to the end of their sentencing terms, they would be collected each day from the prisons to be used as cheap labour.

Upon arrival at Infoplan, we would seek out a work gang which would quickly move our heavy cargo of files from the car to the appropriate microfilming facility inside the cavernous building, saving us a half hour or more of backbreaking carrying. These 'bandits' were always most obliging and very keen to assist, I suspected, because it made a change from digging trenches,

---

[60] You go and fetch the bandits Bakkies, I'll wait at the car.

removing weeds and any other tedious tasks. I would speak to these men as we walked from the car park to our destination, always intrigued as to their crimes, which ranged from shoplifting, to possession of 'dagga'[61], and of course the inevitable 'reference book'[62] offenders, which constituted a large proportion of these work gangs.

---

[61] Cannibis/Marijuana

[62] The document was an internal passport for black people, designed to 'control' migration of black people to urban areas, containing details on the bearer such as their fingerprints, photograph, the name of his/her employer, his/her address, how long the bearer had been employed, as well as other information. Employers often entered a behavioural evaluation, on the conduct of the pass holder. An employer could only be a white person. The pass also documented permission requested and denied or granted to be in a certain region and the reason for seeking such permission. Under the law, any government employee could strike out such entries, basically cancelling the permission to remain in the area. A reference book without a valid entry then allowed officials to arrest and imprison the bearer of the book.

17. Dompas

Pass laws were designed to control the movement of Africans under apartheid. These laws evolved from regulations imposed by the Dutch and British in the 18th and 19th-century slave economy of the Cape Colony. In the 19th century, new pass laws were enacted for the purpose of ensuring a reliable supply of cheap, docile African labour for the gold and diamond mines. In 1952, the government enacted an even more rigid law that required all African males over the age of 16 to carry a 'reference book' (replacing the previous passbook) containing personal information and employment history.

Africans were often compelled to violate the pass laws to find work to support their families, so harassment, fines, and arrests under the pass laws were a constant threat to many urban Africans. Protest against these humiliating laws fuelled the anti-apartheid struggle—from the Defiance Campaign (1952–54), the massive women's protest in Pretoria (1956), to burning of passes at the police station in Sharpeville where 69 protesters were massacred (1960). In the 1970s and 1980s, many Africans found in violation of pass laws were stripped of citizenship and deported to poverty-stricken rural 'homelands'. By the time the increasingly expensive and ineffective pass laws were repealed in 1986, they had led to more than 17 million arrests.[63]

The colours of the trees and the fallen leaves varied from just off-white and yellowing to various degrees of orange to crimson, fawn and beige to golden brown and burnt sepia, mother nature boasting a kaleidoscope of earthy coloured spectrums. At a time when that dead heat of summer would subside, the rains sought to fall elsewhere and the Highveld would become dry and sparse. Petrus grinned broadly, revealing a gap where his two front teeth had once lived, as he

---

[63] *https://overcomingapartheid.msu.edu/multimedia.php?id=65-259-3*

explained that the falling leaves were the reason he and the 'bandiete' were collected now on a daily basis to rake up leaves.

"It felt," he said, "that they were raking up the leaves each day only to rake the 'same' leaves which had fallen the day before." A pleasant Zulu fellow about 30 years of age, he and I would chat every time we arrived and his work gang were around in the gardens. One day he explained to me that his real name 'Siyanda' meant 'we are increasing in number', alluding to the fact that he had many siblings, 'Okokugcina'—'Final One'—born when Siyanda (Siya) was about 6, giving him 8 siblings.

'Siya' as he was known, then succumbed uncontrollably to fits of laughter as he relayed : "Nee my Baas," his body continuing to heave with the comedy of what he was trying to tell me, and he continued: "Dan kom nog een,... 'Iphutha', is sy naam... 'Mistake!'"[64] Siya and his mates eagerly watched my face to gauge reaction... and when I laughed, they knew that the story had hit its mark.

Candid conversations would reveal that Siya was a repeat offender, his 'pass' book (known by black people as a 'dompas', or stupid pass) offences, usually involved him being in the city without the appropriate signature from a white person, be it a boss or a someone in authority overseeing his 'location'.

"But," he said, "it was difficult," because there were no jobs for Zulu men in the countryside, and he needed to be in the city to find work. A catch-22 situation indeed, but surely not an offence to result in the prison system being overcrowded, due to so many pass offence arrests.

Siya and his mates talked freely when not within earshot of their overseer, a black prison warder who seemed to display very little sympathy or empathy for his charges, seemingly disapproving by nature, when in fact, all the 'bandiete' in his detail were simply normal young men who had been criminalised by a legal framework which would have been laughable had its consequences not been so dire, incarcerating men and women en masse. Notwithstanding the indignity and trauma of being jailed, they were subjected to all manner of prison 'rituals' and sexual abuse.

Their perspective on life and demeanour would be forever altered—for the worse. Many of these so called rural 'migrants' had seldom or never been confronted up close by white people, so for most, their earliest impression of 'whites' would be coloured entirely as a result of their arrest by white policemen.

---

[64] No boss, then came another one... Iphutha is his name—'Mistake'.

These arrests, as I had witnessed on many occasions as a small child, often brought tears to my eyes as I saw men and women being physically beaten with 'sjamboks', sometimes attacked by German Shepherd police dogs, as some would scatter and run for their lives, the remaining unfortunates then roughly manhandled into pickup 'trucks' which had been modified to hold several people under lock and key.

As suddenly as these 'roundups' had begun, they would be over, leaving mostly 'white' audiences either appalled or more likely grinning at the spectacle, inane comments accompanying the sniggering, such as: "Yes, the bastards must go back to where they came from, they have no business here!" Within moments people continued about their business, comfortable in the knowledge that the streets were safe again!

These were vivid scenes etched in my mind forever, absolutely unforgettable, as I had witnessed this drama on numerous occasions. The most telling would have been when, on a few occasions, I had noticed a stationery police van outside a house two doors from my childhood home in Highland Road, when closer inspection would reveal through the 'grids' on the sides of the 'lockup holds' on the back of the van, many pairs of darting, silent eyes.

The driver of the van, a very large, portly young Afrikaner policeman, a neighbour and older brother of a boy in my sister's class at primary school. He would often invite his family to come outside to see, no doubt for some entertainment, and perhaps to feed the collective soul, providing comfort, as he was responsible for taking these illegals off the streets, crime prevention at its finest.

The family, including Mum, Dad, Brother and his Ouma would peer into the darkness of the van, smirking, wagging the index finger at the 'criminals', staring for a few moments at the 'fruit' of the policeman's labour, congratulating him, and talking excitedly amongst themselves as they all retired back into the house for a cup of tea, leaving his black assistant policeman in the passenger seat of the van. Thereafter, the load would be deposited at the Cleveland police station, no doubt for 'processing'.

As a boy of perhaps 5 or 6, my family would see the distress I experienced when seeing these 'roundups', and they went to great lengths to explain to me that this was a vital cog in the maintenance of law and order, ensuring the safety of our suburbs and cities. While the trauma of these events remained with me each and every time I witnessed them, I suppose that slowly, a part of me began to accept the 'need' for such police activities.

This was just a small element of my attitude programming, orchestrated by Mum and Dad, grandparents, and parents of my friends. Adulthood, it later struck me, provides a maturity and circumspection, absent in young children, making them more susceptible to suggestion and propaganda. Consequently, the most efficient weapon in the armoury of a racist government is the perpetuation of the grand myth through schools and media. Mum and Dad, as had their parents, naturally long since succumbed to the fear-mongering and, quite frankly, bullshit expounded by our so-called legitimate government.

Somewhat hypocritically, Mum would hire a boy (actually a man) without the 'reference book' to work in our garden, on the advice of others, on the basis that their 'illegal alien' status rendered these 'boys' quite tame, afraid to draw attention to themselves for fear of being reported and arrested. Given that they were 'illegal', their wage requirement could easily be negotiated at a very low level. 'Legitimate' black people in the cities harboured a dislike of these folk who carried no pass books, since they would be said to be stealing jobs, undercutting rates of pay and wages.

The 'dompas', and accompanying pass laws became the most hated symbols of apartheid, since the real purpose was to provide a simple tool for the authorities to micromanage on the ground, their blatant gerrymandering. In turn, control of movement of masses of people at the behest of government became the focus of the typical policeman blindly obeying his masters' instructions.

You had a pass book or you didn't, there was no grey area in the mind of a policeman. A pass book was up to date, signed and current, or it wasn't. A breach was the easiest thing for the most simple-minded policeman in the world to recognise, not requiring any thought or the ability to reason in the abstract, the merits or otherwise of the social engineering on a grand scale undertaken by the Nationalist government.

Arriving at Infoplan one morning, the 'lack' of 'bandiete' almost seemed overwhelming, since they had become such a familiar sight. Instead of the usual 'work-gang', there were it seemed scattered all around the grounds and gardens just a few men in the unmistakable green garb we had become accustomed to seeing. It seemed, that the government had overturned the laws, making reference books a thing of the past. Prisoners like Siya, we were told, had been processed and released fairly quickly.

At the time, I had no idea how many arrests had been made in the name of keeping vagrants off the streets under the guise of enforcing the pass laws. Modern technology, of course, has made research into these matters far easier, suggesting that some 17 million arrests were made to enforce the laws, which, of course, is simply mind boggling, given that in the 1970s the black population of South Africa was around 20 million people. From a purely logical point of view, it follows that many adults were arrested on numerous occasions, giving no credence whatsoever to those whose laws sought to dissuade black people from coming in from the countryside to the big cities.

To submit to the theory that these laws had any effect on the millions of people who flouted them would be to admit to bungling, on a grand scale. The lawmakers, we shudder to think, in their 'wisdom' wasted millions upon millions of police and prison officer man hours, clogging up the courts and prison system costing the taxpayer, probably billions, over time, when a billion was still deemed too difficult to compute. So, the billions now spent have amounted yet again—nought.

18. By Jingo-Military, Industrial, Economic Polity!

According to Prof Sampie Terreblanche, a former member of the Broederbond, what was initially networking created opportunities for 'circles within circles'. A similar argument can, of course, be made about other exclusive 'clubs' that are the preserve of the elite—golf clubs, country clubs, the Freemasons etc. However, the Broederbond was different in that it had a near monopoly on political power. This, combined with its support for white capital, meant that it had the power to set policy that would direct the thinking of the NP and ultimately the white parliament and Cabinet. It became the hidden hand that steered the white establishment and was perhaps only paralleled in power and influence by P.W. Botha's State Security Council in the 1980s.

By the 1970s, the Broederbond had fulfilled its 1918 mission of alleviating Afrikaner poverty. The organisation had become a powerful network of patronage, which meant that Broeders had access to contracts and to quotas in which the minister had discretionary power. Author Hennie Serfontein goes on to argue that the Broederbond was originally an 'underdog' organisation concerned with the interests of impoverished Afrikaners. However, once a significant part of the Afrikaner community became wealthy it continued to promote Afrikaner interests—i.e., the interest of the 'top dogs'. Terreblanche argues that when a 'top dog' organisation acts as if it is still involved with the interest of the 'underdogs', it is almost inevitable that a culture of nepotism and corruption will set in.

Women giggling with delight, urbane background music, sumptuous fare—this was dining at its finest. 'Bakkies' as he had come to be known, fellow national serviceman and now friend of mine, had been entertaining us, and then proposed a toast, *"Prost!"* he held his glass up as it clinked against mine, '*Min dae Steyn*'[65]. We had completed the first year of national service, and we were now into year 2 on the theoretical 'downhill slope', and of course, freedom. It would have been a Thursday… no… perhaps a Monday, or… I suppose it could have been any day of the week. Certainly, this was the life… yes Sir!

A few glasses of the Cape's finest wine would be enjoyed on occasions which one might suggest were a little more than frequent. Fine gourmet meals selected from a menu that made choosing difficult, notwithstanding a resplendent ambience in an opulent venue, completed by the subtle, sometimes dramatic background strains of Bach's Concert for Violin, or perhaps a more upbeat aria from 'Die Fledermaus' courtesy our very own Mimi Coertse and Ge Korsten.

More and more often we enjoyed highly subsidised meals each time we visited the fabulous staff restaurant in the glittering new office complex housing a 'company' called Infoplan. It was an architecturally designed glass monolith proudly occupying the northerly aspect of a suburban hill to take advantage of the warm sun in winter and relative cool in the summer. It was conveniently positioned close to Waterkloof, Waterkloof Ridge and surrounding upmarket areas bursting with mansions to house the Afrikaner elite, many of whom would cruise the short distances to work in the building, along the magnificent Jacaranda tree-lined avenues in their gleaming, luxury German vehicles.

Their homes of course, were in good hands during the day as uniformed black maids would clean house and meticulously attend to laundry, nannies would take care of toddlers, gardeners would see to it that landscaped grounds remained pristine; garden fountains, Japanese Koi ponds and swimming pools kept sparkling, all adding to a real quality of life for the families lucky enough to enjoy a magnificent lifestyle, proudly inviting visitors to share in their good fortune in the evenings and on weekends.

Pre-requisite trophy wives of course, had the important task of attending to their grooming; manicured fingernails, toenails, heels and soles balmed, hair, skin, waxing, requiring an endless array of professionals to provide pampering and the latest gossip. Vital shopping for fashionable shoes, clothing, hats, handbags, complemented by svelte figures and firm thighs, tummies and bums, courtesy a personal trainer at the local gym—it was an exhausting regimen all

---

[65] A typical Afrikaans expression used by conscripts, as the number of days remaining before the two years of duty would conclude. Literal translation would be 'few days'!

needing to be wrapped up by the time the school bell rang so mums could collect their precious progeny.

The menu and dining facility was for the convenience of a multitude of staff and visitors to the company, including Bakkies and me. Infoplan, as we understood it, was a private company run by civilians, whose function it was to synthesise, secure and house government, quasi government and military information using the latest computer, micro-fische and fire-proof storage facilities, so naturally it made sense that the company was in bed with military intelligence, and possibly every other intelligence agency in the country.

As it happened, Bakkies and I had heard through conversation that the microfiche 'cameras' at Infoplan were far superior to our own at DMI, which were effectively well past their sell by date, overseen and operated by a poor Afrikaans fellow named Sarel who spoke no English at all, and who was in his own words: "*gestrem,*"[66] I assumed, as the result of an accident, since he bore many visible scars, and walked with difficulty, reliant on a crutch, his gross motor co-ordination very obviously limited.

Conversations with Sarel, always brief, light and somewhat superficial would reveal that there had been a measure of brain damage, so to all intents and purposes this was sheltered employment. DMI plans had been to retain microfiche records of every security file in the cavernous strongroom while 'hard copy' in the care of Tannie Lategan, as she kept vigil over her beloved 'kluis', microfiche records provide easy, efficient storage and convenient access aided by a bank of microfiche readers.

The official line read: "As the internal strife in the country and overseas sanctions had intensified, more and more 'civilian' companies were established to provide support to the military." The growing deluge of applications for security clearances had resulted in a backlog of files in Sarel's office escalating from a few piles, to mountains of files and papers which would evoke the anger of the normally placid head of counter intelligence on the 8th floor, a particularly large man who loved to eat, and who displayed on his epaulettes—on parade days when uniforms were worn—the insignia of a Brigadier.

Bakkies and I, having previously visited Infoplan and, of course, it's staff restaurant on a few occasions for other purposes, cooked up a plan to make meaningful inroads into Sarel's backlog of files which had really sent the entire

---

[66] Handicapped or disabled.

8th floor administration into a 'tailspin', since records were difficult to locate in the absence of a system to track files which were simply stashed atop piles in his office, more and more each day.

Files it seemed also were going missing, causing additional delays in the process, which simply enraged the Brigadier as well as people needing access to them. We approached the Brigadier with an idea to requisition a pool vehicle and devote a few hours at a time on days when we felt we weren't particularly busy, to transport files to Infoplan for microfilming, ostensibly at a rate far more quickly and efficiently than was currently being done. This was deemed a brilliant idea, and the 'Brig' as we respectfully referred to him called up the appropriate authority at Infoplan with the request to utilise their facilities. In my mind, anything was better than sitting in the offices in Vermeulen Street, and so it happened that Bakkies and I were left to our own devices, the Brig having really given us a free pass.

Others weren't permitted to interfere in the progress which we were seen to be making in a very short space of time. A bonus, not mentioned before, was that the place was crawling with attractive young women, hardly an ordinary one amongst them. These were secretaries, assistants and typists, and it was abundantly clear and pretty obvious to me that recruitment specifications apropos qualifications and experience were definitely secondary relative to the attractiveness of candidates in this, a chauvinists' haven.

One did wonder about these professional men needing trophy wives as well as gorgeous, immaculately groomed young female assistants and secretaries… So, a tiny bit of 'work flow study' calculation revealed that we needed just a few hours a week to keep us busy, until we were due to be discharged from the army. In true military, and indeed, government service tradition, splitting the three-or four-hour shift with a much-needed lunch break was never questioned, as we soon became regulars in the staff restaurant. We would eat our fill, enjoying juicy steaks, tender pork ribs, seafood, lamb dishes, and fine wine at lunch most days of the week, for the price of a sausage roll and a Coke.

On Wednesdays it seemed, a far more relaxed atmosphere invaded the place, as the restaurant would become a little less busy, a little earlier than usual. It seemed also that the folk appeared to be in no hurry to get back to work. While it took some weeks for us to notice the trend, we would find ourselves getting back to our microfilming later and later with the passing of each Wednesday. It was on these days when there seemed to be fewer senior male managers about.

The unusual phenomenon was never discussed, but was only revealed to us by a young lady, who in hushed tones explained that 'Hoerskool Waterkloof', The Waterkloof High School, was directly adjacent to the Infoplan complex.

Wednesday afternoon was prized as the day when the school rugby teams would play against rivals from all over the city, and sometimes even teams visiting from other parts of the country. Suddenly, it all made sense. The Infoplan car park remained full, while the 'managers' walked across to bask in the winter sunlight and the glory of their gladiatorial sons, proudly surrounded by work colleagues as all in attendance savoured the spectacle, drinking in the camaraderie of this, the most traditional of civilised Afrikaner pastimes, the highlight, of course, being the school 1st XV encounter, discussed for days before and after. This was certainly the way things should be done!

19. Bakkies

"The landscape in Willemsdorp has become a terrifying and inescapable symbol of his (the white man's) inability to confront the uneasy paradox of his presence in Africa."

Herman Charles Bosman's allegory in defiance of his Afrikaans speaking peers' broad brushstrokes, painting the South African small town not as pastoral domesticity of colonial settlement, but rather an ideological immoral, scourge on the landscape.

Bakkies, now a firm friend who spoke no English at all, was a master story-teller, an Afrikaans Herman Charles Bosman,[67] originating ironically from the very area described in Bosman's stories. He was, as was I, not a lover of the army, the two of us having been in the same G3 platoon back in Oudtshoorn, transferring at the same time as me to Kimberley. Bakkies had been one of the 'train riders'. Again, we had been in the same platoon, and at the time not really friends as such, but I did always have the impression that he was a gentle, good guy.

In Pretoria, at the DMI building, I found myself in an office adjacent to Bakkies, and I only later learned that having seen me standing guard at some of the DMI installations during my stint with 'The Guard', he had been instrumental in persuading Lt Homan to move me to the 8th floor, possibly even expediting

---

[67] An English-speaking school teacher who had spent time in the 'Groot Marico', a rural region in the Western Transvaal, living and working amongst simple Afrikaner folk who despite their simplicity were world wise, somewhat world weary, yet brimming with an abundance of life lessons and morals. Bosman had created some wonderful composite characters whose stories he relayed through a fictious elder of the 'tribe' Oom Schalk Lourens (Uncle Schalk Lourens) in his books, short stories which were later adapted for stage plays.

decisions around my security clearance. Not overtly anti-government, I did detect that Bakkies was an Afrikaner cut from a different cloth, and consequently we really enjoyed each other's company during our time in Pretoria.

Lunchtimes at Infoplan simply became a part of our daily routine, when Bakkies would have me, and others at our table doubled over with laughter as he regaled us with wonderful stories of his childhood and home town, and as a really engaging teller of stories, he could entertain folk for hours.

The art of storytelling in rural Afrikaner communities was certainly alive and well, conveying to the audience a rich and proud heritage, which I recalled from my days as a young boy sitting at the feet of my Oupa. Bakkies would launch into a jarring, gravelly dialect unique to his 'Western Transvaal' hometown, west, northwest of Johannesburg and Pretoria, fairly close to where Nkosi Nkwenkwezi would have crossed the border at Gaborone into South Africa some months earlier. Bakkies' forefathers had been hardy, pioneering folk, who detested the yoke of English domination, and in a bid to escape such, had 'fled' to an area, beautiful in some parts, inhospitable in others.

Here, they put down roots, established farms, farming communities and co-operatives. Towns sprang up, with schools and churches to ensure continuity for their deep-seated beliefs and culture, and, it seemed, the British had no interest in the area or its people. My own grandmother (Ouma) had been born and raised in the area and it was her mother, grandmother and the womenfolk of the area who had been through the hell of the British concentration camps during the Anglo Boer War.

The war and its consequences had gone some way to reinforcing the generational disdain these folk felt for the British, so it should have come as no surprise when Bakkies and many like him, had no desire at all to learn to speak English. It was on these farms and in these towns that the Afrikaner would experience the ebb, the flow, of success and failure as bumper harvests would provide joy and the confirmation that their forebears had done the right thing by settling in these places; some years bringing failure of crops due to poor rains or pestilence.

It was at these times that farms and the consequent poverty would be abandoned in favour of life in the big cities where opportunity seemed to be more plentiful. Many did, however, survive and prosper, by the grace of God it was said, their very existence and relative abundance, the result of their unshakeable faith in the Almighty, as well as sweat and toil.

Without doubt, the sweat and toil would have contributed in no small measure to success. Not well documented, however, was the sweat and toil of the black labourers on these farms and in the towns. Time honoured, there evolved jobs for whites, and jobs for blacks which almost always consisted of the rigorous, laborious back-breaking work reserved for the less educated. The black people in this area had been dispossessed of their land by the Boers and other European settlers, much of which had been occupied by various tribes, some sources suggesting iron age settlements in the area dating back to 600AD.

The Royal Bafokeng, whose history dates back to the 12th century, seeing them migrate and settle in the Western Transvaal (now known as The Northwest Province) area around 1450. These 'workers', really were invisible people, in that they owned no land or fixed property,[68] and were subject to statutes and laws in South Africa which conferred upon them inferior education, no political rights, no rights to utilise or enjoy any public spaces or amenities reserved for white people.

In fact, draconian, brutal measures were instituted against black people suspected of flouting the rules or laws, or were seen to be vocal in remonstrating against the status quo or deemed guilty of instigating or fomenting insurrection. Sadly, this racist template which was known as apartheid was not unique to Bakkies' Western Transvaal, but had permeated South Africa in its entirety, slowly at first, then ever quicker, like the spreading of a plague, post the 1910 inauguration of the Union of South Africa.

An observation of Bakkies, led me to believe that he harboured no obvious hatred for black people, he simply was indifferent to the existence of these invisible people, which I found puzzling and disturbing, as though he knew little of these folk and had never had any kind of revelation. Not even on a minor scale, had it occurred to him that he knew little of those whose land his forebears had occupied, and whose people they had essentially enslaved[69] for over 100 years. Such is the gut-wrenching, diabolical nature of the country borne of the divergence of her people and the need for domination of one over another.

---

[68] The Royal Bafokeng clan did in fact, buy their own land back from white settlers in later years.

[69] Whilst these people may not have been enslaved per se, they were left with very little choice but to work for white employers for low wages sometimes referred to as 'slave wages', often under appalling conditions on farms or in the towns.

20. The Darkest of Days...

An ANC MK operative, Robert McBride and his 'comrades', or accomplices, dependent on which side of the spectrum your sympathies manifest, were responsible for a planned, targeted bombing of two Durban bars, the area known as a hangout for personnel from nearby SADF Natal Command and a local police station. Facing the media in later years he expressed remorse for his actions, acknowledging the cold-blooded nature of what he had done, he certainly appeared to be saddened by his own actions causing untold pain and devastation to many. This act was one of many in the bitter struggle for South Africa's soul.[70]

"On 14 June 1986, a fierce explosion rent through Durban's beachfront strip, killing three women and wounding 89 other people. It was 9:30 on a drizzly Saturday night when the explosion, identified as a car bomb, caused devastation at the hotel's two bars, Why Not? and Magoo's, the former a popular haunt for Durban's security branch and police force."

"The secrecy and corresponding distrust that is a hallmark of guerilla tactics has left its mark on South Africa's psyche. Closing ranks and protecting their own was a policy practiced by both sides of this asymmetrical battle, and the constant mantra of 'don't ask, don't tell, follow orders' meant the line of responsibility was constantly blurred. The power of a police and security structure unfettered by accountability had long been in evidence: in this case, the torture of MK operatives, the enforced betrayals and coerced statements. The retaliation of those oppressed by Apartheid's racism was dangerous, clandestine and desperate. In his Section 29 inquiry in 1997, McBride succinctly summed up South Africa's 1980s of discontent: 'It wasn't exactly

---

[70] The writer.

how we are sitting here, where there is no war going on outside. I think it's important I must mention that to you'"[71]

The earth shuddered, the dreaded sound of the mighty explosion assaulting the ears, buildings shaking, followed by the shock wave indiscriminately carrying flying, lethal glass daggers. There was blood on the walls, tables, serving cabinets,… shrieks, patrons of Nino's Italian coffee and sandwich bar found themselves centre-stage in a midday nightmare, some staring blankly into space, glass shards embedded in walls and flesh, some folk running, abandoning their carefully constructed gourmet sandwiches, not wanting to wait around for the next explosion or whatever was to follow.

A calm followed, soldiers from South African Medical Services across the road, ambulances and police starting to arrive, the general hospital and police HQ only a few minutes away. This was Melle Street, the unfortunate diners caught in the blast of a bomb positioned to damage a military installation, SAMS HQ, on the corner of Melle Street and Ameshoff Street.

The intention timed, I suspected, also to kill and maim pedestrians at the usually busy intersection, when large groups of staff from mostly Libridge and Liberty Life Head Office would have escaped the offices at lunchtime, many of them crossing at that intersection enroute to a myriad of eating establishments and coffee shops in the centre of Braamfontein, a bustling business precinct adjacent to the Johannesburg CBD.

Workers typically leave offices at 1.00 for lunch. My guess was that the bomb had been deliberately timed to explode at about 1.05pm, when the surrounding stretches of road and the intersection would have been busiest. As it happened, the weather was somewhat inclement, and it seemed that there was no one at the intersection, while patrons at Nino's ordinarily seated outdoors to take advantage of the sunshine, were mostly indoors when grey skies threated to put a damper on Friday afternoon lunch, possibly even the ensuing weekend. So, it seemed that the threat of rain had probably saved countless lives on that day when I had been employed at Liberty Life for only a brief period.

I had learned quickly that the regimented world of teaching at a state school was not for me, and after 2 short years, having fulfilled my contractual

[71]   *https://www.dailymaverick.co.za/article/2015-06-25-mcbride-the-trc-secrets-lies-and-legacy-of-deadly-bombing/*
Robyn Leslie and Deborah Matthews. 25 June 2015.

obligations, I resigned and was quickly ushered into the glamorous, high flying world of corporate insurance and investment. Housed at the Liberty Life Management Academy in the Libridge building, I was on a trajectory which could only be described as an exponential learning curve and accompanying career path, and frankly, life was now lived at a frightening pace, in which we worked hard, sometimes late into the night, and then we played hard, no place for the squeamish.

Friday afternoons were frequently reserved for long lunches or 'team building activities', almost always followed by drinks late into the night. At about 12.30pm on that particular Friday, all on the 4th Floor, filed past my office, every now and then someone poking a head in with a "C'mon we need to be there by 1.30."

"There was an outdoor 'Paintball' venue, to fight mock battles with pistols in the bush, north of the CBD in Northriding, an easy 20 minutes on the motorway, traffic permitting."

"On my way… " I responded, desperately trying to meet a deadline for a Friday 'close of business' report, knowing full well that we would not be back that day. The offices now deserted, I was thankful for the peace and quiet as I quickly completed my report. The report was left with his secretary to place on the desk of John Pettit, Senior Divisional Manager and Head of The Academy. Returning to my corner office, I couldn't help noticing that the weather had taken a turn for the worse.

Glancing at my wrist watch, I recall engaging in some mental arithmetic. It was 12.50, and I had often timed the walk to my car in the basement carpark of the adjacent Liberty Life Head Office building, usually about 6–8 minutes, dependent on how busy the lifts were, and if the red traffic light to cross Melle Street caught me or not. Then there was about 2–4 minutes to escape the basement, so I calculated worst case scenario that I should be on the road approaching the motorway by about 1.02 or so. That left me a little wriggle room to get to my destination in time.

What I could not factor in was the duration of the call following my office telephone ringing on my way out. My answer was no doubt curt, betraying my exasperation, as I pleaded with the caller to call me on Monday. "This will only take a few minutes," I was told, my short sharp response leaving the caller in no doubt that "I do not have a few minutes!"

I had managed to deflect the call, not having lost too much time, as I hurriedly left, glancing at my watch and 're-calibrating' my ETA. *I'm still ok,* I convinced myself, as I fortunately did not need to wait on a lift, or the traffic light, or indeed, any traffic in the basement carpark. I drove out of the building having crossed the road on foot about 25 metres from where that ANC bomb would explode. I did not hear the explosion, not because I was far away, but probably because I had a habit of driving while listening to very loud music.

Speeding down the M1 Motorway northbound, I do know that I missed that blast by a matter of minutes, having driven out of the basement, exiting the building about 40 metres or so from the site of the bomb blast. I learned of the explosion only later that evening, and it was in the days after, that I started to piece together the puzzle, realising that I may well have died that day had I allowed a last minute telephone conversation to continue.

The detail of the shocking event was relayed by a few who had had the misfortune to be dining at a favourite of Liberty Life folk-Nino's Italian Coffee and Sandwich Bar. There were no fatalities that day, and what had been experienced was, unfortunately all too common, often not even making it into the newspapers or the news on radio or television.

This incident represented the bitter, metallic, sanguine flavour which permeated South African society in the latter part of the 1980s. In 1985, the apartheid government had declared a 'state of emergency', giving government, the organs of state, the military, police and the judiciary far-reaching powers beyond the realm of that which could be construed as reasonable, rational or moral.

What followed was a widescale frenzy of arrests, torture, assassinations and strikes across sovereign boundaries to subdue the ANC. The torture resulting in the death of Bantu Stephen Biko in 1977, almost somehow paled into insignificance as the apartheid apparatus seemed to go on a spree; detaining, questioning, torturing and killing at will. This it seemed, was a last-ditch attempt to regain leverage over society through force and fear at a time when South Africa had become a pariah state with very few friends, now subjected to punishing international sanctions, sending an already troubled economy reeling.

As a response, the ANC quickly adopted a stance of fighting fire with fire, and the country would be subjected to 'bombings' on a regular basis. Initially such sabotage had not involved the taking of human life, restricted to strategic installations and sites, but that changed, in line with the hardening of attitudes within the ranks of the apartheid regime. The ANC responded in kind, viewing innocent bystanders as collateral damage. Venues which were perceived as predominantly 'white' became what was felt was fair game; sports stadiums, shopping complexes, 'whites only' eating establishments.

Rudimentary research reveals well over 220 bombings or grenade attacks in South Africa between 1986 and 1989; it seems, more than the total IRA incidents recorded in the UK over a similar period. Ordinary citizens both black and white, seemed to take this grizzly new phenomenon in their stride, in that it had become the new normal by the year 1990, the people of the South adding to their desensitisation in the face of violence surpassed only in war-torn countries.

21. "Heeeere's Andrew!"

A few days later, thousands of protesters marched in cities and in townships around the country to commemorate Chris Hani. In Cape Town, Port Elizabeth, Durban and Pietermaritzburg angry youths went on the rampage. In Umtata, enraged mobs attacked the South African embassy, badly damaging it. More than 70 people lost their lives in the violence, but without ANC intervention, many more would have died.

Nobel peace laureate Archbishop Desmond Tutu, who also worked non-stop to calm tempers, described the time after Hani's death as "one of the most scary moments in our country's history. If we didn't go up in flames then, I don't think we'll ever go up in flames at any other time. It was the worst moment in my life, and for many of us," he told AFP in an interview. "I loved him very deeply. He was a very positive influence on the young."

Pallo Jordan, a former minister under Mandela, now chairperson of parliament's foreign affairs committee, also remembers the moment he learned of Hani's death. "It was like the sky had come down," he told AFP. "The country was on a knife's-edge. Had the ANC leadership not intervened, we might have very well had an explosion of anger."

The Nelson Mandela Foundation: Padraig O'Malley, an Irish peacemaker, 9 April 2003.

"… and what of the ANC?" Andrew Feinstein mused, in his typical, considered approach. Betrayed as always by his non-verbal action, he gazed at nothing in particular. Then it became clear that he was synthesising his thoughts, never rushing, slowly, deliberately formulating narrative for maximum effect. I would delight in these early morning scrambles to get into the city to hear Andrew, I would drive down, level after level of ramps in the Fedsure carpark at No1 De Villiers Street, into the bowels of the earth, seeking that elusive vacant parking bay. A scurry to the lifts and then to the somewhat Spartan basement auditorium. This was certainly the largest meeting room in the building, and often I imagined the meetings that had taken place here, employers at large companies, faced by their adversaries from the trade unions, squaring up to squeeze out better terms for their members, group medical benefits, death benefits and pension pay-outs. Employers fighting tooth and nail to keep company costs as low as possible to keep shareholders from being spooked, in a volatile climate of political uncertainty.

I had worked in the insurance environment for some six years. Having left Liberty Life, I had been with the Fedsure Group for about four years, in which I had risen through the ranks rapidly, and was now an agency manager with Fedlife at Hurlingham Office Park in Sandton, an upmarket suburb of Johannesburg. Fedlife, a well-established company, but not quite on the scale of Liberty, Sanlam or Old Mutual, exuded a special dynamism, since it really felt like family, and the board of directors had exponential growth on their minds.

We believed that we were on the road to fortune and, of course, we were bulletproof. Functions were held, and meetings were called from time to time, requiring personnel and managers from the outlying suburban regions to attend at a centralised venue at No 1 DeVilliers Street, the Fedsure Head-office in the city centre proving ideal.

Andrew Feinstein, an academic and political commentator, had been a regular speaker in the auditorium from time to time, providing audiences with, what I believed to be, invaluable insights into the fascinating machinations and dynamics inherent in the negotiations between key players and stakeholders involved in the cat and mouse business of arriving at a political dispensation which would be acceptable to black people, white people, and all political movements seeking democratic virtue, for the first time in the troubled history of our country.

Andrew would tell of the myriad of pitfalls impeding the progress of 'the negotiations'. A veritable ball of string, tugged tentatively on one side, would threaten the entire construct, giving way to chaos, as the African National Congress, the National Party, the biggest of the players, thrust and parry, sought to gain a foothold, as the future of the country and its people hung precariously in the balance.

The 'superiority' of the white man, hitherto enshrined in volumes of race-based laws was about to be dismantled and consigned to the history books, Afrikaner Nationalists clinging for dear life to some vestiges of assurance that their people would at least be treated with a measure of respect after the 'fact'. The 'fact' now becoming a vast technicolour artwork in the minds of millions, depicting a black state president and a black 'ruling class'. For most, it was a picture that was wildly vivid and bright, unashamedly complete in the boldest of cheery shades; for some, the hues mutated from shades of grey to jet black, tinged with red, underpinned by a vast sea of dark uncertainty, sinister in its makeup, fuelling unbridled fear in some quarters.

With nothing to distract me in that auditorium, I listened intently to a man who could only be described as the quintessential 'urbane' intellectual. Andrew displayed a rare grasp of the South African condition at that juncture in our history. Always objective, succinct, yet with the right measure of emotion, he would relay tales of the dynamics of the players in the modern day thespian drama, and how erstwhile enemies were forging relationships, giving enormous hope to the jousting parties, these, once dashed when right wing Afrikaner groups would drive military vehicles through the glass foyer of the negotiating venue, in a show of force, voicing their displeasure around the status quo.

News would filter into the theatre, of ostensibly government backed Zulu militias going on the rampage, killing Xhosa people or those seen to be ANC supporters, demonstrating a faux uprising of the invisible hand of a mighty 3rd force. The murder of Chris Hani[72] by right wing extremists, derailed talks.

Indeed, there were some in certain quarters who, having felt betrayed that their own emissaries would enter into talks with the enemy, were now enduring lonely abandonment. It was these disenchanted souls from each extremity of the political spectrum who would gleefully go to war to seek nourishment to quell their own disillusioned desires.

Andrew would provide articulate, sober commentary on events unfolding, and their repercussions back at the HQs of the various negotiating parties. He would talk of progress in the negotiating halls at times, and at others, how the entire process had regressed, coloured by disappointment and suspicion. Conciliatory demeanour would give way to rage, while cool heads were needed to rekindle optimism and reason. Our orator would keep us informed, it seemed without adding or subtracting spice of any description.

Such information for me certainly, was a good thing, and while I enjoyed the entertainment, it was Andrew who did a marvellous job of conveying the gravity

---

[72] Chris Hani (28 June 1942–10 April 1993), born Martin Thembisile Hani, was the leader of the South African Communist Party and chief of staff of uMkhonto We Sizwe

of the situation, while affording a dignity to all parties under the microscope, his pinpoint accuracy leaving us in a pleasant state of cautious optimism as he wrapped up each time. I would always try to have Andrew's ear for a few minutes after each session, as I simply enjoyed talking to the man who contributed in no small measure to my immensely positive stance on a post-apartheid South Africa.

The atmosphere on the streets was tangible, although invisible. The good people of South Africa felt a foreboding, a mist shrouding all in apprehension, an emotional humidity, warning of impending disaster. Any milestones, or indeed progress of any description reached during the political negotiations, now seemed irrelevant as the people of our country felt that perhaps the match providing the initial flame to the tinder box, might well have been lit, and like a runaway veld fire, might engulf the country in a protracted, bloody civil war.

One of the country's most loved and popular figures (mostly amongst black people), Chris Hani, in a working-class neighbourhood, had walked down his driveway to pick up his daily newspaper, when he was brutally gunned down in a 'hit and run' assassination undertaken by a self-styled anti-communist Polish immigrant, Janusz Walusz. Aided and abetted by a middle-aged right wing white South African politician Clive Derby-Lewis.

Derby-Lewis, to my mind, had never constituted a threat in any way to the political future of South Africa, as I had close friends who discussed visiting his daughter at his home, not far from where we lived, and becoming entangled in political debates with him, enraging him when they were easily able to get the better of him, illustrating just how lacking the evidence and doctrine supporting his narrow view of the world had been. Notwithstanding his hateful, one-eyed white supremacist monologue, it seemed that he was simply not a nice person, convinced that 'he who baulks the loudest will triumph'.

Distinctly, I recall driving through the dry country side, returning to Johannesburg after visiting my friend Nic in Rustenberg. Late on that Saturday morning, the music playing on the car radio stopped abruptly. A stern voiced announcer read aloud a sequence of events, and to my dismay, we were left in no doubt that Chris Hani was dead, assassinated by white, right-wing extremists. Thoughts racing, I barely remember the remainder of the drive home, my mind now out of control as my thoughts seemed to bounce this way and that. That very evening, Nelson Mandela, although not yet the president of the country, assumed the mantle of leader of the people, all the county's people.

Broadcasting on radio and television, he referred to Hani as one of the greatest freedom fighters this country had ever known. He went on to say: "Chris Hani championed the cause of peace, trudging to every corner of South Africa calling for a spirit of tolerance among all our people. We are a nation in mourning. Our pain and anger are real. Yet we must not permit ourselves to be provoked by those who seek to deny us the very freedom Chris Hani gave his life for."

Mandela's impassioned plea for people to remain calm seemed to be well received by black and white alike, as he concluded by insisting emphatically that: 'This killing must stop' and then, 'No-one will desecrate his memory by rash and irresponsible actions'.

While many did go on the rampage, sadly some 70 people losing their lives, many were angry at what had happened, but the situation was relatively quickly stabilised as protest marches were peacefully dispersed, and in a short space of time, a calm normality seemed to return to the streets and countryside. Mandela had gone some way to entrench in minds, his worth as an orator, through his words, and a leader through his actions during a crisis.

Equally as important, he was beginning to win hearts and minds of people who previously despised him, viewing him as nothing more than a terrorist. White people started to colourfully refer to Mandela with affection, as the 'Madiba Magic' and this began to gain traction. 'Madiba', a term of endearment, respect and familiarity, became the new 'nomenclature' of this benevolent presence, who like a saint, was easily able to brush away from his shoulders the dust and pain of some 27 years in the white man's prison, forgiving without prejudice or malice. The beginning of the miracle we had hoped for, for so long?

Andrew would continue to regale us with wonderful tales of the talks behind the scenes, as the country marched inexorably toward a constitution cast in stone, guaranteeing equal rights for all. The negotiations which seemed to be little other than organised chaos in the early days were now morphing into a robust process, allowing nothing to stand in the way of progress and ultimately freedom for all in a fully democratic electoral procedure, which if I needed any further persuasion would see elections take place on my birthday.

If it had been thought apartheid was an immovable object, now was the time for ostriches to remove heads from the sand. Time marched on, elections were 'just around the corner' and sadly for us at Fedsure, Andrew Feinstein was no more.

22. Christine

Alexandra, informally abbreviated to Alex, is a township in the Gauteng province of South Africa. It forms part of the City of Johannesburg Metropolitan Municipality and is located next to the wealthy suburb of Sandton. It is commonly known as 'Gomorrah' among local residents. Alexandra is bounded by Wynberg on the west, Marlboro and Kelvin on the north, Kew, Lombardy West and Lombardy East on the south. Alexandra is one of the poorest urban areas in the country. Alexandra is situated on the banks of the Jukskei River. In addition to its original, reasonably well-built houses, it also has a large number (estimated at more than 20,000) of informal dwellings or 'shacks' called imikhukhu.[73]

The gentle knock on my office door I recognised immediately, as I instinctively glanced at my watch, "Yep," subconsciously I would have thought, "As usual, bang on time," 10.00am on the dot. My office was first on Christine's round, as the smell of the rich aromatic coffee entered the room, and eagerly I peaked at the tray to see if she had included my favourite morning treat, 'Romany Creams' chocolate biscuits. Commonplace in South Africa for many years in the workplace had been the ever-welcome presence of the 'Tea Girl', later known as the 'Tea Lady', which was more politically correct, the term 'girl' being derogatory.

The Tea Lady would typically dispense tea or coffee to the entire office twice daily, and when a client or visitor arrived at the office, she would be asked to provide the warm beverages and possibly some biscuits. Christine, or Chris as I called her, played a game every day, as she tried to conceal the biscuits for as long as possible, giving the impression that there were indeed none. As they were revealed she and I would both laugh out loud, a twinkle in her eye. On days when

---

[73] Wikipedia

she'd run out of snacks, she would appear visibly sad, and the game on that day would be a mutual show of us both pretending to be on the verge of tears.

The delivery of my morning 'tea' would almost always be followed by a minute or two of 'banter', when I would enquire after her wellbeing, and that of her children, and I would show an interest in their schooling and activities. Christine, an attractive Xhosa woman, shared a special bond with me: we had been born on the same day, but due to where we were born, the circumstances of our births, and pigmentation resulting in us having different colour skins, the differences in our lives were evidence that we had we had emerged from two very different worlds.

Given that our offices housed only about 17 staff, tea duties did not occupy much of her time, and she had been tasked with tidying, vacuuming carpets, general cleaning and dusting each week. My own army experience had taught me to fill a day so as not to look idle, and not attract more workload. I had observed Christine in action and quickly recognised the signs. Christine had always displayed a cheerful disposition, and given her nature, she revelled in the popularity of the office staff. Christine lived in Alexandra, a satellite slum township, originally only for black people, north east of Johannesburg, and I was well aware of the difficulties associated with her getting to and from work each day, given that she was reliant on taxis.

A taxi in Africa is a far cry from a taxi anywhere else in the world, transporting millions of black people en masse to and from work each day, in vehicles which are designed to carry up to fifteen people, but somehow manage to squeeze in more. The industry historically was run as a syndicated 'mafia', with taxi wars resulting in hundreds of deaths over the years. As with any other industry, profits drive the activities of the players, and one perceived way to enhance profit is by spending as little as possible on vehicle maintenance, resulting in thousands of vehicles being overloaded and unroadworthy. Commuters took their lives in their hands on a daily basis, but felt that they were without choice in a country which had never provided efficient, reliable transport for the masses to adequately address transportation needs.

After having Christine work for us for a few months, I called a meeting with her to make her an offer. I knew that she rose at 5.00 in the mornings to prepare sandwiches and get her kids ready for school, leaving to walk to a taxi rank at about 6.00 to ensure she secured a seat on a taxi to Johannesburg Central or Sandton City, and then a second taxi to the rank in Randburg, finally finishing with a long walk to the office. She would return home at a late hour, to cook, assist kids with homework, clean her little home, wash herself and get to bed at around 11.00.

I knew also that Christine was a single mum raising young children, and compared with other people in a similar situation to her own, had done well to secure a job with Fedsure, where she was shielded from abusive bosses by a very active, progressive HR department, and a liveable wage. I suggested that she was free to leave work when she felt she had finished up all her duties for the day, as opposed to marking time until 5.00 pm, never implying that she had paced herself.

Christine gave a wry smile to suggest that the 'game was up', but at the same time gratefully acknowledged and accepted the offer. After a few days of implementation of the new schedule, Christine would leave the office about one hour earlier than before, and arrive home between one and a half and two hours earlier than usual, since she now travelled outside 'of peak time'.

This she told me had changed the complexion of her life, giving her meaningful time with her children at a time when they really needed their mum. I recognised in this woman, an inherent, rare type of intelligence, and realised that she as a black person working in an office full of 'whites', had learned to 'play the game'. Again, I recognised the signs, thinking back to my own army experiences.

Christine would be whatever we wanted her to be, if it meant that she had a job, albeit menial, earning better than average, and not having too bad a time of it. Some-time later, after having made some investigations, again I called her in for a meeting, with an offer. I put it to her that she was wasting her talents and having spoken at length to HR, conveyed to her that they were willing to meet with Christine and collaborate on a personal development programme to provide skills training, and on-the-job learning in our offices, in administration, typing, computers and general office procedure and etiquette.

This, with a view to fast track her initially into a position as an administration assistant somewhere within the organisation, and then to jointly agree on an outline for a career path. Christine, although very composed, seemed pleased, and so she reached her crossroads, and we started to see a little less of Christine in the offices. I lost track of Christine's movements in the offices while she trained and had commitments in the city at Fedsure Head Office for a few months, I had my own issues occupying my days.

Life for me was somewhat hectic, and I had made a promise to myself that as the agency manager I would be the first one at work in the morning, and often the last to leave in the evening. The company had a philosophy of recruiting high calibre individuals, some of whom held high paying positions, sometimes accountants, lawyers, senior managers. But the industry had taught us that the failure rate for new consultants was high, and in order to improve on those woeful statistics, dynamic go-getters were employed. In order to survive in a tough industry, the combination of a top-notch person and detailed training and development programmes providing the secret to success.

The role of the agency manager was to recruit, train and supervise these folk until they gained experience and became successful. It seemed that former schoolteachers were well suited to this role, and so my life had taken a new turn. I had grown to love my work, which also involved playing 'hard', partying with my staff to 'blow off steam' which gave me deeper insight into the people I was assisting to 'survive'.

I would meet their significant others, and we all became a 'family' in a sense. When a consultant failed, there was almost always a financial consequence, so it became important for me to learn to take the knocks in the trenches with my people. A rollercoaster ride indeed, the highs being truly amazing, and the lows—well, desperately disappointing, the relationships not always ending amicably.

Safe to say though that on the whole, life for me was good. I had married a lovely lady who had become something of a high flier in the advertising industry. Sadly, we were later divorced—due, maybe because to two busy, social careers conflicting? I was conscious of the need for balance, so in addition to working hard and playing hard, I regularly attended a gym, ran a few times a week, and continued, as I had for most of my life, to play league tennis at a high level. The nature of my work meant that the financial rewards for success were bountiful, allowing for a lovely home in Sandton, BMWs, dinners in the best restaurants, and certainly multiple holidays each year.

One fateful morning, however, I received a call from HR asking after Christine, saying that she had not been present for training over the last two days. Casting my mind back, I didn't recall seeing her at the office for a few days. I rang her home, and talked to her. Nothing could have prepared me for what she was about to tell me. People in her neighbourhood had reported witnessing

Christine's 12-year-old daughter being abducted by five or six men, and she had been missing for two days.

What frightened me was the 'matter of fact' tone in which Christine described to me the sequence of events which had just rocked her world. I told her not to return to work until there was resolution. I called HR and asked if there was anything they could do by way of providing counselling and support for Christine and her children at home. They agreed to call on her and assist in whatever way they could. So, the waiting began.

Each day I would be in touch with HR, the police, and of course, Christine herself. While very willing, there was not too much that HR were able to do, while the police one feels, could have acted quickly and decisively, but seemed to lack the will to act, leaving one with the impression that this was simply one of hundreds, possibly thousands of grizzly crimes which for them were no longer abnormal.

The devastating end to this chapter tells the story of a mother who never did accept help from anyone, and when her daughter returned home after some two weeks it was revealed that this 12-year-old girl had been repeatedly gang raped on a daily basis by several adult men until she saw her opportunity to get away. To the best of my knowledge the perpetrators were never sought by the police, no assistance was accepted by the family, and a little girl and her mother faced the rest of their lives trying to deal and come to terms with this nightmare.

Christine's demeanour when she returned to work was one of indifference, and I couldn't help thinking that what her daughter had been through was not perceived as very unusual (societal norm shift?) as I might have imagined, while I felt sick to my stomach. The consensus amongst black people with whom I sought to discuss this was that she was lucky to be alive. Was she really though?

This event had for me constituted some of the most barbaric behaviour I had ever encountered in my life, and continues to return to my thoughts from time to time. In later years I became more alarmed at the rape statistics and society's attitude to rape in South Africa, and indeed throughout Africa. More evident as time went on, was the lack of government funding in many areas of life. It would in time come to light that police were grossly underfunded, understaffed, overworked and utterly demoralised. Such underfunding would contribute in no small measure to the alarming proliferation of crime in the country.

23. A Country's Catharsis; Heal Thyself

"The primary focus of the commission was on victims. It received more than 22,000 statements from victims and held public hearings at which victims gave testimony about gross violations of human rights, defined in the Act as torture, killings, disappearances and abductions, and severe ill treatment suffered at the hands of the apartheid state. Those who had suffered violations at the hands of the liberation movements—by members and leaders of such groups as the African National Congress, the Inkatha Freedom Party, and the Pan-Africanist Congress—also appeared before the commission."

"The commission received more than 7,000 amnesty applications, held more than 2,500 amnesty hearings, and granted 1,500 amnesties for thousands of crimes committed during the apartheid years. An important feature of the TRC was its openness and transparency. The public hearings held by the TRC ensured that South Africans became aware of the atrocities that had been committed during the apartheid years."[74]

After a restful sleep, I would take the lift down to the ground floor each morning. I always looked forward to a hearty breakfast, relishing eating in the dining area of the old Holiday Inn on St Georges Mall. I would savour the experience of a full English breakfast, then relax with a cup of coffee and a cigarette while watching folks of all shapes and sizes scurry in the darkness through the mall to their places of work. The city, being so far south of the Equator, seemed doomed to see the sun make an appearance only at about 8.00 am during the coldest winter period. This was not a 'mall' as we know it, but perhaps a beautiful old town centre 'square' as would be found in any old European city.

---

[74] Truth and Reconciliation Commission, South Africa. *https://www.britannica.com/topic/Truth-and-Reconciliation-Commission-South-Africa*

This particular 'square' however, was nestled cosily in the heart of old Cape Town, under the watchful eye of an aged stone edifice which was St George's Cathedral, and some magnificent European structures housing many old, established institutions like Syfrets and the Old Mutual. Although, a relatively young country, here, one felt infused with a sense of history, reminding one of the early days when European sailors were reluctant to brave a landing in the 'Cape of Storms'.

Later, it would be the Dutch and then the British who would vie to gain a foothold on the Cape Peninsula and fertile surrounds. A town sprang up like a well nurtured sapling, growing then into a city, against conceivably one of the most dramatic, beautiful backdrops on planet Earth.

As I finished my coffee, I recall glancing at my watch while estimating perhaps a 20-to-30-minute walk to my first appointment for the day in Waterkant, near to the recently completed Victoria and Alfred Waterfront. It was now a little after 8.00am, yet still quite dark, unusually so. My table being almost up against a window, I glanced up to the sky and realised that a dense rain cloud hovered overhead, resulting in a change of plans. I would enjoy a leisurely second cup of coffee and drive my rental car to my appointment.

It was at that moment when a chattering group of about seven or eight people appeared in the dining area, the central figure being a diminutive cleric whose face beamed permanently, revealing snow white teeth severely contrasting with his ebony complexion. I knew this man to be Bishop Desmond Tutu, and I soon realised that his 'ensemble' were the members of no less than the famed Truth and Reconciliation Commission.

I had moved on from the Fedlife Agency Division, but remained with the Fedsure Group, having been offered the coolest job imaginable; National Sales Manager, Fedsure Trust. John Field, an Australian Chartered Accountant, had gained a great deal of experience in the South African commercial and industrial property scene prior to buying a 'dormant' PMB (Participation Mortgage Bond) company, and a Trust Company licence. He had been of a mind to 'go it alone', when the PMB Association of South Africa hinted to him that from their perspective it would be preferable for him to join forces with a significantly larger entity, providing more visible financial buoyancy and thus perhaps more credibility in the 'shark-infested' waters of public investment.

Investor funds would be utilised to finance lenders purchasing or developing good quality commercial and industrial property. Robust lease agreements in place with sound tenants, and stepped rental income completed the picture. Life Insurance on the lenders would minimise the risk to ourselves, and 'sinking funds' structured through life insurance endowment policies would be set up to further dilute risk. It was very tidy indeed, and John saw a natural symbiotic relationship between a PMB company and a large insurer, which led to a meeting between himself and Fedsure.

This evolved into a long-term relationship and the baptism of Fedsure Participation Mortgage Bonds, and 'sister' company Fedsure Trust. Having a 'big player' acting as business partner provided the added benefit of being afforded a bridging facility in the event of funds being in short supply if there were an abundance of borrowers with good available 'stock'.

I had been tasked with employing life insurance brokers throughout the country, and was later approached to head up the finance broking team, a role which, although daunting in the early days, I came to relish, learning very quickly to deal with the vagaries of the world of high finance and the precarious existence of commercial and industrial property developers. My role for some years now involved a lot of travel, and so it had been that I came to find myself in Cape Town on that particular day.

I would look forward to quiet Sunday nights at home in anticipation of the whirlwind week ahead and for some years, I would eagerly watch a highlights package broadcast by SABC TV on Sunday evenings, providing the most sentient moments at the Truth and Reconciliation Commission hearings captured during the preceding week. Although the subject of much debate, I was of the firm opinion that conceptually the 'commission' was a really good idea, providing an opportunity to perpetrators of injustice or crimes against humanity back in the days of apartheid, what seemed a genuine opportunity to 'come clean' vis a vis their deeds.

Such deeds ranged from blatant racist dealings with people, to incarceration of suspects and torture, and then to murder or even mass murder, supposedly in the interests of the security of the country. The commissioners were chosen based upon their standing in the community and it seemed, their wisdom and ability to be both circumspect and objective in the face of information and evidence which would come to light over the next few years.

This information unearthed events and acts so callous, brutal and indeed heinous, that even those with the most hardened hearts would have tears brought to their eyes, or worse, experience the physical heaving, as bile would rise involuntarily, literally making one feel 'sick to the stomach'. It seemed that the commission was successful, in many instances, in forcing racist white supremacists to face their demons, by recounting their horrific deeds in the presence of their 'victims' or families of their victims, and begging forgiveness. One felt that some of these people had genuinely seen the error of their ways, but sadly, not all, some paying lip service to the process.

The commission had the power to grant full amnesty, or not, which rendered those in the 'dock' still liable for prosecution. Naturally the structure was viewed by some as fundamentally flawed, but then again ANC members and other activist groups who had accusations of wrongdoing levelled against them were invited to participate, and so seek forgiveness and/or amnesty from victims and the commission.

Breakfast the next morning found me sitting at a table next to the commissioners, and I was easily able to overhear the conversations as the banter vacillated between light hearted and some serious consideration of the previous day's events. Contrary to my nature, I stood up, made my way directly to Demond Tutu, and stammered: "Excuse me sir, you don't know me, but I know exactly who you are," adding, "For what it's worth, I think you people are remarkable, and doing a particularly difficult job very, very well indeed."

The man who had recently stepped down from the position of Archbishop of Cape Town, gently took my right hand in both his hands, smiled and unhurriedly looked me in the eye announcing: "Well, thank you,… that is most encouraging, and refreshing for all of our ears."

I felt a genuine warmth emanating from this man, and then I was on a roll, asking: "May I shake the hand of Mr George Bizos?"

The rest of the commission playfully displayed a mock disappointment that I wanted only to shake the hand of the man who had gallantly defended Nelson Mandela during the infamous 'Treason Trial' which would see Mandela and his cohorts unceremoniously sent off to be imprisoned on Robben Island for more years than they probably anticipated. It was said that Bizos may have saved Mandela from the gallows, by persuading him to temper his final speech before sentencing, when, it was said, that Mandela was preparing to lambast all and sundry, unconcerned about his own wellbeing.

I counted myself most fortunate that day to have met some of the pre-eminent South Africans who could without fear of contradiction claim to have put the needs of the people ahead of their own. This chance, albeit brief encounter, buoyed me for quite some time, and certainly fuelled the optimism I had felt for the future of the country since the 1994 elections, providing a 'shot in the arm' which would keep me going for some time.

Moved on from the *Reconciliation Commission, South.*

24. These Are My Principles, But If You Don't Like Them, I Have Others!

There's nothing in the streets
Looks any different to me
And the slogans are replaced, by-the-bye
And the parting on the left
Is now parting on the right
And the beards have all grown longer overnight
I'll tip my hat to the new constitution
Take a bow for the new revolution
Smile and grin at the change all around
Pick up my guitar and play
Just like yesterday
Then I'll get on my knees and pray
We don't get fooled again
Don't get fooled again, no, no
Yeah
Meet the new boss
Same as the old boss[75]

Amazing, I thought, as I urged my BMW to go faster, when the speed limit on the motorway connecting Johannesburg and the country's capital city, Pretoria, was 120kmh, yet speeding along in the fast lane at *140kmh* one would be harassed by vehicles tailgating and flashing lights, demanding that one speed up or get off the road. Even then, the adjacent lane would seem no slower, as I glanced to my left looking into the steely eyes of the driver alongside. My mind

---

[75] 'Won't get fooled again' Roger Daltrey—The Who

drifted to matters more general as I conceded and drove at the speeds demanded by my fellow road users, concluding that policing in South Africa had deteriorated to the point where the 'small' things went unpunished and the rot had set in.

Consequently, the 'big' things also went largely unpunished. Official crime statistics each year suggested that the vast majority of crimes went unsolved, from traffic law violations, theft, housebreaking, to rape, murder, and corruption. The police, it seemed, simply were not doing their jobs. It had been argued that the judicial system had become ineffective, the courts backlogged, and understaffed while facilities holding awaiting trial prisoners were hopelessly inadequate.

I had, much to my dismay, heard and read of many stories of policemen themselves, blatantly involved in criminal activities ranging from overseeing car-jacking syndicates to accepting bribes, and aiding in the disappearance of criminal records, so abetting fugitives from the law and awaiting trial criminals, to the extent that hundreds, if not thousands of guilty parties would walk free each year, the hands of the judiciary bound, while the good people of the country looked on, speechless—helpless.

This sadly was, 'welcome to the new South Africa', the white supremacist dream of the apartheid era despatched into the political wilderness. The fears of the old white Afrikaner, and in fact many white English speakers had come to fruition. The ANC and black rule had come to pass, and generally things weren't looking good.

It had been thought that the Aparatchik amongst the ANC leadership would be kowtowing to their masters in Moscow, leading to the downfall of South African society as we knew it. Now there were no masters in Moscow, since they too had been given their marching orders. The devil had disguised himself in a very different cloak; a cloak not too dissimilar from that which had adorned the Broederbonders and their favourite sons in their quest for power and riches, no matter the human cost.

My destination and meeting on this particular day were to drastically change my view on the country and the new, apparently inept, ANC government. General public confidence had been systematically corroded to the point in which one had to consciously stop oneself spewing a jaundiced tirade against them at the slightest provocation. Arriving in Pretoria, I made my way to the eastern suburb of Silverton, exiting the motorway not too far from our escapades at Infoplan some years prior, and following a good old-fashioned map book, I located the entrance to my destination in good time for a 7.30am meeting, thanks in no small measure to the intercity motorway turned race track.

A dusty schoolyard, and standard government school buildings it seemed, housed the offices in which I would meet with Mr Nel. A long. A neat row of jet-black VW Golfs stood, proudly displaying their licence plates: Scorpion 1, Scorpion 2, Scorpion 3 etc. Being a 'car man', I was first intrigued, and then impressed as I inspected these spotlessly clean, gleaming 'pocket rockets' which I knew to be Golf GTIs, the envy of many a young man, and indeed some of the ladies.

I had somehow contrived to avoid entirely, the main entrance to the building, unintentionally wandering into the back end of the structure, whereupon I was greeted by what could only be described as well organised mayhem—people of all shapes, sizes, colours and genders. The smell of this Spartan place was familiar, it was that almost musty, woody institutional 'fragrance' which attacked my sense of smell. Not altogether unpleasant, it ushered in a small measure of comfort that I recalled as a small boy at the primary school which I had absolutely loved.

Any resemblance to a school ended abruptly as I was invited into the little office of Mr Nel, Gerrie Nel. The early morning meeting had been arranged several weeks prior, due to the extreme lack of availability of time in Gerrie's diary. Gerrie was possessed of a steely handshake. Not a particularly tall man, he seemed younger rather than middle aged, his eyes reminding me of eyes I had seen before, crystalline and questioning in their intensity. He offered me a cup of tea and a biscuit while gesturing toward a chair at what could be mistaken for a school teacher's desk, overflowing with files and documents.

As Gerrie walked around the desk to his own chair, I noticed the old metal filing cabinets, bursting to contain their contents, and a black gown hanging from a hook on the back of the door, waiting patiently to be snatched down at a moment's notice for duty in the courtroom.

Having left the Fedsure Group after some 10 years to set up my own company, I had met with many senior officials and heads of departments in the new government in my role as an insurance broker, since our biggest market constituted government employees, due to generous employer subsidies of premiums for some insurance products. It became painfully obvious to me, and to an ever more cynical public, that BEE1 and Joint Ventures between private sector and government were playing their part in no small measure in creating opportunities for cronies to take advantage of situations to easily enrich themselves and family members with a minimum of fuss, and not too much concern around detection.

Offices of senior government officials and heads of departments I had noticed had a lot in common, other than the obvious. It would all start when one arrived at many of the offices. One would often be confronted by what could only be described as an 'ante chamber', housing one or more attractive, well-dressed young ladies, personal assistants, or secretaries perhaps. The doors to the office of the 'boss' was always bold and beautiful, perhaps mahogany or a lighter Cedar. Entrance to the chamber itself would reveal a very large desk, accompanied by a throne like chair, two ornate, slightly inferior chairs completing the cluster.

Meetings seldom took place at that desk, but one would find oneself seated in a plush burgundy leather lounge suite to the side of the cavernous office, the centrepiece being a coffee table to match the desk. Often original paintings would adorn the walls, and trendy *Habitat* magazines would try to outdo glossy books or colourful periodicals singing the praise of the government department in which one found oneself, boasting countless successful projects over preceding months and years. Whenever the opportunity arose, I would thumb through these books and periodicals, marvelling, inviting the occupier to tell me more.

Sadly, a pattern emerged, and conversations revealed that many a costly project had become simply another failure, written off to experience. Kibbutz-type farming initiatives failed due to lack of proper agricultural training, irrigation projects due to underfunding, small manufacturing enterprises as a result of poor logistics supply chain management, and so it went on. The realisation struck that many of these senior people seemed to be transitory, not remaining in positions for very long, moving on to the next best thing for more money and a grander title—the BEE[76] go-round, as it became known. These were the early days in the development of the class of the young, black nouveau riche.

The office of this white Afrikaans speaker redefined 'Spartan', as Gerrie's command of the English language impressed more and more as we spoke. Although reluctant at first, he spoke freely, and I detected in the man a rare

---

[76] Black Economic Empowerment

sincerity, warmth and a visible determination to match his steely handshake, his humility belying his monumental achievements. This was clearly a place where sleeves were rolled up and real work took place. No matching desks and credenzas, no fancy coffee table magazines or books, this was the hub of the machine to find and prosecute dishonest fatcats, and derail the gravy train which had become the main artery of collusion between unscrupulous private sector elements and dirty government officials, a situation becoming more and more untenable as time went by.

Gerrie, a lawyer by profession, had been a founder member and lead prosecutor of The Directorate of Special Operations (DSO), known also as the Scorpions, a team of investigators, lawyers, intelligence and financial experts, they were handpicked from the best South Africa had to offer. This division was created to be **independent of the SA Police**, **apolitical**, with a mandate to combat white collar crime, government corruption, and international crime including drug smuggling and human trafficking.

Walking through the halls of their HQ, as I sometimes did, one sensed a refreshing, invigorating energy. Largely young or at least, apparently youthful, well presented, obviously proud people of all hues, there being no place or time here for racism or sexism, as both male and female went about their business at a rapid pace, without a moment to lose, a glint in the eye. This was the stuff of fiction I remembered thinking at the time. Rarely catching sight of Gerrie after that, yours truly became the Scorpions biggest fan, following their exploits and progress.

These people provided the nourishment which honest Joe Citizen thrived upon, reinforcing the belief that the country would become the giant of the continent, leading the African Renaissance. I grew to know many of these people, visiting their homes, meeting their families, and quietly feeling proud to be associated with this unique, highly effective product of South African innovation.

I read human interest pieces about them after dangerous forays and successful convictions, sadly, anonymously, due the nature of their work and the need for secrecy. As an insurance broker, I had been the beneficiary of an extremely valuable and intriguing referral when I was asked to call Gerrie Nel who had enquired about a group insurance scheme for his staff.

The Scorpions became famous for their fearless raids of homes of high-ranking politicians within the ANC. Following investigations of alleged

162

corruption in the case of the **South African Arms Deal**, raids were commenced at the houses of then Deputy President Jacob Zuma, former Transport Minister Mac Maharaj and Durban businessman Schabir Shaik. In his book *After the Party*, Andrew Feinstein describes the arms deal, suggesting bribe money to the tune of up to US$200,000,000 changing hands in the upper echelons of government, thus 'epitomising all that is rotten at the heart of the ANC'.— Andrew Feinstein.

The scandal had been sparked when after the conviction of Shaik on 8 June 2005, the Scorpions raided his home on 18 August. This time, it was part of a couple of raids in the investigation of corruption in the trial of Zuma3, which started in October 2005. Raids were also conducted at the homes of Zuma himself, which were heavily criticised by COSATU (Council of South African Trade Unions), accusing the Scorpions and the judicial system of being manipulated and influenced to take biased political decisions and actions.

Just a few days before the raids, COSATU[77] had asked the government to drop charges against former Deputy President Zuma and to reinstate him without delay. The Scorpions had pioneered a new approach, which combined the activities of intelligence, investigation and prosecution, with an enormous emphasis on watertight guarding of information combined with unprecedented efficiency of all activities undertaken in those humble yet hallowed halls. With the Scorpions' success in high-profile cases, public confidence grew in their ability to make inroads into organised crime.

Money laundering and racketeering were added to its list of directives and they succeeded in obtaining the first ever convictions for racketeering in South Africa. By February 2004, they had completed 653 cases, 273 investigations and 380 prosecutions, of which, 349 resulted in convictions, representing a conviction rate of 93.1%. This constituted crime fighting as had never before been experienced in South Africa, or possibly anywhere else for that matter.

Interestingly enough, as mentioned previously, Schabir Shaik went to prison, and Mr Zuma later went on to become President of South Africa amid disputes as to precisely which words had been used by the presiding Judge Hilary Squire to describe the nature of the relationship between Zuma and Shaik (client and financial adviser) during the course of the trial.

---

[77] Congress of South African Trade Unions

Earlier in his career, Gerrie Nel had been a junior prosecutor in the trial of Janusz Walus, and Clive Derby-Lewis, when they were found guilty of the murder of Chris Hani, the event which almost derailed the negotiations between the national government and the ANC and others, bringing South Africa to the precipice of a civil war at a time when delicate treading was paramount to the stability of the country, prior to the 1994 watershed elections. He had headed the council for the prosecution when self-confessed drug dealer Glenn Agliotti was put on trial for the murder of mining magnate Brett Kebble.

This trial had led to the arrest of Chief of South African Police and **Head of Interpol**, Jackie Selebi, followed by a conviction for corruption, thanks to the investigative efforts and determination of Nel and his Scorpions. No mean feat, since every effort had been made to thwart the investigation, including the arrest of Nel by Selebi's South African Polices Service, in a blatant attempt to intimidate the Scorpion boss and his team. Suspiciously, the Scorpions were disbanded in 2009, it was said, by forces within the senior ranks of the ANC government who were in the sights or about to be in the sights of Nel and his indefatigables.

A sad, sad day indeed. Any country or society that could be assured of such fine crime-fighting results would surely cling to so valuable an asset, taking great comfort in the knowledge that the complete eradication of major crime no longer constituted the impossible dream. Of more concern of course, was the question: "what did these people have to hide?" One wonders who they are, and the extent of their criminal behaviour. We can but surmise. They have successfully shooed the bloodhounds away from their respective doors and one doubts whether posterity will fully reveal their identities or their activities, which led me to begin to fear for the future of South Africa.

In more recent times, Gerrie Nel led the prosecution in the State's case against 'Blade Runner' Oscar Pistorius for the death of his girlfriend Reeva Steenkamp, securing a conviction for manslaughter. I had been aware of his exploits in the Janus Walusz, Clive Derby Lewis debacle, when he successfully prosecuted the two for the murder of Chris Hani. This man, somehow, just commanded respect in his own quiet, understated way.

In later years, Gerrie, resigned from government employment unexpectedly, and suddenly he would leave the National Prosecuting Authority to take up a role as Head of Private Prosecutions for Afriforum,[78] fighting for the rights of minority groups in South Africa1. This move was met with much surprise in many quarters, as Nel had, certainly to me, oozed 'apolitical', now throwing in his lot in with a highly visible, ostensibly white, 'Afrikaner' outfit.

Every fibre of my instinct screamed it's a response borne of 100 years of history that this constituted betrayal personified. Interviewed on this subject, Gerrie refers to his love of and belief in nothing, but 'facts'. The truly rational person however, would recognise this and fight tooth and nail in support of any minority group grappling with an overpowering overseer, who would deny basic human rights to a workforce excluded from the workplace based upon skin colour.

Sadly, in some areas, the ANC has sunk to the levels of their predecessors, instituting legislation which governs human rights on the basis of skin colour and even ethnicity. Under the apartheid government, Indians and so-called coloured people (people of mixed race) were afforded a diluted presence in the country's parliament, and of course, the underlying crime committed by these people was that they weren't 'white enough'. The numbers of these groups were significantly less than 'white South Africa', so they simply couldn't constitute a political threat.

Under the new and improved government, these folk aren't 'black enough', so, they remain in a wilderness of sorts, not being considered for many vacant jobs, or excluded from the tender processes for government or quasi government procurement.

---

[78] AfriForum is a South African civil rights organisation focused mainly on the interests of Afrikaners, a subgroup of the country's white population. Wikipedia

25. Supping with the Devil
at a Very Old Table

'Sup with the devil'[79]—To associate or deal with a particularly malicious, immoral, or unscrupulous person or people; to commit malicious, immoral, or evil deeds.

Gazing across a shimmery sea, I stood hand in hand with my wife of 4 years, Michelle, whom I had met at Fedsure. The gentlest of breezes, whispering to us the promise of a lifetime of warmth, adventure and excitement. We stood as one, eyes fixed on nothing in particular, yet everything that was beautiful about False Bay at the southern tip of Africa. Such a clear day revealing to us a maritime vista most spectacular—a mirror like ocean, ever divergent white trails from distant boats, criss-crossing each other, Seal Island—a speck in the middle of this vast bay belying the daily drama of the Great White Shark waiting in ambush for the ever vigilant seal, and clear as clear can be, the mountains encapsulating the quaint harbour village of Gordon's Bay some 25 km away, obscuring the horizon directly across the water, yet a good few hours' drive by car.

It was that magical week between Christmas Day and the New Year's parties. Holidaying in the Cape with such fine weather was hard to beat, some of the most spectacular beaches on planet earth, world class wine farms, fine dining from seafood to French or Cuban fare, entwined in a most dramatic tapestry of mountain and ocean, it was all there, and more.

A day trip planned, Michelle had contacted old friends, for whom she had worked as a teenager, not seen in many years. She and her young family would be welcomed for lunch by Peter and Denise, at their beautiful cottage, high on

---

[79] 14th Century saying

the hill overlooking the romantic old settlement which was Simonstown, an operational naval base established for British fleets in 1680.

Our hosts, unable to contain their joy, had wept as they hugged Michelle, whom they'd not seen for about 15 years, and hugging me—I was simply an extension of their young friend as they welcomed us and our children into their home. The finest Franschoek wine uncorked, all drank to a wonderfully emotional reunion. As Denise added the finishing touches to her gourmet meal, Peter joined us outside in the sunshine as we sipped at the Cabernet Sauvignon, marvelling at their home, the views and indeed the beauty and quality defining their lives.

They had lived in Johannesburg, and when their adult children had moved on, the two found themselves living the dream in a state of semi-retirement—yes idyllic, a reward for a lifetime of hard work and a fair amount of sacrifice. Peter pointed out things and places of interest across the water, and closer to home, vessels in the docks of the naval yard, some older boats bristling with armaments while apparently newer vessels, mere shells, bobbing innocently in the water as they awaited their fate which was being contested by media, politicians and the public at large.

We sat down to a memorable luncheon, Peter and Denise proving to be the perfect hosts, lovely people, all the while enjoying conversation ranging from our lives in Johannesburg, trials and tribulations of business, and, of course, the perennial political and current affairs, both locally and abroad.

It had been a few years prior to the holiday which we had planned in Cape Town, when a group of people in the halls of power found themselves sitting around a table, negotiating, demanding, conceding, a veritable verbal thrust and parry. The meeting, one of a series, was no ordinary meeting, and the people, no ordinary players. Old apartheid tribulations and the once indomitable Broederbond now fading in the memory, but equally, the glamour, the love, the warmth of the Nelson Mandela era was also over.

The time to roll up sleeves and sully the hands had arrived, and 'sullying of the hands' was the very thing on the table, a beautifully ornate table, a hangover from the days of old when dark suited middle aged white Afrikaner men would gather in the majestic parliamentary halls to discuss what it was that was needed to grease the wheels of the South African economy and the palms of those on the take. This very table no doubt, concealing some telling secrets of old, now party to some modern-day secrets, nothing really changing, other than the gender restrictions discarded, the players representing all across the racial spectrum. But there was no danger here, tables won't be coaxed into revealing talk.

Now the talk around this table, much like that in days of old, was similarly, behind closed doors, and as before, centred around that which generates the flow of money, even though money in and of itself not being the topic of conversation. The new democratic South Africa was, it would seem, in desperate need of fighter aircraft to stave off dastardly northern enemies lurking in the skies above. Surreptitiously, uninvited, and at a moment's notice other enemies it was feared, might emerge from the depths of the Indian or Atlantic Ocean in great numbers, armed to the teeth, intent on pillage and conquest.

These enemies might come from any one of many, many pernicious kingdoms with intentions so murderous as to leave the new ANC government with no choice at all but to purchase gun-boats, armed flying machines and submarines without delay. So it came to pass that in order to ensure the security of sea and sky, negotiations ensued as President Thabo Mbeki, the embodiment of anglicised, urbane sophistication, grasped the helm firmly, while names like Thompson CSF, BAE and SAAB began to garner traction in the minds of those around the table, the seed being planted to provide the country with weapons to ward off non-existent enemies.

His charges—the darlings of the world, the good people of the Rainbow Nation of South Africa as it had been dubbed—remained totally oblivious, as he and Messrs Shaik, Zuma, Modise et al supped with the devil, the makers and distributors of material, that which kills so easily in frighteningly large numbers, always for sale to those who can afford it and are willing to learn the rules and embrace the clandestine enrichment game.

Now it is rare it would seem, that a reasonable, intelligent person in a position of trust and authority over his fellow man, would awake one morning with a firm resolve to change course completely and without deliberation jump onto a gravy train thus lining his own pockets, alongside his comrades like pigs with snouts grunting and snorting while scoffing away at the trough for fear of losing out on a bumper feed.

This related to merely one question, amongst many, which I asked myself on the drive from Peter and Denise, back to our holiday apartment in Melkbosstrand. I had recalled reading of the procurement of frigates, submarines and fighter aircraft by the South African National Defence Force a short while before, but until I had seen those 'shells' bobbing innocuously on the water first hand, I hadn't given much thought to the so-called 'Arms Deal'.

With the new political landscape of the ANC now beginning to grow comfortable in its own skin, South Africans had little cause to suspect that anything untoward was afoot. The new political dispensation had been occupied by three separate and distinct entities: those who had been incarcerated on Robben Island (affectionately known as the 'islanders'); those who had returned from exile in Angola, Zambia, Tanzania, Scandinavia and various other countries which had supported the ANC and provided shelter for its members; and of course those who had remained in South Africa to fight from the ranks of the trade unions or as MK operatives doing whatever was deemed necessary to intensify the struggle against the apartheid regime.

There had, of course, been a measure of enmity and mistrust between the groups, the 'islanders' viewed as old men who had lost touch with the youth on the 'ground', the exiles being tainted as perhaps a little cowardly and arrogant, and the 'stayers' looked down upon by the former exiles as less educated and therefore somewhat inferior,—some exiles had achieved master's degree level and beyond at prestigious overseas institutions catapulting them to the ranks of international intelligentsia, or so it seemed. Despite the differences that existed between them, there had developed a uniting sense of purpose and a refreshing energy, which flowed through the new ruling party as differences were set aside for the greater good of the country and her people.

It had seemed that the endeavours of ruling politicos would now centre around the benevolence of the work being done, and trying to unravel the difficulties faced by the ruling party in 'righting the ship' from a fiscal point of view, given that the economic baggage inherited from the apartheid government could not simply be jettisoned along with race-based laws and draconian policing methods. Contrary to views held dear by many white South Africans, the old National Party had dug quite a hole for itself and the country, resulting in foreign debt constituting an alarming proportion as a ratio of Gross Domestic Product, effectively resulting in the new government being mightily hamstrung before even embarking on its new course.

The fiscus needed to continue to prop up the legacy of debt created over decades by the predecessor before consideration could be given to social upliftment programmes, the promise of which had for decades been the clarion call of the shadow government in exile, as well as a rallying point while on the campaign trail preceding the first non-racial election in 1994, in a sense making liars of them before they left the starting blocks. This was starting to become evident in the face of slow progress now highlighted in the media.

It was against this backdrop that the story began to unravel itself. Those who, having been supportive of the ANC and sympathetic to the financial dilemma faced, now found themselves questioning the moral fibre of the leadership of the organisation. Uncertain as to who had started the ball rolling, or exactly where and when, the spectre of something very ugly had begun to rear its head. It had, in fact, been our worst fear that was now slowly appearing to become reality, the fear that the new improved government could be guilty of mismanagement and heaven forbid, a new era of corruption.

Returning home to Johannesburg after a magical holiday in the fairest Cape, that distinct dry, dusty smell of the Highveld settled over us as we carried our luggage from the car into the house. While Johannesburg could never be described as beautiful or indeed even attractive, for us it remained home, and definitely provided a certain buzz, a magnetism which had drawn people from Europe through the 1970s and 1980s to enjoy a really good standard of living, with jobs aplenty, magnificent homes in upmarket areas, world class shopping malls, fancy cars, fine dining at a ridiculous number of restaurants, yes, and a standard of living to rival that of cities in Europe or the United States.

Life in the big cities, particularly Johannesburg and Cape Town, had been kind to a good many white people for a long time, and now things were changing, and starting to emerge was an urban, nouveau riche, a stratum of previously disadvantaged black people. White liberals embraced these newfound friends, revelling in the freedom and indeed success of these folk, announcing that this was what they had been fighting for, for so long. Sadly, still confined to misery, there remained millions of black people living below the poverty line.

Jobless and with no hope of finding work, rural people now flocked to the cities, where before, this migration was fundamentally illegal without the right 'paperwork' (dompas). An oversupply of unskilled labour, too few jobs, and no social system to speak of, resulted in squatter camps springing up on the periphery of every city and town in South Africa almost without exception. Squatter camps which housed people in makeshift shelters, long-run tin roofs stripped bare, wood and cardboard, and even old plastic packets provided the materials for peoples' homes, as hundreds of thousands of families lived in these polluted, crime-ridden settlements which lacked fundamental sewerage, electricity or running water facilities.

It had been said of Diepsloot, a camp north of Johannesburg, that when someone died, the poverty-stricken family, lacking funds for a proper funeral, buried the corpse beneath the shack. This seemed a stretch for the imagination, until a TV documentary aired interviews with shack dwellers who confirmed the stories, and mangy underfed dogs were filmed carrying around in their mouths, bones which constituted without question, human remains.

The luncheon at Peter and Denise had, for me, set the 'cat amongst the pigeons' as my mind returned again and again to the useless bobbing shells which were frigates and dry-docked submarines, offering less defence capabilities than an Avenger speedboat towing a slalom skier on a warm Sunday afternoon along the Vaal River. I recalled the new government had spent billions on defence, and now saw for myself the fruit (or lack thereof) of what seemed a frivolous waste of precious taxpayers' money, and lots of it by all accounts.

This was to be merely the tip of the iceberg, for what was to follow would scar the country forever, and sadly, would be instrumental in plotting a course down a dark road. I had always been aware that there had been some token resistance to the arms purchases in the halls of parliament, the basis of which had centred largely around the cost of the material, the budget back in the day limiting expenditure to R8 billion (US$ 2.7 billion, mid to late 1990s) while the proposed packages amounted to some R30billion (escalating it was suggested in later years, to somewhere north of R100billion).

While being alarming, in and of itself, this information was freely available in the public domain, and it appeared that the only 'crimes' which had been committed related to undue influence to overspend, and perhaps a lack of due diligence, infused with a generous helping of naivete.

As the layers of the onion were peeled back, slowly, systematically, the ugly truth would reveal itself as it was deduced that the well-intentioned were deviously taken by the hand and gingerly led through a maze, perfected and replicated over decades, the end of which led the unsuspecting prey into a sticky spider's web. The web which they did not foresee nor understand was unforgiving in the extreme, for once you were entangled in it, there was never a way out, and the coup de grace—talking about it or 'spilling the beans'—would result in a monumental fall from grace, one way or another, the worst possible outcome rendering one guilty of breaching legislation protecting secrets of state.

The most senior people in government were later implicated in an arms procurement programme that took on a life of its own. The rumour mill suggested that the main protagonists had been and continued to be swept up in a merry-go-round of personal payments and extreme generosity towards those who assisted in oiling the wheels of the machine.

Chief protagonists were rumoured to be the state president himself, Thabo Mbeki; his deputy, Jacob Zuma; Joe Modise, founder member of MK and now Minister of Defence; Shamin 'Chippy' Shaik, head of procurement for the SA National Defence Force; and Schabir Shaik, brother of 'Chippy' and erstwhile confidant and 'Financial Adviser' to Jacob Zuma. The phrase 'thick as thieves' sprang to mind, when cursory investigation revealed that four Shaik brothers had been very active in the ANC in exile, and close to Jacob Zuma, who had been the intelligence head of the ANC in exile.

Far larger than life, the ever-popular Zuma had, over time, been adorned in a cloak as untouchable, a mantle which would simply intensify with time. It seemed that Schabir Shaik, entrepreneur extraordinaire, might have started the ball rolling when it so happened that he bid on a lucrative contract to supply to the South African Navy, patrol boats. To the trained eye, this would, of course, smack of collusion, since, as highlighted before, his brother was the head of acquisition for the South African National Defence Force, not forgetting that Schabir had the ear of the Deputy State President, Mr Zuma. Schabir's company Nkobi Holdings entered a joint venture with Thomson CSF, a French defence company, under the banner of Thomson Holdings.

Suggestions emerged that Jacob Zuma would receive from Thomson CSF a stipend of some R500,000 per annum, with no confirmed end date, for which he was required simply to bat for Thomson-CSF in the parliamentary chambers.

26. Hush, Hush or We'll All Fall Down!

'The point at which the ANC lost its moral compass'.[80]

No doubt the days and weeks ahead of the 1994 democratic election were heady times for those who had devoted their entire existences to 'The Struggle'. Their selfless efforts finally paying dividends, many still shaking their heads in disbelief, never having contemplated that liberation might happen in their lifetime. Heady indeed, followed by an indescribable euphoria when the reality set in that black people now occupied the highest offices in the land, free to plot the course for the future of all South Africans. The effervescence of Nelson Mandela, his overt reconciliatory demeanour, his signature colourful shirts and his willingness to engage with ordinary people, very quickly made him the darling of the world, and the attitude of many white people in South Africa who had demonised him, softened.

This was either the result of a public relations masterstroke, or indeed a man with the qualities of a saint, who could be sure, but what could not be contested was that he was the right man for the job at the time, albeit the existence of some truth that he represented little more than a figurehead. The realities of the new dispensation would, like a cold slap in the face, jolt the new leadership into reality as Madiba (Mandela) enjoyed the privileges of international elder statesman, travelling the world and entertaining foreign dignitaries, as everyone wanted a 'piece of him', while the realities of polity at the coalface was delegated to others by design or by default.

Arms deals of course, are nothing new to arms manufacturers and arms dealers, well-versed in the dynamics and techniques required to peddle their wares. They would sit around the negotiating table and muddy the waters by impressing those 'less in the know'. While many of the South African

---

[80] Andrew Feinstein 2007

government negotiators could not be accused of being blatantly dishonest at the outset of the transaction, or unintelligent, one surmises that they would not have woken up on a fateful, definitive, day in time, with thoughts of bribery and bounty uppermost in their minds while they enjoyed their morning muesli, then hugging their wives and children before departing for parliamentary obligations.

Bribery and bounty weave their way slowly into situations, not revealing themselves or the true nature of their character until much later in the stanza. Traffickers of bribery, do not boldly announce the complexity of their intentions in early stages of relationships, or indeed ever, but colour their schemes as good and gracious, victims discerning the realities too late, at a time when the need to censor clouds minds, the entrapment complete, now controlling bank accounts, body and mind, barn door well shut, the dark horse nowhere to be seen.

Muddying of the waters is both a science and an art, and is not at all easy to identify should you be among the ranks of the uninitiated. And so it was that a host of defence contractors systematically got the better of the South African government, using their conduits including Mr Schabir Shaik. Parliament was convinced by the protagonists that the arms deal which entailed the purchase of combat aircraft, training aircraft, patrol boats and submarines was the best deal on the table, despite being the most expensive deal on the table.

Competitor tenders were deemed to provide products that were satisfactory, yet at a fraction of the price, but the seed had been planted, and it had been explained that the expensive deal on offer was the best option due to 'financial offsets', a word borne of a new lexicon, that of the world of the arms trade. An offset very simply infers that should you spend a dollar on my product, I will reinvest back into your economy, funds for purposes of construction of manufacturing plants, or any entity which will contribute significantly to your economy.

Slowly at first, your economy will enjoy fruits, later ratcheting up valuable revenue worth many multiples of the initial investment in our product effectively negating the initial cost of weapons of war. So for the uninitiated, the material would almost, almost…, be free of charge. How nice, and to think that these defence contractors have such a bad reputation.

I had had occasion to have a series of long conversations with an old school friend of mine, Mark, confirming the sinister nature of the truth behind the sale of arms to 'third world' countries. Mark, now based in the UK, had taken it upon himself to better understand the ever-evolving intricacies of international crime syndicates and their involvement in financial and political impropriety within former colonies.

Having grown up in South Africa, he could lay claim to a better than average understanding of the dynamics of the process of colonisation and 'decolonisation', its inherent consequences, as well as an understanding of the methodologies of organised criminal groups targeting countries which had reasonably stable economies but whose neophyte governments were politically fragile in their naivete. Topping their shopping lists were countries throughout Africa, the South American continent and the newly dismembered USSR. For international criminal organisations, the playing field had just opened up beyond hope or expectation.

It could be argued, that one of the most effective and efficient of the so-called international crime syndicates can count amongst their number, ostensibly legitimate organisations involved in the arms trade. Their efficiency and efficacy shielding behind government secrecy acts relating to national security, protecting them from nosy media and the public in general, and in fact, governments' own internal watchdog structures with little to no recourse.

Such protection provides not only a shield, but by implication renders the governments in question complicit in the ensuing shady deals. Mark went to great lengths to stress that the offset system was little more than a symbolic 'sleight of hand', the dexterous seller easily gaining an early foothold in the sales process, providing additional comfort by way of contractual assurances that in the event of a default, the seller would be bound by punitive financial penalties.

In point of fact, the offset agreements in third world countries had seldom, if ever, been honoured, penalties paid in lieu thereof, the price of such being factored into the initially agreed costs, so the buyer received nothing more than a token refund or discount and little else. It seemed that the entire sales strategy of the purveyors of death and destruction was constructed on the foundation of a ruse, future long term revenue generation for a struggling economy, not being part of the game plan at the outset.

A puzzled, vacant look would be the standard reaction when I raised the subject of the 'arms deal' in conversation with friends, family or acquaintances, which I had found to be hugely alarming. It took a while, but the realisation struck, that having seen first-hand those useless shells bobbing on the water in Simonstown, purchased at great expense to the taxpayer, I had been alerted to the shameful smoke and mirrors trickery employed by the various arms manufacturers and dealers.

What the general public and I hadn't been aware of where the layers of illicit transactions beneath the surface, enriching all who were complicit in the flawed decision-making process which had been driven by invisible coercive forces; the finer detail of which would come to light only much later.

Alarming indeed, since I had no doubt, along with millions of other South Africans, originally been persuaded that the navy and air force had desperately needed to upgrade equipment, and the concept of **'financial offsets'** seemed to be a logical, almost philanthropic gesture on the part of South Africa's newly acquired international friends. We had also been of the opinion that the procurement process had been kept clean by way of special committees providing checks and balances, the way of the new government ensuring transparency, thus not being tainted by the ways of their miscreant predecessors.

Further investigation, however, would reveal (and was later confirmed by Andrew Feinstein in his book *After the Party*),[81] that some US$200 million had been paid by the arms companies in question in three portions, one to the ANC to assist in funding their 1999 election campaign, another to 'agents' along the way who had 'facilitated' the transaction, the final one third being paid to individuals within the government structure. (In communications with Andrew as recently as March 2023, he suggested to me that his estimate was now closer to the US$350 million mark.)

Naturally a little of the bad news later had managed to seep from the 'closed ranks', resulting in the need to be seen to 'do something', and it was Tony Yengeni (chief whip of the ANC), for accepting a luxury vehicle at cost price, and Schabir Shaik, for 'corrupting' Jacob Zuma, who would find themselves 'fall

---

[81] Andrew Feinstein *After the Party*: A Personal and Political Journey Inside the ANC (2007)[20]

- The Shadow World: Inside the Global Arms Trade (2011)
- Andrew Feinstein now resides in London, where he is Executive Director of Corruption Watch UK and chaired the Aids charity Friends of the Treatment Action Campaign, and lectures and writes on South Africa and the global arms trade. He is now considered an ANC dissident and critic, with his memoirs, *After the Party*, being severely critical of the political culture of the ANC. He describes the ill-fated arms deal as the 'point at which the ANC lost its moral compass'.

guys' at the sharp end of the wrath of the ANC, both ultimately spending very little of their predetermined sentencing time behind bars, Tony Yengeni escorted to prison by a legion of followers as a celebrity might be cheered and cherished en route to the Oscars.

Schabir Shaik was found guilty of fraud and corruption, and following presiding judge Hillary Squires' announcement that there existed 'overwhelming evidence that the relationship between Schaik and Zuma was a corrupt one'. Schaik was sentenced to 15 years in prison and Zuma was dismissed from his position by the State President Thabo Mbeki. So, one half of the corrupt relationship went to prison, the other half did not, Zuma later becoming the President of South Africa. Two scapegoats, lots of snouts in the trough, the smell of the thing was one to overwhelm the senses, but a veil of silence had been erected around this orgy of money grabbing.

Later, Andrew Feinstein, who had been an ANC parliamentarian, was put to work to uncover any and all impropriety relating to the arms deal, by no less than Jacob Zuma himself. After making much headway, his evidence, it would seem, threatened to bring down not just parliamentary structures, but the ANC itself. Soon, it was made abundantly clear that his investigations had become unwelcome, and that he should cease forthwith. Sadly, the dark side of these events only came to light later, in 2007.

27. The Zimbabweans

- *Poverty affects 76.3% of Zimbabwean children living in rural areas as of 2020.*

- *Roughly 74% of the population lives on less than $5.50 a day and the average wage is $253 per month.*

- *Half of Zimbabwe's 13.5 million people live below the food poverty line and about 3.5 million children are chronically hungry.*

- *Approximately 1.3 million Zimbabweans were living with HIV as of 2016. However, the number of HIV cases has been declining since 1997 because of improvements in prevention, treatment and support services.*

- *About 60% of rural Zimbabwean women face period poverty, meaning they lack access to menstrual supplies or education. Girls who experience period poverty miss an estimated 20% of their school life.*

Some estimates suggest that the numbers of Zimbabweans living in South Africa could run into the millions; the vast majority having fled their home country due to poverty, hyperinflation and the Gukurahandi, a black chapter in the annals of Zimbabwean history when it was reported throughout the 1980s that some 20,000 people were murdered in Matabeleland by President Robert Mugabe's 'personal' army, the 5th Brigade, trained in North Korea.

Many people in the region were reportedly sent to Pol Pot style 'Re-Education' camps. [82]

By 2018, 'Statistics South Africa' revealed that more than 30.4 million South Africans, 55.5% of the population, live on less than $2.50 per day, some 24 years after the fall of apartheid. The same year, international credit rating agency adjustments condemning the country's status to that of 'junk', made life tougher for everyone, the poor bearing the brunt.

Despite numerous initiatives, commissions and task groups, unemployment is in excess of 30%, South Africa's youth caught in an inescapable poverty trap, seeing those between 15 and 24 unemployed at a rate of over 60%. One of the most enduring legacies of apartheid is the grinding poverty suffered by the country's majority black population. Post-apartheid, black South Africans continue to be worst affected by poverty, and their numbers are growing.

The apartheid government wasted billions on a proxy border war, diabolical homeland infrastructure and 17 million arrests and imprisonment of ordinary people for 'reference book offences'. The unwitting ANC inherited a growing debt from its apartheid predecessor, then going on to waste billions on reconstruction and development programme scams, and a tragic episode of unnecessary expenditure on military materiel. [83]

His trembling right hand unable to keep the weapon steady, betraying some nervousness and an obvious lack of confidence, the 9mm pistol wavered ever so slightly. His facial features were unusual. He was not a South African, possibly a Zimbabwean, young, probably between 19 and about 22. There was absolutely no doubt in my mind, that only one of two things would happen as I looked deep into his eyes while he deliberately aimed his weapon at my forehead. They would need to kill me in order to gain access, or I would fashion a way to get them out of the house.

Of one thing I was absolutely certain, I was not going to let them get to my family. The pace of events changed dramatically, everything now happening for me in really slow motion, no doubt instinctive survival mechanisms at play. In a matter of what was probably no more than a few seconds, my mind raced, and in

---

[82] The writer, October 2021
[83] The writer October 2021

that short time my thoughts confirming the positioning of my family in the house, two-year-old Bianca asleep in her cot in her bedroom, my wife Michelle on the couch in the sunken lounge to my left, who may or may not have seen the weapon, and five-year-old Son James, now asleep on the couch next to his mum.

We had just eaten dinner. James was allowed a late night to be with Mum and Dad. As usual on Saturday night, we had just settled down to watch a movie on television. The external door of the adjacent, open-plan dining room left ajar for air on a balmy summer night, I had heard the shuffling of feet as I jumped from my seat to encounter the two just as they were about to enter the house.

The intruder's right arm was locked straight, the pistol held 'side on' as was often shown in the American gangster movies. He had stopped and taken aim as he stood in the doorway leading from the outdoor patio. Fleetingly, my mind recalled Johan, a friend gunned down and killed in his office while counting out cash for pay packets, my own cousin Andrew shot and killed in a supermarket hold up, and the previous occupier of our house, shot dead in the driveway of our home.

So many thoughts—my military training (despite being a reluctant conscript) had taught me that a weapon is held upright, right arm slightly bent to absorb the 'kick' of the firing weapon, while the supporting hand would provide stability under the handle of the weapon, reducing movement, ensuring the accuracy of the shot.

His accomplice, due to insufficient space to enter two abreast, was directly behind him, the two dressed in dark trousers and black leather jackets both brandishing what appeared to be standard military or police issue 9mm Star pistols. Instantaneously, I convinced myself that if he pulled the trigger, the weapon would recoil, and because of the lack of hand support, the trajectory of the round would be way off the mark. Had he taken aim at my stomach or chest, I would probably have been a lot less confident, as we were separated by only about two metres.

The sudden infusion of confidence, buoyed by the assumption that if he had planned to shoot, he would have done so by now, I heard his instruction, "Don't move!" and I recall thinking: *Yes, definitely a Zimbabwean accent.*

I put my hands into the air and stopped, and I responded: "Don't worry, I'm not moving," as I waited for just a brief moment.

I followed with: "See, I'm not moving." I then said to him confidently: "Don't worry, I'm ok. Are you ok?"

The question must have confused his thought processes, but given the nature of our crime-ridden society, I had learned the importance of keeping everyone calm, in a sense, assuming at least some control of the situation. His accomplice who was a little shorter than him, seemed frustrated, bobbing his head this way and that, in a vain attempt to get a sense of what was happening. It was evident the sequence wasn't panning out the way that they had planned, frustrating them, the result of which could go either way. I thought to test the water, confident that he probably wouldn't pull the trigger, and if he did, he wouldn't hit me anyway.

A third choice had crept in; the very real possibility that the weapons weren't loaded. The thoughts continued to stream through my mind in the short burst of that few seconds, memories of reading and hearing how these home invaders had made the rape of women and children, even babies, while the men of the house were bound, gagged and forced to watch, a mandatory rite as part of their home invasion.

Realising I was a fair bit taller and a little heavier than my would-be assailant, I instantaneously stacked up all these considerations. His accomplice proving totally ineffective, I made the determination that the odds were in fact, in my favour and to add to my confidence Michelle, now clearly aware of what was happening, had the presence of mind to remain quiet and out of sight, switching off the lamp in the lounge, which in fact had been the only burning light inside the house.

A light burned on the outdoor patio now, illuminating only them, me now in darkness. Taking the sudden darkness as a cue, I stepped again toward him. When I started a second step, his mate lost his nerve, turned and ran. I continued forward, the barrel of his weapon now almost up against my forehead, and I asked him outright: "What are you going to do now that your friend is gone?"

My next thought was to step toward him, grabbing his wrist and the weapon as my elbow and right arm would pin his right arm to my body, and he would no longer have a target to shoot at, and I would wrest the weapon from him. Within seconds this was no longer necessary, as he turned and ran, Michelle having grabbed a remote 'panic button' to activate the alarm siren, which would wail mercilessly for the next 60 seconds, upsetting the children who cried inconsolably after the commotion, and then learned what had just happened.

The serialised post mortem of this awful event yielded much to me about so many things. For the very first time I appreciated my military training, imagining a very different, tragic outcome had I not confronted my attacker with confidence. Those miserable months spent in Oudtshoorn might have been the very thing that saved my family and me from unspeakable horror.

One doesn't have any inkling as to what your response might be to certain given situations, until such time as you are confronted by the horror. I had been close to being car-jacked on a few occasions, always on my own though, so, typical of South African machismo, these events I would 'dine out' on, me being the one who could identify a potential car-jacking or as we called it 'hi-jacking' at 100 paces, they would never catch me!

Men loitering in groups outside a shop, carpark or at a traffic light, to the casual observer would go unnoticed. However, in South Africa my first thought would be that their presence, usually accompanied by furtive glances, was a dead giveaway of their intention to hold up a driver at gunpoint with the aim of stealing the vehicle. Taking evasive action became something of an art, and I recall sometimes not even relating the story to others, given that these incidents became fairly commonplace. Armed intruders in the home, a person's sanctuary where women and children take comfort in the certainty of safety, presented a vastly different experience.

Hope beats eternal in the breast of the optimist, who in a normal society, when a crime has been committed, calls the police without hesitation. And so, it was with me on that fateful night, the optimist in me simply assuming that the local police station would despatch a vehicle without delay. The station police would, one might think, respond to an armed invasion of a home with utmost urgency. South African police, I learned that night, finally confirming my suspicion that they were understaffed, ill equipped, poorly trained and devoid of morale.

Our local police station, Douglasdale, had not long before consisted of a caravan and some rudimentary furniture. The good, civil-minded people of the suburbs of Fourways, Douglasdale and surrounds, very conscious of the alarming increase in crime statistics, both locally, and nationally, had over time raised substantial funds and given of their skills and time to build a 'state of the art' station, housing a commander's office, charge office, administration offices, holding cells, a kitchen, a safe for weaponry, changing/locker rooms, toilet and ablution facilities with showers.

Donations by the local community, and some residents volunteering themselves to be trained and utilised as unpaid police reservists sought to ease the burden placed upon the police, 'our police'. Douglasdale police station was possibly the envy of the force around the country. This was the same police station I had called on that fateful night.

I had been trained back in the day in a corporate environment, that the telephone is the umbilical cord to paying customers, upon which any company is dependent for its very survival. When the telephone rang, it was not acceptable to allow the instrument to ring incessantly, but to be answered quickly; 'Cheerful, Chipper and Polite' at all times went the lesson, followed by appropriate tempo and volume, all the while articulating in order to be clearly understood, thereafter listening to understand, so that the channel of communication was opened to pave the way for the most positive outcome at the conclusion of the interaction. It followed, that I had developed, naively, an expectation that management at any institution dealing with the public would have taken 20 minutes to train their frontline staff on the fundamentals of telephone etiquette.

On that fateful night, it became abundantly clear to me that after ringing for a quite some time, the telephone was answered by a policeman wo was audibly agitated by having to answer the phone at all; his objective was not to provide service to the public in his precinct, but to get me off the phone as quickly as possible allowing him to return to his conversation with his colleague, who continued to talk to him anyway while he was on a call. Given what had transpired in our home just a few minutes earlier, and my state of mind, I found myself gritting my teeth to contain my anger, particularly since the man was barely audible, inarticulate, and most importantly, totally disinterested.

I pressed him, and eventually, reluctantly, he conceded that an officer would be despatched to our address as soon as a vehicle became available. About 45 minutes later, a lone officer arrived, and after taking a cursory look around the house, asked if anything had been stolen. "No," I responded, and then it seemed he was about to leave, when I asked why he was leaving without so much as taking a statement.

He was genuinely surprised at my insistence. "Because," as he put it, "nothing was stolen. Why do you want to make statements and open a case?" Seemingly bemused. He produced a pen and an official statement document, his inability to write and spell even the most fundamental words, quickly evident. I asked what his home language was, the response to which was an indignant: "I am a Zulu," which prompted me to suggest that he write the statement in in his home language.

He agreed, and I realised that this presented just as much of a challenge. The officer in question was a Sergeant, and while I almost felt sorry that I had inadvertently focussed a spotlight on the fact that he was, for practical purposes, functionally illiterate at worst, semi-literate at best. This was an indictment of the police structure, demonstrating to me first-hand that the policeman sitting at our dining table, visibly frustrated and embarrassed, had been the beneficiary of an inferior education, courtesy of a flawed system dating back over 50 years. Poorly educated and trained personnel were clearly being thrust into positions of authority and responsibility which were way beyond their levels of competence or confidence.

Bed time that night produced its own new fears, as I ensured that every external light on the patio and in the garden were left to burn until daybreak, providing me with at least some confidence that I could see out, but no-one could see into the house. I would be startled at every sound, which would prompt me to quietly climb out of the bed to patrol the house yet again, staring out of every window for a few minutes, anticipating the return of the gunmen.

The dining room being fairly central, allowed me to observe the outdoors through the windows of the kitchen, dining room and office without moving. Here I would stand without moving, with three good vantage point views of the garden, sometimes for half an hour at a time or more, night after night, as the fear took hold of my spleen and grew unabated within me, when one might have thought it would in fact subside.

Having always been totally opposed to a weapon in the house, I wished now that I could feel the comfort of the heavy 357 Magnum army issue 'cannon', I had so reluctantly been forced to adopt 24 hours a day when I had been in the Military Intelligence. That cold, steely, heavy encumbrance that I had despised so much would now be the only thing which might provide me with any comfort, since I had seen the devastation that the weapon could cause, and recall being sickened at the time. It was that devastation I longed for, since that would keep my young family safe, news of which would spread like wildfire, deterring even the most hardened of would-be home invaders.

I had never experienced this kind of indescribable fear in my life before, and I probably exacerbated my delicate state of being, with my reluctance to admit to or talk of it. So, quietly and in a state of isolation, bed time each night for me became an ordeal to be survived, the only comfort being to hear the easy breathing of my wife and 'babies' sleeping fitfully without a care in the world, while I patrolled the house, barely sleeping for several months.

The gunmen never did return, and we bought a 'new' home in the area, dubbed the fortress by friends and strangers alike. An automated driveway gate, an eight-foot wall built of concrete blocks, topped with an eight-strand electrified, alarmed fence providing our first line of defence against criminals. A motion-detecting system of infrared beams in the garden were activated by a central control panel at sunset.

External doors and windows protected by anti-burglar bars aided by electronic sensors, and motion detectors within the ground floor rooms of the house were all activated at bed time. A cast iron gate at the top of the stairwell leading to the first floor, effectively isolating all bedrooms upstairs from the rest of the house, provided for me the comfort I had sought. Our first nights in our new home delivered the first peaceful sleep I had experienced in several months.

Finally, I was able relax in the evenings, entirely comfortable in the knowledge that my family would not fall victim to gun-wielding criminals in our new-found safe haven.

Despite any misgivings, I might have harboured about the country of my birth, I still loved everything about 'my country', illustrated to the tee, by the tense, electric anticipation and distinctive smell of the Highveld before a pending thunderstorm, as the black cumulonimbus cloud would build overhead, slowly at first, then suddenly. Day would seemingly turn to night, as we would scurry indoors, lights would go on in the house, the tension quite tangible.

Convective cloud systems would produce large drops of rain, thudding slowly onto the roof, and gaining in frequency. It would build to a noisy crescendo, and then there would be the blinding, terrifying lightning, striking the earth as thunder would fill the sky, punishing the ears, hundreds of thousands of gallons of water despatched from above, and then more lightning, flash after flash. We knew that the fewer the seconds between the thunder and the lightening, the closer the lightning was to striking our trees or the house.

I would catch myself subconsciously counting the seconds between the flash and then the 'boom'. Large raindrops would often make way for hailstones which would fall down mercilessly, sometimes the size of pigeon eggs, sometimes as big as golf balls or larger, driving motorists and motorcyclists undercover for fear of damage or injury, while severe wind gusts would bend the largest of trees like blades of grass, threatening to rip the roofs from buildings.

Like insects hiding from a predator, we would 'batten down hatches', and when the clouds had been drained of their life-giving, devastating ice and liquid, as suddenly as the unstoppable force of nature had foist herself upon the unsuspecting world below, the sun would peek through an eerie silence, shooing away the cloud, and within minutes the entire sky would manifest as a magnificent, flawless, azure dome, complimented by warm sunshine, bathing the earth in a golden glow.

Dogs barking, cars back on the streets, children chattering in their gardens, life would carry on having barely skipped a beat, the whole thing might have been nothing but a dream. We had once again been reminded this was Africa, a tough continent, not for the faint of heart, but the Africa which flowed unashamedly through our veins for several generations, perhaps making us 'tough' people.

As much as I loved our frequent thunderstorms, I loved my life, more so now that I had successfully seen to the safety of my family in our new house, which besides being a 'fortress' was truly a magnificent home with a huge, manicured, treed garden; large swimming pool, tudor-style 'pub', children's playroom, and ample accommodation including a wing of offices for us to run our business, separate from the general living and 'inviting' indoor and outdoor entertainment areas, and a flatlet with kitchen and bathroom for our housekeeper—'Happy'.

Business was treating us well. Our young children were at a good school, memorable holidays to the mountains or the seaside were frequent, and frankly, we could not have asked for more. We were certainly living the dream, still confident that our new government would 'right' the ship, promising a bright future for all. I certainly was conscious of and grateful for everything that I had, and everything I could offer my family. I knew that we were truly fortunate in a country where, sadly, most people existed in the shackles of 'crushing destitution'.

The domestic staff whom we employed were representative of these 'poor' people, and always mindful of our good fortune, Michelle and I tried as hard as we possibly could to assist these folk in the upliftment of themselves and their families, assisting youngsters with funding for schooling, college and clothing, attempting to find jobs for others, and generally going out of our way to show these people as much humaneness and kindness as we possibly could. Heartening was the fact that despite their extreme difficulties, we always found them all to be somewhat philosophical toward their plight, and without question, they were mostly just good, decent, people who found themselves in the wrong place in history.

Memories of the treatment of the maids who had worked for our family when I had been a child, might have resulted in a layer of guilt within me, which festered and grew over time, causing me to overcompensate in my dealings with our staff, for which I made no apologies.

28. Vincent

By 2018, 'Statistics South Africa' revealed that more than 30.4 million South Africans, 55.5% of the population, live on less than $2.50 per day, some 24 years after the fall of apartheid. The same year, international credit rating agency adjustments condemning the country's status to that of 'junk', made life tougher for everyone, the poor bearing the brunt.

Despite numerous initiatives, commissions and task groups, unemployment is in excess of 30%, South Africa's youth caught in an inescapable poverty trap, seeing those between 15 and 24 unemployed at a rate of over 60%. One of the most enduring legacies of apartheid is the grinding poverty suffered by the country's majority black population. Post apartheid, black South Africans continue to be worst affected by poverty, and their numbers are growing.

The apartheid government wasted billions on a proxy border war, diabolical homeland infrastructure and 17 million arrests and imprisonment of ordinary people for 'reference book offences'. The unwitting ANC inherited a growing debt from its apartheid predecessor, then going on to waste billions on reconstruction and development programme scams, and a tragic episode of unnecessary expenditure on military materiel.[84]

"You are my sunshine... My only sunshine..." the little voice strained through the speakers, competing with the babble of a few hundred chattering voices. Determined, the little voice persisted, until the crowd went eerily silent, as the voice now took control of not only the stage, but also the entirety of the school grounds, buoyed, confidence growing all the while, mesmerising the audience who had stopped everything they were doing to savour the richness washing over them, purity directly from heaven.

---

[84] The writer October 2021

A little golden haired angel, five-years old, singing with the confidence of an accomplished star, causing the hairs on the back of my neck to stand as the realisation struck me: it was my daughter Bianca who had insisted that she go onto the stage to persuade the announcer to allow her to sing. Everything in the world now was unimportant, as the warmth and beauty of that strident voice emanating from a little, little person caused time to stand still, capturing the hearts of all in attendance, a reminder of the beauty of simplicity in our mad, rushed lives. Thunderous applause accompanied the little mite's descent from the stage and continued as she scurried to grab the hand of her mum.

Our extended family had gathered, as we had the year before, to enjoy the festivities and the 'big walk' for fund raising at our children's school, Bryandale Primary. The familiar smell and sound of spicy boerewors sizzling above the flames—a traditional South African sausage—to be eaten on a fresh bread roll with a variety of sauces which would run down the chin.

The juices from the sausage would soon render the bread roll into nothing but a drenched, messy, 'hold in the hand' trap, as those delicious juices would embarrass one, dripping onto the floor and clothing if not eaten quickly enough, always a challenge when the sausage was too hot to handle, having just been taken from the fire and hot coals. Later, the smell of hot chips, or warm donuts might tempt; the children well aware that that Mum and Dad were pretty relaxed at events such as this, and would almost aways get whatever they wanted.

After all, the money was going to a good cause. There would be drinks and snacks, rides, and fun activities at the 'fair' which would accompany the main event.

We would sit, under the shade of giant oak trees, snacking, chatting amongst ourselves, greeting and chatting to parents of other kids, the weather perfect—sunny with the gentlest of breezes—as our children in their element ran freely with their schoolmates, returning from time to time to ask for a coin for a ride, or a snack, or perhaps to buy hoops to throw in order to win a prize. Consciously, I sat on the spectator stands overlooking the sports-field, not a care in the world, absorbing the atmosphere, a very real contentment washing over me as simple days such as this would punctuate the richness of our lives.

It was our third 'big walk' and the school was becoming an integral part of our family life, providing for me, a new, fun, challenging activity; assisting with coaching of our son James' cricket and soccer teams. This had been one of the elements of the teaching environment I had really missed when I had moved on to the corporate world. Yes, we had certainly become part of the greater Bryandale School family. A cursory glance around the school would illustrate the metamorphosis which South Africa was experiencing, as children, parents, aunts and uncles, grandparents were represented across ethnic spectrums.

This was not, as it had been years before, a whites-only government school in the leafy northern suburbs of Johannesburg. The expensive European cars arriving at the school in the mornings suggested that most of the kids, regardless of ethnicity or creed, were from 'well to do' homes, so this essentially remained a school for privileged kids from the northern suburbs, with its doors thrown open to all. I guess that this gave me comfort, for this was the South Africa I had hoped for, for so long, and it all just seemed to fit into place so neatly! The rose-tinted lens through which I had started to see the country's evolution was no doubt, a construct of my own mind, for my own benefit, in keeping with my deeply ingrained positive outlook on life and the future.

Basking in the mottled shade of the enormous, old oak trees, my contentment was interrupted by the musical ringing of my mobile phone. Glancing down, I thought I recognised the number, but never having been one for fastidiously storing contact names and numbers, I could not be sure. "Pete, can you talk?" Enquired the earnest voice of Beryl, Michelle's step-mother.

In an instant, I knew something was amiss, terribly amiss, Beryl was one of the most jovial people I knew, and this certainly was not the voice of that jovial person. I had absolutely no idea what to expect, as I moved away from my family to take the call, assuring her that it was okay to talk.

Michelle's brother Stephen had recently started a restaurant in Honeydew, a peri-urban area consisting of mostly five, or ten-acre hobby farms, and some light industry. It was an area earmarked for future urban/suburban sprawl, so a large restaurant, offering good value for money fare, certainly seemed a good business prospect. Stephen was on the lookout for kitchen staff and waiters, so knowing that Vincent needed a job, we mentioned this to Happy. He would have been about 23 or 24 years old, the son of our housekeeper, 'Happy', Vincent was an introverted young man from Soweto, having grown up in Venda, a dusty, poor 'homeland'.

Unemployed, inexperienced, with a very limited command of English, his prospects for work were largely restricted to manual, menial labour at best. Happy had indicated that he would 'grab' whatever he could get, so we arranged that Vincent meet Stephen for an interview. Stephen reported that despite a passive, quiet demeanour, Vincent had displayed a keen sense of humour, and Stephen felt that Vincent was, despite the myriad stumbling blocks faced in his lifetime, willing and able to be trained. It also came to light that Vincent was partially deaf, and had relied on a hearing aid, no doubt contributing to his apparent lack of confidence.

Vincent gladly accepted the job as bus boy/dishwasher for a wage, and given that he lived far from the restaurant, travel money for taxis to and from work. Also agreed upon, was that Vincent would train under the head chef, to become himself, a chef. Stephen often remarked that Vincent had become one of his favourites, and by all accounts, Vincent was delighted to finally have a job, and enjoyed working for Stephen.

"Vincent is dead!" was what I thought I heard, so naturally my first instinct was that I had heard incorrectly, I quickly retorted: "What was that Beryl?"

To which she responded: "Sorry Pete, you heard correctly… Vincent is dead, he was murdered last night."

"What, how… Beryl?"

"Sorry Pete, I have no detail other than Stephen just got the call from the police a few minutes ago, after he had started to wonder why Vincent hadn't arrived for work this morning." Michelle, the children and I had got to know Vincent when we'd invited him to come to our home to do some casual jobs. He'd always shown his gratitude for some extra cash and a meal, and although he was a difficult one to get to know, the family were in agreement that he was a shy, nice guy. I slowly, reluctantly returned to the group who had not really noticed my absence, and here suddenly I was burdened with this shocking news which would no doubt put an end to the day's festivities all too suddenly. My mind raced.

"Perhaps it's a hoax, perhaps it's mistaken identity… Not Vincent, but some other poor unfortunate, no… no… no, there will be some rational explanation, since Vincent was little more than a quiet, harmless soul, who'd want to murder him?"

My reluctance to interrupt and in so doing, cut short a wonderful family outing on a beautiful sunny day, was overwhelming. More overwhelming, though, was the burden of the horrific news which I felt the misfortune of having to process and then share, all the while continuing to wear my contented face.

As though it was the most natural thing in the world, I quietly asked Michelle to walk with me, desperately trying to be unobtrusive. A little way from the others I told her of the call, as the colour drained from her face. She too in an instant had processed the information, and with a silent acknowledgement of the circumstances, suggested that I remain at the school while she would call Happy to prepare her to be picked up, and in the car on the way to the police mortuary in Honeydew she would relay to her what I had been told.

Quietly, we re-joined our children and family, Michelle nonchalantly excusing herself, saying that she needed to collect Happy to attend to a family matter, her demeanour not betraying any emotion or detail, as she hugged and kissed each child promising to back as soon as she could.

It's known by different names around the world; in Brazil, a Favela, in other parts of the world, a shanty town; and in Southern Africa it's a Squatter Camp. It is said, that in the squatter camps, which number in excess of 2000 in South Africa, a remarkable sense of community exists largely born of the shared commonality; all poor black people[85], mostly unemployed, transient, living in the most squalid of circumstances without running water, electricity, very limited communal toilet facilities, unsealed roads which quickly transform into muddy quagmires when the rains begin to fall.

Rudimentary structures, hastily cobbled from materials which can easily be scavenged; plastic tarpaulins, plastic containers or boxes, plastic bags, corrugated iron sheeting seemingly a luxury if found, all provide that which is necessary to create a tiny, leaky, home on a sand floor, which some people brush and polish to create a semblance of a hard floor. In such a 'home', the single room serves different purposes at different times of day and night, from being a 'lounge' during the day it will transform into a kitchen for cooking in the late afternoon, thereafter a dining room, and finally a bedroom, in which sometimes an entire family might live.

It was in such a squatter camp in which Vincent had 'chosen' to live. He had learned that it was substantially cheaper to live in a shack (slumlords collected rent each week from those living in 'his' shacks) which was walking distance from the restaurant, than to commute to Soweto, resulting in a saving of time and money each day.

---

[85] Many years after the 1994 elections, the situation regarding the squatter camps housing black people under the apartheid government has not improved, but in fact worsened. Under the new government, many thousands of white families also find themselves in such squatter camps.

192

It was rumoured that the camp in which he found himself had been inhabited mostly by Zimbabweans at a time when a fair amount of xenophobic hostility had been levelled toward not only Zimbabweans, but all and sundry from neighbouring countries and elsewhere in Africa. It seemed entirely possible that Vincent's killer/s had meted out some xenophobic retaliation of their own, but of course, no one knew for sure.

Whoever had killed Vincent had certainly harboured no 'sense of community' when they sat him down on a large plastic container which had held HTH, a chlorine powder for swimming pool maintenance which very possibly had its origins at our home. The large inverted container had been used as a chair, the attackers binding Vincent's feet and his wrists behind him. His head and upper body drenched in petrol, the fear, the sensations and finally the pain Vincent would have experienced as the inevitability of that flame became all too real, to me were unimaginable.

Unimaginable, unfathomable to the point of defying even a base level code of morality which defines us as human. The extent of the evil or hatred in a person's heart required to do such a thing led us to suspect that a message was being sent. To whom, and why, we had no answer. In an attempt to make sense of the murder in general, and the brutal method in particular, in my mind's eye I reached a somewhat impalpable conclusion.

Perhaps after so many decades, more than a century of 'legitimised' oppression by colonial powers and then 'white' republican rule maintained by a brutal iron fist, the collective psyche of black people had been desensitised to violence in general, including that to which 'normal' societies would react with horror, such as savage murder and large scale rape of females regardless of age.

After many generations, desensitisation, exacerbated in no small measure by widespread poverty and the absent parent syndrome, life had become so cheap and devoid of meaning, that societal norms had shifted, evil and hatred being superseded by cold, callous indifference, black society averting eyes, reacting to this new 'norm' with a deep breath and silent resignation.

Those guilty of ending Vincent's life were never sought, no investigation eventuated, Happy never talked of the heartbreaking incident, urging us to not speak of it, particularly when we wanted to follow up with the police. In a state of desperation, she did her best to explain the 'rogue element' which existed underground, a communications network concealed from white suburban society, a conduit for news and threats, black domestic workers and gardeners unwittingly being sucked into the vast web of 'intelligence', criminals strategically positioned to pounce when opportunities presented themselves.

Sometimes threats would be used to coerce staff to provide insight into the workings as well as the comings and goings of white households in order to plan burglaries or armed invasions. Disgruntled employees, wanting to get back at the 'master' or 'madam' of the house, may well have seen an opportunity for self-enrichment as well as a bit of old-fashioned vengeance, resulting in complicity in home invasions, often leading to torture, rape and murder. Happy insisted that it was this web which was not to be fed, since retribution against her family, or possibly even our family was a very real possibility, hence her reluctance born of deep-seated fear.

The far-reaching tentacles of criminals active in these neighbourhood networks, knew no bounds. We had harboured suspicions for some time that in South Africa, 'bent cops' existed. Happy alluded to a police force operating on the periphery of the underground network, not to aid in policing, but almost as an auxiliary resource at the disposal of criminals operating in the shadows.

Having not really understood before, now it made sense that not only was Happy reluctant to have a civil case opened or pursued following the death of the unfortunate Vincent, she was vehemently opposed to it, fearing for herself and her family. The episode highlighted once again the parallel societies which exist in South Africa, domestic workers and gardeners occupying the same physical spaces as their white suburban employers, yet separated by light years in so many spheres of life. Urban black South Africans putting on award winning acts in the presence of their white employers for the sake of apparent deference, while many harbour disdain or worse—hatred for those same employers, at the same time safeguarding the secrets of the 'underground network', which quietly, deftly, remains fully operational 24/7.

29. A Mighty Thunderstorm

The security industry in South Africa which provides alarm systems, security gates, electric fences, security sentries, and armed reaction security personnel in South Africa, is estimated to be worth an annual turnover of US$6-billion (2021), much of which is spent by the South African Government paying private contractors to do work which should be undertaken by the South African police. [86]

The annual policing budget for South Africa in 2021 reflects a similar allowance of approximately US$6-billion [87]

Sleep came easily to me, the memories of that fateful night when I had stared down the barrel of a gun in my own home had all but dissipated, as we had taken the necessary steps to get on with our lives in the best way we knew how. There was, however, just one thing which lingered, but even then, we had become accustomed, yet again as a result of a long period of desensitisation. Frequently after dark we would hear gunfire. Some nights, two, three or four shots shattering the stillness of the night. Some nights we would stop momentarily as we heard what sounded like an exchange in a protracted firefight.

Some nights we heard the crack of small calibre handguns, some nights the tap tap tap of automatic assault rifles, sometimes distant, sometimes way too close for comfort. *Safety in numbers*, I would always console myself, ours in amongst hundreds of homes, probably the best fortified house on the block. Then add to the mix two huge German Shepherds, having slept lazily for most of the day, now roaming the garden, evading detection just beneath the external infrared sensors, invisible to the naked eye, set a little higher to detect the

---

[86] The Writer.

[87] *(http://www.treasury.gov.za/documents/National%20Budget/2020/enebooklets/Vote% 2028%20Police.pdf)*

presence a grown man. Many other homes would be targeted for invasion or looting before our fortress was considered an option.

Scouring of local newspapers, TV or radio news broadcasts yielded no information whatsoever about these nocturnal gun battles we were privy to, and worse, had become accustomed to. In time, I started to give a little more thought to that which was obviously abnormal. Subconsciously I wondered also just how much people could tolerate, particularly the millions of uneducated, unemployed, poverty-stricken black people who had been promised the earth by the ANC before elections in 1994.

Now, 12 or 13 years later, it was a very small proportion of black society who could honestly say that they were financially and socially better off than before. People wanting to break into my home, certainly was not surprising, and while I dreaded such an event, on a certain level, I felt I understood such actions.

Sleeping fitfully one warm, clammy summer evening, I was awakened in the small hours of the morning by a wild wind whistling through the house. Throughout the summer months, we slept leaving our bedroom window ajar. A slit of a window, it was way too narrow for even a small child to squeeze through, much less an adult intent on mischief. The breeze contributing to a continuous flow of fresh air, aiding in a comfortable slumber. Not at all alarmed by the wind, my mind instinctively acknowledging the pending thunderstorm.

I turned over in bed, rather looking forward to sleeping through the coming half hour or so of violent flashes in the sky, thunderous confirmation that the electricity despatched from above had found and made contact with some metallic object above ground or perhaps a deposit of ore concealed for millennia beneath the earth's surface. Following the script to the letter, the thunderstorm went through its prescribed stages as it had done since I was toddler… until one of the lightning strikes aligned itself perfectly with a crash of thunder, and without a moment's hesitation I knew that this was not some distant strike, but the house being struck.

Instantaneously, the alarm was sounded when both internal and external sirens wailed, the cacophony deliberately designed to cause pressure on the eardrums and, it felt, the brain itself was under attack—the security measures had been breached.

It was impossible to know precisely what had happened as I glanced at the alarm clock which informed without malice that it was 12.48am. The children, wide-eyed and terrified, came running as their mum gathered them up in her arms, all taking shelter in our bed as I stabbed at the alarm control panels to deactivate the wailing sirens, in so doing, shutting down the entire security system. Venturing out from behind the huge, double locked steel gate protecting the sleeping quarters, I locked it behind me calling to Michelle to take the key.

Switching on lights and walking through the house I saw no obvious damage, leading me to suspect that perhaps it had been the high voltage lightning strike which had simply caused a system overload triggering the alarms, one connected to the electrified perimeter fence, the other linked to all door, window and internal sensors. Returning upstairs, I fed the code numbers into the control panels, whereupon a siren wailed, indicating that it was the electrified fence which had been compromised.

A cursory inspection of the garden revealed, to my horror, the devastation of a large, heavy bough from a mature tree, possibly 10 metres in length, having crashed down on the electrified fence, the damage concealed by a mountain of leafy debris. What was visible, was a tangle of wires, like the strings on a guitar fret having been cut through with a sharp blade. My thoughts running, kept returning to the obvious, our first line of defence had been decimated.

Without consideration for my predicament, the rain was still pelting down, but fortunately the lightning and thunder seemed to have moved on to wreak havoc in some distant suburb. Returning to my warm, dry cosy bed no longer an option, I imagined calling up someone in the morning to repair the damage, only to be reminded that there would be a wait of a week or more making it imperative to 'book well in advance'.

Collecting a ladder and a saw from my workshop, I set to work in the deluging rain, cutting and removing the unwanted debris from the top of the wall, hoping that the wall itself had not been damaged. The security 'floodlight' mounted on the side of the house provided ample lighting at least for the first part of the job. About an hour's toil revealed no structural damage to the wall or indeed the posts which hosted the wiring, much to my delight.

Having had no working knowledge of an electrified fence, I stood back, and figured that the wiring could easily be fed through the 'system' of 'wheels' on each post, and wires that were snapped could be re-joined with tiny metal clasps, which I had recalled seeing in the workshop, having always wondered what they had been for. Now it all seemed so obvious. The rain had slowed, and working with the aid of a mechanic's bright lead light, voila, our first line of defence was quickly, proudly up and running, evidenced when the entering of code numbers into the control panel in our bedroom was met with a welcome, stony silence.

Final inspection of the fence was met the familiar '... hum...' of a live electrified fence warning of terrible bodily pain should you chance your luck, accompanied by a screaming alarm promising to wake the entire neighbourhood. By the time I got back to bed, it would have been about 3.00am. Our bed was now occupied by two sleeping children and their mum, so I went to sleep in James' bed. Very proud of myself and my resolve, and in an instant, I was in dreamland, once again, not a care in the world.

Waking the next morning the events during the thunderstorm seemed like nothing more than a dream. Business as usual, I woke the children at 5.30, brushed teeth, dressed them and combed hair before venturing downstairs for breakfast. At about 6.15, I would start chivvying them along to the car, making sure that they had been to the toilet, washed hands and that they had not forgotten their packed lunches, or anything else they might have needed for school for the day.

Leaving home before 6.20 would ensure that we would not be late for the bell signalling the start of the school day. Our mornings had become ritual, as we would go through the absurdity of sitting in stop-start traffic to cover six km in 45 minutes.

This time, I had always used to play different types of music from my collection of CDs, encouraging the children to sing along. In this way they became familiar with a wide variety of genres and artists, from the Reggae of Bob Marley, the Beatles, the Rolling Stones, Roy Orbison, David Bowie, Iggy Pop, Black Sabbath, and from Slade to the Disco/New Romantic/Techno eras. Some mornings I would share with them music that their grandad loved; Elvis, Buddy Holly, Gene Vincent or Dean Martin and Frank Sinatra.

We would interrupt our music sessions at 7.00 to listen to the morning news on radio which would sometimes ignite conversation, I always hoped, to spark enquiry and stimulate engagement. For me, these daily school runs came to represent an important component in the development of my relationship with my children.

Discussions emerging from news broadcasts would range from issues of racism, to conflicts or wars around the world, economics, matters of social responsibility and, of course, many other topics. I continued to drive both children to school for a number of years, for which I made no apologies, until they passed driver licensing tests, and drove themselves. As inevitable as it was always going to be, I couldn't but help feeling that a little privilege had been taken from me when I wasn't quite ready for it.

My mind returned from time to time to the evening when I had repaired the electric fence, and it later struck me that the fear of a home invasion had not left me, our new 'safe' home, nothing more than a 'band aid' to plaster over the fine cracks in my mental state, not visible to others, but certainly very obvious and real to me, as I subconsciously began more and more to find fault with my surroundings.

30. Task Forces, Talking Heads and Echo Chambers

Epiphany: a usually sudden manifestation or perception of the essential nature or meaning of something. (2): an intuitive grasp of reality through something (such as an event) usually simple and striking. (3): an illuminating discovery, realisation, or disclosure.[88]

I almost choked on my coffee, as he talked. "My kids are off to Australia next month, and as soon as they're settled, the wife and I will follow!" said Chris in a way which could only be described as 'matter of fact'. "Yep," he continued, "this country is finished!" I watched his face; carefully concealing my disapproval—no—disdain—for what I had just heard. Chris and his business partner Cornel, were, as far as I was concerned, more rooted to the African continent than anyone else that I knew.

Chris, a longstanding insurance client of ours had grown up on the dusty West Rand, on the gold mines which followed a roughly east-to-west crescent on the outskirts of Johannesburg. He had gravitated towards the Freight and Logistics industry and of late, he and Cornel had started up a business, combining their years of expertise in the field of logistics to run an apparently lucrative business with a great deal of promise for the future.

Between the cities of Johannesburg and Pretoria, just off the 'high speed' motorway, lay a new, well-planned suburb boasting modern homes, schools, office complexes, hotels, shopping precincts, a wonderful sports stadium where many international cricket matches had been won and lost, as well as its very own man-made lake as the focal point. Named after Hendrik Verwoerd, assassinated Prime Minister of South Africa and 'architect of apartheid',

---

[88] *https://www.merriam-webster.com › dictionary › epiphany*

'Verwoerdburg' was testament to the industrious Afrikaner and his advancement.

To the black people who worked here (they weren't permitted to own property in the area up until the 1990s), the naming of the place would no doubt have been akin to calling a suburb in Tel Aviv, 'Hitlerville'. Reason later prevailed, and the name was changed to Centurion, and many nouveau riche black families moved into the area because of its convenient location and multitude of amenities.

It was at a coffee shop at Centurion, basking in the glorious autumn sunshine, enjoying bottomless cups of rich Mocca Java, or Arabica coffee, that we would have our meetings from time to time overlooking the 'lake', where Chris' comments seemed totally out of character that day. This was their preferred meeting venue, to which I had no objection at all. I always looked forward to and enjoyed meeting with the two directors of the company. Chris particularly, speaking with a gravelly accent, was an earthy, dyed-in-the-wool 'South African patriot', Cornel similarly, although more urbane, was quite simply a sophisticated Afrikaner.

While we always had good lengthy chats about the state of the world, it was always pleasing to get down to business, since the exponential growth of their company meant that the shareholder life and disability insurance for the partners needed to be upgraded at significant expense, obviously translating into very generous commissions to me, following their declaration of healthy profits each financial year end.

It was on this particular day, after Chris has dropped his bombshell, that I had pressed him for more answers. I had generally had no interest in people when I had learned of their intentions to emigrate, so had never pressed anyone before. In fact, people talking of leaving my beloved South Africa embittered me to the point in which I had no desire to speak to them at all.

This was perhaps a little different, since it meant the loss of a very good client, and truth be told, I had come to hold Chris' opinions in high regard, as an intelligent person and a 'battle hardened' businessman. The answers he provided were certainly thought-provoking, as Chris talked of his adult children, with children of their own, struggling to procure suitable employment due to BEE, excluding white people from even being interviewed for positions in government and private sector.

He talked of his son procuring a number of offers of employment in Western Australia, the challenge being to decide which one he wanted. After a spate of violent incidents in the upmarket suburb in which he lived, he stated with some intensity that his wife resented being alone, feeling fearful at home during daytime hours while Chris was at work, sometimes well into the early evenings. I certainly couldn't fault what I was hearing, particularly in light of my own recent experiences. I certainly, had never so much as entertained the thought of leaving my home and my country.

One of my best childhood friends, Nick, had talked of uprooting his family and emigrating to Perth in Western Australia where he'd investigated business opportunities a number of years before. A close old friend of Nick and I, Jonathan, whose family home had provided my earlier enlightenment, had relocated to New Zealand some years prior, and I recall thinking that he had acted impulsively.

More and more over the ensuing weeks and months, my awareness of people emigrating, or even talking of emigration, was now heightened. No doubt the incidence of emigration or talk thereof was no different to before, but I felt that I was less critical of those wanting to flee. Life continued, and I didn't consciously give a great deal of thought to the subject again.

Democracy had been alive and kicking for well over 10 years now, a drive through the countryside revealing government attempts at providing brick homes to the masses, as here and there one would see clusters of new homes in neat rows, visible overhead cables providing electricity to each abode, which although tiny in size, still conveyed an air of respectability since they were built of brick, had proper roofing, and internal plumbing for running water and toilets.

Sight of these would give one hope that the masses would soon be homeowners, homelessness and squatter camps a thing of the past. RDP housing this was called, the Reconstruction and Development Programme. Encouraging to the casual passer-by, this was government delivering on promises, there now being no reason for doubt of any description. The following months were, perhaps, the point at which my patriotism really started to wane, as I would need to buy expensive tyres for my car on an all too frequent basis, having damaged tyres by hitting potholes in roads, almost it seemed, on a daily basis.

This for me represented a local government which either did not have the funds for basic infrastructural maintenance, or lacked the will to repair roads, representing a much larger set of problems relating to infrastructure. The phrases 'Rolling blackout', 'load shedding' and 'power outage' entered our everyday lexicon. These all relating to frequent episodes of no electricity in the home, shops, factories and offices for several hours at a time, sometimes even days.

It seemed that power stations had not been adequately maintained, and the supply chain for coal, one of the most important ingredients for power stations had been corrupted by politicians and 'tenderpreneurs' who lacked the wherewithal to plan, source, or transport the top quality coal efficiently to keep the lights on. Further, it seemed that there had been a gross miscalculation that the infrastructure could supply necessary power to the existing grid as well as the rapidly growing new areas requiring electricity.

Those within the ANC responsible for infrastructure should have been well aware that a priority in 1994 should have been the fervent maintenance of power stations, and indeed a robust strategy to construct more power stations for future demand. None of this was considered back in 1994.

Sadly, the corruption evident in supply chain management of coal, saw unbridled corruption in supply chains elsewhere, somewhat reminiscent of the old homeland days. With this, and a decline in standards generally, more and more cracks within the new government began to manifest and, sadly, most of that for which it was responsible.

The promise of RDP homes for all had started with a 'bang', as we encouraged all of our black staff to register, their names now officially on the 'list', excitement mounted, the joy tangible. Then as the years went by, RDP scams came to light, in which developers were making off with funds intended to realise the dreams of thousands of people needing a place to call home, resulting in half-finished projects.

Other developers handed over keys for homes that were poorly constructed, leaky or sometimes even hazardous and uninhabitable. Some RDP projects were plagued by corruption when tenders were granted on the basis of 'backhanders' or providing friends or family with the contracts. None of this augured well for the RDP, which had, in principle provided hope and certainly seemed like a good idea. It was as usual the poor who bore the brunt of government mischief, folly and lack of oversight. Happy and her family came to realise over time that owning a house was but a pipe dream.

Each time a new social problem was highlighted, usually by the media, the new game in parliament seemed to be one of creating a moniker to counter the problem, turn it into an acronym, create a committee or task team to investigate the problem. The committee or task team would dissipate organically over time as parliamentarians would be redeployed as re-shuffle after re-shuffle took place within cabinet.

After no further real evaluation or consideration the matter would go cold, fading into obscurity and without further ado, expiring quietly... eventually erased from the collective memory. Where the matter was of grave importance, the irksome collective conscience of society or the media would haunt government, who would skilfully find or manufacture a diversion, often inciting the masses, the have-nots, to take to the streets, creating a 'something must be done' narrative, the original problem hopefully forgotten.

Unwittingly, the ANC, through their mismanagement, lack of action, and corrupt practices have, on a platter, given credence to the white racist forewarning, framing the decades leading up to the first democratic elections. With unadulterated glee, the white racist struts without reserve, the words 'I told you so' having become their 'post-apartheid' mantra. As hard as one tries to reason with these people, the fact that the ANC inherited a lemon, is precisely what they don't want to hear.

What the ANC certainly don't want to hear, are success stories, the likes of Singapore proving that with no natural resources to speak of, after independence, the leadership took a country of functionally illiterate people, through meticulous planning, intelligent innovation, and hard slog to amongst the highest GDPs per capita in the world, while consistently ranking amongst the least corrupt societies on the planet. Not to suggest that Singapore is by any means perfect, but they certainly can boast achievements to be emulated. Why not us?

Despite our privileged existence, a culmination of recent events started to consume much of my thinking. I was becoming fearful for my own safety, but more so for the long-term safety of my wife and children, not least of all, future prospects for my children and their children. I had become a little brittle in my dealings with others, always on edge, and manic about locking up the house at night, ensuring that alarms, beams and electric security fence were in working order and correctly set.

Waking in the early hours of the morning hearing noises in the house or garden, my heart would race, ruling out any more sleep, I would long for sunrise. I would become quite anxious when Michelle wished to visit with friends at night, knowing of the dangers lurking on the streets. Our children were not allowed out of our gates, and had seldom walked on a sidewalk, always being driven by car to friends, school or shops. Ensuring the safety of my family became an obsession which was front of mind more frequently than ever before.

31. Juxtaposition and a
Whole New Epiphany

"Perhaps because the challenges we face in our country are so daunting, we are also tempted by shortcuts. We tell ourselves that if we invent a new acronym, or write a new empowerment charter, we can avoid some of the back-breaking work that sustained progress requires."

Helen Zille.[89]

It was a few months later in that year, driving home one afternoon from a business appointment that I felt the urge to stop at a café for a cup of my standard Mocha Java coffee, wanting to relax for a few minutes and have some time to gather my thoughts before returning to the hustle and bustle of the office and home, where I would have to complete my work for the day, go for a training run, then collect James from his Karate class. As I sat outside at the 'Mugg and Bean' in Ferndale in Johannesburg, the weather began to turn, a thunderstorm threatening, forcing me to drink up and get going, or I would be drenched getting to the car once the deluge started.

---

[89] Zille is a white former journalist and anti-apartheid activist and was one of the journalists who exposed the cover-up around the death of Black Consciousness leader Steve Biko while working for the *Rand Daily Mail* in the late 1970s She also worked with the Black Sash and other pro-democracy groups during the 1980s. In the political arena, Zille has served in all three tiers of government, as the Western Cape's education MEC (1999–2001), as a Member of Parliament (2004–2006), as Mayor of Cape Town (2006–2009), and as Premier of the Western Cape (2009–2019). Zille became an outspoken critic of corruption, cadre deployment and general mismanagement within the ANC ruling party. Ironically, she is of Dutch descent, her political views diametrically opposed to Hendrik Verwoerd, late Prime Minister of South Africa, also Dutch by birth. Wikipedia 2021

Turning on the car's ignition, I heard the distinctive voice of Helen Zille, as she spoke during a fairly lengthy radio interview, her voice very calm and reassuring as always. Helen was the outspoken leader of the Democratic Alliance, opposition party to the ANC, and Premier of the Western Cape. She spoke of the decline of the South African democracy, describing how a person looking into a mirror each day for five years will not consciously notice the ageing of the face.

Comparing your mirrored image to a photo taken five years ago will, of course, reveal the ageing and wrinkles, and so it is with the systematic deterioration of the political and social landscape subsequent to the democratisation of our country, as day by we do not consciously see the decline in our society. She made very clear and definite reference to her fear for the future of our democracy and indeed our very survival. Such erudite and direct comments from a high-profile politician is rare, and given my unconditional historical support of this woman, I interpreted her message as a subliminal "get the hell out if you can!"

If I were ever to be confronted and asked about a 'moment critique' in my life, I would respond unconditionally that the end of the short drive home lasting 10 minutes or so, on that afternoon, contained that defining moment and turning point in my life.

A sudden sense of urgency had crash landed in my world and we needed to get out of South Africa quickly, before it was too late. Hastily, I drove home, parked the car and rushed to Michelle's office, and standing in front of her desk I backtracked momentarily, thinking I had gone mad and expecting her to think the same. I don't have any idea why New Zealand sprang to mind, but I recall saying something like: "Let's get out of this hellhole and go to New Zealand!"

She looked up from her computer, and without so much a flinch, asked, "When?"

"As soon as possible," I responded, and she: "Done!"

"Seriously?" I asked.

"Seriously!" said she.

New Zealand is a small, remote country consisting of two major islands in the South Pacific, just off the coast of Australia where there are millions of sheep, lots of rugby players, and people talk with an accent similar to Australians. The land was stolen from the Māori by the white settlers (just like in Africa), but the

Māori had ostensibly 'forgiven' the white folk, and now everybody gets along 'swimmingly' was about all I knew, or **thought** I knew about New Zealand.

I had always felt a tiny bit of animosity towards the New Zealand rugby team—the All Blacks, given my love for the Springboks, and that had been pretty much where my relationship with New Zealand started and ended. In a sense, perhaps I subconsciously hoped that some research into New Zealand would disappoint and we would be forced to come to terms with our bundle in South Africa. We had heard that the procedure for immigrants to Australia was fraught with obstacles, and furthermore the apparent 'cut off' age for consideration was 45, and I was about to turn 46.

The UK for me had never held much appeal, and beyond that I couldn't picture any other country that would be a pragmatic destination for us as immigrants. So with much purpose, Michelle and I immersed ourselves in researching what we considered could one day become home for us and our children.

Within a few days, I had my 'Damascus Experience', suddenly convinced that New Zealand was exactly where we needed to be. The Internet had made it very easy to look up all aspects of life in Aotearoa, 'The land of the long white cloud', and we were convinced that we should submit our 'expression of interest' to the New Zealand immigration offices in London. With an incredibly low rate of unemployment, strong economy, low crime rate and stable political history, from a point of view of pure logic, New Zealand made sense.

A myriad of photographs called up on screen, caused us to marvel at the sheer beauty of the place, from beaches to forests, mountains, fjords, rivers and lakes. This was paradise, who knew? Research revealed that New Zealand takes great pride in being one of the 'cleanest' countries in the world, her people showing a real lack of tolerance for land, air and water pollution, as well as an ethos which places family above all else.

Sports mad, the country punches well above her weight, standing shoulder to shoulder with much larger adversaries in all manner of sports and activities, I felt that I would certainly fit in, and of course our children being eight and five years of age, would adapt very quickly and easily. Reading reviews of emigres who now found themselves on one of the two main islands, the tone we detected seemed to convey to readers that this was a country where one could breathe clean air, sleep easy, enjoy the great outdoors, and raise children to be fine upstanding citizens without a care in the world.

Like an impenetrable fortress, the islands were surrounded by thousands of kilometres of ocean, creating the world's largest moat, keeping criminals and undesirables at bay, leaving good, wholesome folk to get on with the business of living their best lives.

'Ambivalence' is a word that rolls easily off the tongue, but to explore the deeper context of the word is to dust off a large old leather chest, prising it open to rediscover that it is jam packed with memories of a lifetime, a happy childhood, emotions represented on a wide spectrum, a host of experiences and hundreds of faces and names flitting through the mind like a series of slide shows when we were kids. More happy times than sad, the memories can overwhelm, calling my latest decision into question.

I felt that I was now a proud South African, a mix of Dutch Boer and Cornish English; I, like my family, was the mongrel which never ails, tough as they come, having inherited the best genes from both breeds, we'd survived and prospered on this beautiful but unforgiving continent for four generations. Relegating in my mind, those who emigrated as fearful, ungrateful and weak, I had always harboured a disdain for the 'traitors'.

Any potential for vacillation, on my part, was snuffed out as quickly as it had sought to take root, courtesy of my wife. Her steely resolve to emigrate had set in and become immovable, now cast in stone as she sat me down each morning for a 'meeting', going through her 'to do checklist' which as any immigrant will confirm, is nothing short of overwhelming and intimidating, and, I suspect constituting an apparently insurmountable set of obstacles, putting the kibosh on the hopes of many an aspiring émigré before even getting out of the starting blocks.

Sourcing criminal history checks from the deep, dark vaults of the South African Police Services, unabridged birth certificates dating back two generations, 23-year-old university transcripts, and tax clearance certificates was, we realised, next to impossible, dealing with incompetent record keeping at government and municipal institutions. And this was just the tip of the iceberg.

Michelle and I sat together one afternoon and meticulously completed and submitted the Expression of Interest (EOI), which also provided a good indication that we had sufficient 'points' to make us 'desirable' immigrants. Points relating to the attributes which are preferred in new immigrants 'assessing' as far as possible the likelihood of a successful transition.

All of this activity had been kept secret from our children, friends and family, and between Michelle and I, we agreed that the cat would escape the bag only when the immigration offices confirmed that New Zealand wanted us as much as we wanted New Zealand. Our planning became a tricky business, since we were not far off the end of the year, and we needed to appear to be doing everything necessary in preparation for the beginning of the new year, regarding children's schooling and activities, business plans, staffing, all as though nothing would change, and, of course, planning had to commence on the 'QT', should the 'big move' become a reality.

So, on the surface, life continued as normal, business as usual, the only tell-tale sign of anything out of the ordinary, was Michelle's early rising, quietly sneaking downstairs to her office each morning before the family stirred. I would be woken by the peep, peep, peep sound of buttons pushed on the control panel as she disengaged the internal security alarm system, with a view to checking for emails from the New Zealand Department of Immigration.

Weeks went by, and a hint of disappointment began to show on her face, as nothing was forthcoming, Michelle and I eventually agreeing that if we weren't going to be accepted, the least they could do was to let us know. I had become irreparably despondent, disappointed and saddened. My roots for generations had been in South Africa, and my firm resolve to be supportive of a democratic dispensation, providing the platform for a fighting chance for the millions of indigent black, previously disadvantaged people, had been corroded through a new government which had revealed itself to be more inept than the previous apartheid government, and frankly just as corrupt.

Quietly, I convinced myself that my decision was the correct one, and if it came to pass that New Zealand was unwilling to accept us, we would, undeterred, explore other immigration destinations, steeling ourselves against the potential onslaught of vexed or indifferent confrontations from quarters including friends and family.

The waiting continued, until one morning, tears in her eyes, she woke me gently, and upon seeing the well of tears I knew immediately that our Expression of Interest had been declined. Struggling to get any words out at all, she smiled through the flood of tears as she stuttered: "No, no, we've been invited to apply for residence!" And like two little children we cried and danced around, as happy as can be, a sense of elation as though an enormous burden had been lifted from our shoulders as we would embrace this new adventure, jubilant in the knowledge that we could now venture with our babies to a beautiful, clean, first world environment, where they and their progeny would become rooted to the islands of the South Pacific.

Michelle and I talked incessantly each day about having not shirked our responsibility of being the modern-day pioneers providing a safe haven in which our blood line could flourish and prosper. We had absolutely not the vaguest conception of the magnitude of the task and emotional rollercoaster which lay before us—a story for another time.

32. How to Steal a Country in Broad Daylight, a Beginners Guide

State Capture; a brand new, unique adventure.

A stony silence and a vacant stare are the usual, standard responses when speaking to expat South Africans in New Zealand about headline events in the 'old country'. There are many of us here, and stories abound of how Kiwi kids at certain schools on Auckland's North Shore start to import South African words and catchphrases into their jargon, sometimes much to the chagrin of their parents. Mostly, however, the South African kids who arrived at tender ages, lose their accents, and chuckle at their parents for using old, distinctly South African words and phrases.

When we had travelled to school each day back in Johannesburg, the morning radio broadcasts would end with sports news on radio 94.7FM, as sports announcer extraordinaire, Graeme Joffe would be introduced by Jeremy Mansfield as 'Joffers my boy', which always elicited a smile from James. I would always greet my son, including at some point the phrase, 'my boy'.

At the time it seemed the most natural thing on earth. In New Zealand, James' friends could be seen to eagerly await the inclusion of 'my boy' when I greeted him, whereupon in unison they would look at each other and recite 'My Boy', followed by peals of laughter. This, of course, was done in good spirits, and I always made sure to play along with the long-standing joke, sometimes holding out for effect.

The vast majority of South Africans in New Zealand have neither the time nor the inclination to pay much attention to events in South Africa, the precis of events usually resulting in stern faces and the shaking of heads at functions or events where expats gather to socialise and chat. Most expats tend be white or of 'mixed race', younger than me when making the move, and while there certainly are exceptions, the mean emigration age seems to be early 30s, at a time when their kids are young and impressionable and the realisation has struck that their careers are on a road to nowhere, thanks to the ANC's Black Economic Empowerment (BEE), which recent history has confirmed as little more than a legitimised vehicle for a small number of black businessmen or professionals to scoop up shares and appointments to boards of directors of top companies represented across the spectrum of industry and commerce in South Africa.

Displaying names of black shareholders and directors on company letterheads gives comfort to the BEE rule-makers that said companies are compliant both in the spirit of and the letter of the law. Closer to the 'coalface' BEE has simply regulated employers to exclude white people, Indians and 'so called' Coloureds—people of mixed race, who are now not 'black enough', requiring in many instances that only 'Ethnic Africans' need apply.

Contrary to many of my expat countrymen, I have paid reasonably close attention to events in Southern Africa, having been for a long time a keen student of the history South Africa and her neighbours. One of the most recent unfortunate episodes to bleed the coffers dry and once again sully the names of those running the country has been the 'State Capture' debacle. The word 'debacle' offering no clue as to the magnitude of the wrongdoing which continued under the noses of South Africans. It is said that highly efficient international crime syndicates, run as functional businesses are always on the lookout for new business opportunities, unhindered by geographic or financial constraints.

One thinks of criminal elements, operative in western countries, whose origins are in Russia, Serbia, China, or potentially a host of other countries. Some of these, less than subtle in their approaches to conducting shady business dealings, when for example one considers the brutality of the Russian Mob, or the sinister nature of the Chinese Triads or the Japanese Yakuza. Perhaps, tongue-in-cheek, these it could be argued are at least 'honest' criminals: honest in the sense that they do not obviously masquerade as something which they are not.

Far more sinister, would be a family arriving in the country, ostensibly seeking business opportunities. Such a family was in the guise of a company called Sahara Computers—apparently their first major foray into business in South Africa—seemingly innocent enough, particularly at a time when the imagination of the country and indeed, the world was being seduced by quantum strides in the world of technology and information. From there the tentacles of the Gupta brothers, slowly at first, and then with voracious appetite began to grab at opportunities, some legitimate and some less so. At the time of writing, Part 1 of a 3-part report on the findings of the investigation into 'State Capture', which spanned three years of public hearings and cost over R1bn, focussed on gross public-sector corruption during Jacob Zuma's presidency.

The government estimate is that well in excess of **R3 Billion** was stolen from its coffers during President Zuma's nine-year rule, which ended in 2018. The brothers, it seemed, ingratiated themselves with government officials, systematically corrupting many of them in carefully orchestrated manoeuvres, introducing them to the high life, and enriching family members of the officials, and being so close to the corridors of power, it seems they were able to manipulate decisions made in parliament as well as influencing appointments to government positions. Their best chum of course was Mr Zuma himself. One suspects that the 'success' attained by the brothers possibly exceeded their wildest dreams.

Theft and greed appear to have been uppermost on the minds of the brothers who emigrated from Uttar Pradesh in the northern reaches of India to South Africa in 1993. One does wonder if they had plotted this course from the outset, or whether the smorgasbord of temptations for easy money evolved as the frailties and flawed character of those willing participants in government revealed themselves? The most disturbing facet to this most bizarre of stories, are the lengths to which the brothers would go to achieve their ambitions, edging a country toward widespread insurrection, re-igniting racial hatred, in order to shift public gaze away from their rape and pillage of the economy of South Africa.

33. Dictators, Oligarchs and the Spin Doctor

"South Africa's former president Jacob Zuma along with Indian-origin Gupta brothers, who had 'considerable' influence over him, misappropriated huge amount of public money, including diverting millions of rands to enrich the now defunct The New Age newspaper, according to a probe report on corruption during Zuma's tenure from 2009 to 2018."

"President Cyril Ramaphosa on Tuesday received the first of the three parts of the report of the South African Commission of Inquiry into State Capture from the chairperson of the commission, Acting Chief Justice Raymond Zondo. The report has been made public. However, the government said it will be able to comment on it only after studying all the three parts. The rest of the parts will be handed over to the president by February-end."

"The first part deals with the Gupta family's New Age newspaper, the destruction of South African Airways (SAA) by Zuma's consigliere Dudu Myeni, the capture of the South African Revenue Service (SARS) and the corruption of the state procurement system through the tender system."

"The New Age (TNA) newspaper was started by the three Gupta brothers— Ajay, Atul and Rajesh (Tony)—who migrated to South Africa from Uttar Pradesh's Saharanpur town and are now believed to be in self-exile in Dubai as authorities seek their extradition to face graft charges."

"The report said the Guptas wielded great influence over Zuma, as they set about looting billions from state enterprises before fleeing the country."

"The evidence before the Commission paints a picture of a calculated strategy by the Guptas to appropriate public funds from state-owned enterprises," it said.

It was key to their efforts to have facilitators within the state-owned enterprises (SOEs) and government departments, such as Government Communication Information Services (GCIS), who would ensure that the entities committed millions of rands to the TNA despite there being no discernible value for the entities or government departments, the report said.

The influence they (Gupta brothers) exerted over former President Zuma was considerable. They managed to ensure that a well-performing and principled public servant was removed at lightning speed when he refused to accede to their demands to divert millions of rands of public money to enrich their media business, it added. This was a reference to the resistance that the Guptas met when they tried to coerce GCIS head Themba Maseko to divert 600-million rand to TNA. Maseko was later dismissed allegedly at the instruction of Zuma.

Underlining that Zuma replaced Maseko with a facilitator, in the form of Mzwanele Manyi, the report said that during Manyi's term as GCIS Director-General, "millions of rands were spent on TNA in circumstances where there was no credible readership information nor certified circulation figures for the newspaper."

"It is inconceivable that this would have been allowed to occur if Mr Maseko had remained at the helm of GCIS," it said.

"The Commission also found that senior officials, including some board members at SOEs, were complicit in irregular transfers of huge amount of money to TNA, through contracts that were adjusted to misrepresent the value of the deals to watchdogs like Parliament and the Public Protector through recasting the agreements as something different to what they really were."

"The contracts concluded by the SOEs were often patently irregular and wasteful by definition because their value simply could not be established, the report said. According to the commission, the TNA investigation shows that state capture thrived at SOEs, despite the fact that necessary laws to prevent it were in place. The Public Finance Management Act (PFMA) clearly and definitively made each of the TNA contracts unlawful."

"State capture thrived because the people given power and authority in the SOEs simply flouted its terms. One way to prevent this in the future is to ensure that those who ignored their legal obligations are held to account for their conduct," it said.

The Commission recommended that the role of Brian Molefe—former chair of national rail transport provider Transnet and Collin Matjila and former chairperson of national electricity supplier Eskom—be investigated in the misrepresentation of contracts with TNA by the National Prosecuting Authority, with a view to charges of fraud and/or contravention of the PFMA.

The Commission also recommended that the law enforcement agencies should investigate a possible case of corruption against Tony Gupta, on the basis of the testimony of former Acting Chair of the state-run South African Airways Board—Vuyisile Kona. Kona had told the Commission that Tony had initially offered him R100,000 and later R500,000 in October 2012. After he refused to accept the bribe, Kona was fired from his job.

The Indian Express, 20 January 2022

The dossier had its desired effect. South Africans were outraged by the revelation that a British PR firm had meddled in their nation's politics. To many of them, Bell Pottinger's actions felt not just irresponsible but colonial. On social media, a campaign was launched against Bell Pottinger and its staff. In April 2017, thousands of South Africans marched against Zuma's government, and some protesters carried posters denouncing Bell Pottinger. One poster showed Victoria Geoghegan's photograph along with the slogan "Gupta's Girl."

That month, Bell Pottinger issued a statement claiming that many assertions in the dossier were 'wholly untrue', and that a 'politically motivated' campaign was being waged against the firm. But it conceded that the campaign had worked—Bell Pottinger could no longer be an 'effective advocate' for Oakbay. It was dropping the account.[90]

In my little cocooned environment, each morning, I savour that first cup of coffee while catching up on the news of the world. Cocooned, because a beautiful small island in the South Pacific boasting political stability, low levels of crime and relative racial harmony threatens to render one blissfully ignorant of the unrelenting, jarring realities of life for most of the world's people. Of concern at any given moment are some truly grim events in the Middle East, horror stories of homeless millions attempting to seek a better life in Europe, many incarcerated in internment camps. North and central Africans, fleeced of their very last, often meagre life savings by unscrupulous 'people transporters', only

---

[90] Ed Caesar 18 June 2018, *The New Yorker*.

to find themselves like sardines packed into tins, on boats inadequate to make the perilous journey across the Mediterranean.

Many losing their lives on an unforgiving ocean, many being grounded close to their points of departure, with nothing to show for their troubles except empty pockets. Those who do make it, often offer little to no skill or value to the lands across the sea, and are viewed as liabilities, mouths to fed, troublemakers who should be sent home. Tragic scenes are to be seen on a daily basis, as desperate fathers show us their hungry, frightened children, having endured unimaginable horrors of war, famine or natural disasters. Wives and husbands weep unconsolably at the prospect of being returned to their home countries, or being unable to find employment in order to put food on the table.

We read of India, and cobalt mines in the Congo, where entire families are effectively enslaved by indentured servitude, child soldiers in Africa, and the rise of the Islamic State and the related atrocities. The latest, most alarming of events, of course, is the protracted war in Ukraine, impacting in no small measure on the world economy. Somehow though, all of this bad news remains somewhat abstract for an insular island nation, protected by our relative anonymity, isolation and largely minding our own business. Although my passport states that my nationality as 'New Zealand', my emotions are stirred when I read of the old country.

Despite the many failings of my old home country, I have always, and continue to wish for racial harmony and political and economic progress, so it was a dagger straight into the heart when I read of uprisings, marches and indeed campaigns which were unashamedly, no, proudly, anti-white. 'White Capital', a phrase which took on a life of its own, alluded to a claim that the vast majority of assets and wealth remained in the hands of whites. Students rallied against tuition fees, demanding free tertiary education, the situation erupting into violent confrontations with police, and then the '… must fall' campaign, suggesting that anything borne of colonisation or the colonial era, somehow suggesting that history could be erased and rewritten from an Afrocentric perspective.

While the deep scars of colonisation must be understood by everyone and never forgotten, the campaign was inherently destructive, suggesting that it was white people, and no-one else, who were directly to blame for the plight of the unemployed, homeless masses. While modern technology gives access to many, mass media, social media and information like never before, two natural problems stem from this. Accuracy of information and honesty of contributors can always be questioned.

The unscrupulous can cause immense damage, sometimes very quickly, at other times a slow poison over long periods. It has taken time for many to come to the realisation that nothing can be taken at face value, and we have, of necessity, become fact 'checkers'. The other problem arising in modern times, relates to the indigent masses who have no or limited access to this modern wonder which opens up a worldwide web of information and insight which was not previously available or so easily accessible. These folk wallow in that darkness as before, and rely on media, hearsay and opinions, from friends, acquaintances and political leaders at rallies.

Now, it seems our Gupta brothers would stop at nothing when they decided to 'muddy the waters' to divert attention away from their shenanigans, as Tony Gupta contracted the services of Bell Pottinger to use everything at their disposal to discredit white South Africans, in an effort to persuade all and sundry that the wealth of the 'coloniser' remained the overwhelming reason for the vast majority of black South Africans languishing in a never-ending quagmire of poverty.

Disturbing of course is the fact that an opportunity to direct a racial attack on a now minority group of people, was met with more than just a hint of enthusiasm by a British PR company which in the past had battled for wealthy whites, and white politicians of South Africa.

So far reaching, and toxic was their campaign, that it seemed tangible racial abrasion leading to insurrection or worse on a national scale, was in the offing. It seemed that racial friction was looming to rival that during the darkest days of apartheid, all instigated by a company in England and it's paying Indian customers to keep the South African people from shaking the Gupta Tree.

Happily, one's faith in human nature is restored due to some honest, cool heads, who saw to it that the Gupta Tree was well and truly shaken, and the miscreants are now persona non grata in South Africa, ostensibly welcomed with open arms in the UAE. Bell Pottinger oft referred to as 'audacious', but certainly a tag more fitting would be 'firm for despots and rogues', is no longer operative. James Henderson, Bell Pottinger's chief executive, appeared before the PRCA Disciplinary Committee to answer accusations that the firm ran a "hateful and divisive campaign to divide South Africa along the lines of race."

Fake email addresses were created for a shotgun campaign of misinformation, and a host of other dirty tricks ensued. The actions of Bell

Pottinger contributed in no small measure to renewed racial tensions in a country often teetering on the edge of race-based violence, at a time when the country needed hope based on reconciliation. Officials within government and their cronies who were seduced by these unscrupulous brothers, should be hauled before the courts, their actions tested against a litmus test for fraud.

It is estimated that the theft of money during this dark reign of a 'shadow government' amounted to some US$200,000,000. Again, considering where money could be put to good use, we see such blatant mismanagement of funds resulting in theft, added together, it is not only sad, but diabolical that the systemic usurping of capital continued unabated throughout the tenure of both the apartheid regime, and the 'New and Improved' government which it seems is more and more evolving into a one-party state, having ruled the roost and enjoyed carte blanche for some 28 years.

Yes, as Johnny Clegg[91] put it, we are the 'scatterlings of Africa'. For many of us, we've embraced our adopted countries; our kids may not feel very South African, but rest assured that those of us abroad of a certain age, struggle to halt the flow of tears when we hear the fine music of Juluka, Lucky Dube, David Kramer, Miriam Makeba, Evoid, Mandoza or the beautiful strains of Radio Kalahari Orkes' rendition of *Suikerbossie*. It was David Paton who coined the phrase 'Ah but your land is beautiful'. The land is beautiful, as are its people. Nothing has changed in that regard, and we will be buoyed by the unique spirit of all South Africans.

Corruption, which seems almost endemic throughout many, if not most former European colonies, be they in Africa, South America or Asia, seem to display some similarities. Neophyte political leaders are systematically lured into a game for the first time, by those who have played many times before, having had ample opportunity to hone their skills and fine-tune their craft, almost guaranteeing them a 100% success rate. Once the die is cast, things become more and more murky for the unsuspecting until the trap is sprung, and there is no return. Then like a lie, more lies are needed to protect the protagonists of the original lie, and the spiral has been activated.

The victim, often the state president, must now cling to power at all costs to ensure that his position is not compromised. He must see to it also that those in cahoots are protected or they may become the architects of his downfall. This

---

[91] Famous South African musician RIP, singer, songwriter isiZulu/Celtic/Rock ballads. Known as the White Zulu. Bands—Juluka, Savuka

precarious existence is usually made more palatable by the sweeteners; exotic cars, planes, boats, luxurious homes, gifts—in short, the high life, juxtaposed by not only potential expulsion from the Garden of Eden, but prison time if the dirty truth comes to light.

The instigators in these dramas are frequently allied with the former coloniser, or indeed the former coloniser itself. An economic hitman is sometimes used to pave the way for more dastardly ventures to 'rob' a land of its natural resources, particularly in countries where extractivism remains the primary means of revenue.

Underpinning the nature of people in South Africa is the deep-seated concept of UBUNTU. In South Africa, the Amazulu say: 'Umuntu ngumuntu ngabantu'—**A person is a person through other people**. Ubuntu is that! The very fibre of UBUNTU weaves it's way gently around the construct which is for the greater good of the community. Corruption therefore is something outside the natural state of UBUNTU and consequently if all are true to themselves and their nature, this toxin which is corruption, has absolutely no place in South Africa, where most people fear disrespecting and offending their ancestors, who believed to be omnipresent. Similarly, one might have thought that the previous regime would have feared transgressions of a corrupt nature given the overt, pious submission to 'their' omnipresent, omnipotent Almighty.

UBUNTU.

Bheka kokhokho bakho, kumuntu wakini kanye nekusasa.[92]
Kyk na jou skepper, medemens en toekoms.[93]

Bell Pottinger, RIP. Born 1998 passed quietly in the night 12 September 2017, post mortem reveals cause of death: 'self-induced shame'. At the time of writing, more than half the population of South Africa have no direct experience of living under apartheid conditions, being born into the 'new South Africa' after 1994.

---

[92] IsiZulu. Look to ancestors, your fellow man and the future. The writer February 2022.
[93] Afrikaans Look to your creator, your fellow man and the future. The writer February 2022.

Sadly, that same generation bears the brunt of the youth unemployment rate[94] for 2021 reaching an unprecedented milestone now well in excess of 60%, the overall official unemployment rate being well in excess of 30%. The blight on history which was apartheid, has without question cast a long shadow. The new government, now seemingly entrenched after 29 years, is casting long shadows of its own, effectively ratcheting up the elements of life under which poverty, illiteracy, unemployment, squalor and general hopelessness took root many decades ago.

Fertile ground has been created for the malaise to metastasise, while band aids are produced on a regular basis in the absence of aggressive diagnosis to identify a present disease by examination and observation of signs and symptoms; followed by prognosis to **predict the course of the diagnosed disease**, determining treatment and outcome. While those in government have their minds occupied by arms deals, self-advancement, 'tenderpreneurship', jobs for mates, and other such activities, the business of honest governance and strategy becomes a 'side show' government 'fatcats' becoming adept at covering their tracks and ensuring that there is always a feast in the trough.

Close scrutiny of annual African National Congress leaves absolutely no doubt in the mind of the concerned observer that the actors in this drama must display an unwavering loyalty to the party, or face being ostracised, or even worse, a purgatory of sorts, even expulsion from the ranks of the intelligentsia. Such absolute it seems, supersedes the interests of the nation and her people. The ANC culture which has taken on a life of its own sees the tail wagging the dog, with an alarming disregard for the constitution of the country.

Many elements of the constitution of South Africa, whose very foundation which was crafted on tenets of freedom and equality for **ALL**, by brave men and women following centuries of strife, bloodshed, anger and sadness, has been relegated to the status of 'irrelevant'. The relevance or lack thereof of constitutional 'pillars' has long since given way to the 'Toe the party line' mantra, evident both at the annual national conferences and within the machinations of the alarming speed of moving parts within the government cabinet.

---

[94] *https://tradingeconomics.com/south-africa/youth-unemployment-rate#:~:text=Youth%20Unemployment%20Rate%20in%20South%20Africa%20averaged%2054.21%20percent%20from,the%20fourth%20quarter%20of%202014.*

Epilogue

Dirty, Dirty Dossiers, some really nasty people, truth being stranger than fiction. An epilogue worth reading.

Ed Caesar, The New Yorker, 18 June 2018 wrote:

On 14 January 2016, four publicists from Bell Pottinger, one of London's leading public-relations firms, flew to Johannesburg and met with a potential client: Oakbay Investments, a company controlled by Atul, Ajay, and Tony Gupta, three of South Africa's most powerful businessmen. The Guptas, brothers who had holdings in everything from uranium mining to newspapers, maintained close ties with Jacob Zuma, the President of South Africa, and were notorious for having leveraged this connection for profit and influence. Three members of Zuma's family had worked in Gupta-owned businesses.

In 2015, South Africans staged large protests against Zuma's Administration, calling it inept and corrupt. They also accused the Guptas, who were born in India, of running a 'shadow government' that swung procurement decisions their way and appointed government ministers aligned with their interests. That December, an adviser to BNP Paribas Securities South Africa told Bloomberg News that the relationship between Zuma and the Guptas was 'deeply troubling', noting, "This goes beyond undue influence."

Tony Gupta attended the Johannesburg meeting, as did Tim Bell, one of Bell Pottinger's founders. Lord Bell, perhaps the best-known figure in British public relations, has worked for decades in South Africa, including a stint as an adviser to President F. W. de Klerk, the final leader of the apartheid era. Bell can be charming or cutthroat, as the moment requires. After tea was served, Bell recalls, he sat through "an hour and a half of Tony Gupta lecturing us on how wonderful he was—he'd made so much money, he didn't need to make any more money, he was just a good man, he had empowered brown people, he was very well connected to the government, knew Zuma very well."

Gupta requested Bell Pottinger's help in launching a PR campaign to highlight economic inequality in South Africa. The goal was to persuade South Africans of colour that they were far poorer than they should be, mainly because large white-owned corporations had outsized power. The campaign, Gupta suggested, would not only be beneficial to the country but would also bolster his family's financial position, by casting the brothers not as overstepping oligarchs but as outsiders countering white supremacy.

Bell told me that Gupta's proposal did not strike him as cynical; he found it 'eminently reasonable'. On January 18th, he e-mailed James Henderson, Bell Pottinger's CEO, and described the PR campaign's theme as one of 'economic emancipation', adding, 'The trip was a great success'.

Against competition from another London agency, Bell Pottinger won the account, and Oakbay agreed to a monthly fee of a hundred and thirty thousand dollars, plus costs, for a three-month trial period. In addition to launching the economic-emancipation campaign, Bell Pottinger would provide traditional PR services for Oakbay, including 'crisis communications'.

Bell Pottinger's work in South Africa included the covert dissemination of articles, cartoons, blog posts, and tweets implying that the Guptas' opponents were upholding a racist system. As the brothers' influence over Zuma's government fell under increasing scrutiny, Bell Pottinger's tactics were exposed. More details of the Oakbay account became public, including revelations about the inflammatory economic-emancipation campaign. Soon, one of the world's savviest reputation-management companies became embroiled in a reputational scandal. Bell Pottinger could not contain the uproar, and, in September 2017, it collapsed.

By the time of its demise, Bell Pottinger, which was founded by Bell and his longtime colleague Piers Pottinger, had existed, in various incarnations, for nearly twenty years. Bell began his career in advertising, in the sixties, and joined Saatchi & Saatchi in 1970. Nine years later, he began advising the Conservative leader Margaret Thatcher, and helped shape some of her most effective messages, including the 'Labour Isn't Working' campaign, which attacked the Labour Party's record on employment. Thatcher—or the She-wolf, as Bell affectionately calls her—remains his political lodestar. "The right is called 'the right' because it is," he told me, at his town house, in Belgravia.

It was shortly after Bell Pottinger's implosion, and he related his past and his idiosyncratic world view while smoking a succession of cigarettes. (I stopped counting at eight.) He was seventy-five, much thinner than in his heyday, with hawkish features. He had suffered two strokes, most recently in 2016, and was unsteady on his feet. At one point, his fiancée, Jacky Phillips, entered the room, asking him if he was experiencing a 'sugar dip' and needed a snack. Despite his frailty, Bell's eyes danced behind his thick-rimmed spectacles.

Bell became a publicist in the eighties, advising companies, politicians, celebrities, and royalty, and also foreign governments and politicians. When he started in PR, he told me, "Corporate communications was regarded as like peeing down your trouser leg—it gave you a nice warm feeling when it first happened, but it goes cold and wet pretty quickly." He boasted, "What we did was move the public-relations advisers from being senders of press releases and lunches with journalists into serious strategists."

As a former adman, Bell is adept at exploiting images. In 2006, assassins affiliated with the Russian government fatally poisoned the Russian dissident and former spy Alexander Litvinenko, who was living in London. Bell, working on behalf of Litvinenko, urged his family to release a photograph of him in the hospital. It was a masterstroke. The picture, showing Litvinenko hairless, with eerily yellow skin, instantly became a symbol of the ruthlessness of Putin's regime.

Bell did not hesitate, however, to represent dubious political figures. In 1989, in Chile, he worked on the Presidential campaign of Hernán Büchi, a former finance minister for the dictator General Augusto Pinochet. (Büchi lost the election.) Bell also worked for the Pinochet Foundation, which, in 1998, successfully campaigned against efforts to extradite Pinochet to Spain, where a judge had issued a warrant for his arrest on charges of torture and murder. Among Bell's other notorious clients are Alexander Lukashenko, the dictator of Belarus; Asma al-Assad, the wife of the Syrian strongman Bashar; and government representatives of the repressive state of Bahrain.

Bell is hardly alone in performing such work. London has become a honeypot for the international super-rich, especially in the past twenty years, as the city has emerged as the world's financial centre. A network of services is available to oligarchs, sheikhs, and mandarins with the proper investment profiles.

Lawyers, accountants, fund managers, and real-estate agents have become a kind of butler class to the extraordinarily wealthy, helping them to reinvest or to hide their wealth. (Actual butlers can be hired, too.) Publicists like Bell manage the public images of rich and powerful people from around the globe. In 2010, the Guardian called London the 'world capital of reputation laundering.'

Most publicists are discreet about working with controversial figures, but Bell is vocally unrepentant about it. A publicist, he argues, merely allows clients to have a voice in public discussions that affect them. As Bell presented it to me, access to an expensive London PR firm was a right as fundamental as access to a defence lawyer.

Bell emphasised that he was not without scruples, saying that his 'personal morals' would stop him working for someone as cruel as Robert Mugabe, the former dictator of Zimbabwe, whose regime had killed or tortured tens of thousands of his own people. And Bell noted that he had dropped Lukashenko after the Belarusian President failed to implement electoral reforms. (A partner at Bell Pottinger told me that the Belarus account was easy to relinquish, because Lukashenko's Russian handler had stopped paying his fees.)

Nevertheless, Bell Pottinger reflected its co-founder's lack of squeamishness. According to another partner at the firm, publicists at rival agencies, when debating whether to represent a questionable individual, used to joke that the answer was either "Yes," "No," or "One for Bell Pottinger."

In the summer of 2011, Bell Pottinger executives received an inquiry from a potential client, the Azimov Group, which described itself as an international team of investors in the cotton trade who had links to the government of Uzbekistan. The inquiry should have raised concerns. Uzbekistan's cotton industry was reported to be reliant on government-enforced child labour. The country's leader, Islam Karimov, was a de-facto dictator, and his security services had been accused of manifold abuses, including the torture of political opponents. In 2002, there were credible reports that two dissidents had been boiled alive.

A Bell Pottinger executive quickly replied to the Azimov Group, saying that some of his colleagues would be "delighted to talk to you about how we might best support your enterprise." Two representatives of the Azimov Group soon came to Bell Pottinger's main office, in Holborn. Firm executives told them that they'd take the job only if the Uzbek government pursued a 'reform agenda'. Nobody expressed broader concerns about polishing the image of a dictatorship.

The Bell Pottinger executives proposed a monthly fee of about a hundred and thirty thousand dollars. They boasted about their political connections, noting that one executive at the firm, Tim Collins, had worked with George Osborne, who was now the Chancellor of the Exchequer, and with David Cameron, who had become the prime minister. Collins told the Azimov representatives, "There is not a problem in getting messages through to them." The executives also discussed what they called the 'dark arts' of optimising Google searches and editing Wikipedia pages in favour of clients.

Collins said that Bell Pottinger's goal would be "to get to the point where, even if they type in 'Uzbek child labour' or 'Uzbek human-rights violation', some of the first results that come up are sites talking about what you guys are doing to address and improve that, not just the critical voices saying how terrible this all is."

The meetings, however, were an ambush. The Azimov Group was a fake entity, and the two 'representatives' were undercover reporters from the Bureau of Investigative Journalism. Both were using hidden cameras. A front-page story soon appeared in the Independent with the headline "CAUGHT ON CAMERA: TOP LOBBYISTS BOASTING HOW THEY INFLUENCE THE PM."

After the article was published, PR agencies in London were subjected to heavy scrutiny, and legislators in parliament started a campaign to create a registry of lobbyists, similar to one that exists in the United States. Bell's response was to express outrage at the BIJ's subterfuge. He reported the Independent to the Press Complaints Commission, which rebuffed him. Eventually, he took some heat out of the scandal by ordering an internal inquiry. In an interview with the Evening Standard, Bell promised that 'every person here is searching their souls'

In July 2012, Bell Pottinger, which at the time was owned by a publicly traded company, Chime Communications, went private, in a management buyout. Bell Pottinger was then worth about forty-one million dollars. Bell couldn't afford to take the business private himself, even after he arranged bank loans and an investment from Chime. And so, he invited another publicist at Bell Pottinger, James Henderson, to join the buyout. Bell barely knew Henderson, but he was aware that Henderson had money: he'd made millions of dollars when a financial-PR firm that he'd launched was acquired by Bell Pottinger in 2010.

Henderson, whose features combine sorrow and pep in a way that calls to mind a spaniel, was worried about losing his fortune, but he took the risk. He became Bell Pottinger's largest shareholder, and also its CEO Bell was named chairman. Henderson told me recently that he'd believed in the 'fairy dust' of Bell's reputation, and thought that they would succeed together.

The deal wasn't entirely satisfying to Bell: although he was a more famous and charismatic publicist than Henderson, and was twenty-three years his senior, he held a smaller stake in the company. Henderson, meanwhile, hoped to use his position at Bell Pottinger to become a star himself. "He wanted to be the go-to guy for PR in London," one partner said. "The problem is that, while he's a good businessman, he's not a good manager. He's a bit socially awkward."

Henderson wanted the company to leave behind the 'one for Bell Pottinger' caricature by shifting its focus to blue-chip corporate work. He announced that Bell Pottinger was establishing an ethics committee that would assess clients who might prove controversial. (This may have been a PR gesture in itself: several people at the firm say that the committee met rarely, if ever.)

The buyout required Bell Pottinger to take on sixteen million dollars' worth of bank debt, and Henderson set ambitious targets to reduce that burden. In 2012, the firm represented only one company on the FTSE 100, the primary index of the London Stock Exchange; by 2016, it had seven. It also became more creative in its pitches. Henderson remembers painting a meeting room red in order to impress a delegation from Virgin Money, Richard Branson's finance group. (Virgin's logo is red.) Bell Pottinger won the account.

To the chagrin of many Bell Pottinger employees, however, the firm's efforts to reduce debt were felt most keenly in its lower echelons: employees say that their compensation was mediocre. Henderson's salary, meanwhile, rose to about seven hundred and fifty thousand dollars. He became known for his 'social mountaineering', as two of his employees put it, and often threw parties attended by celebrities and minor royals. In 2015, through a mutual friendship with the Duchess of York, Henderson met his future fiancée, Heather Kerzner, an American socialite who previously had been married to the South African hotelier Sol Kerzner.

Bell, for his part, had negotiated a basic salary of about $1.5 million a year, plus such perks as a chauffeur and what colleagues called his 'pocket money'—bundles of cash for expenses. Bell also demanded a separate office for his division, the geopolitical team, in a town house in Mayfair, the most expensive area of London.

The house featured a commissioned sculpture, 'Ascension', consisting of four hundred tiny naked white bodies suspended from the ceiling. To make up for all the spending, another partner added, Bell "was reduced to more and more scratching around for the despots and other difficult communications jobs from around the world."

Almost immediately, Bell and Henderson clashed. "We didn't agree about how you run a company," Bell told me. At one of their first meetings, he recalled, "I lost my temper with him, because he said something that was really stupid, and I shouted at him. And he got all huffy and said, 'If you're going to shout at me then I won't speak to you.' I continued to lose my temper and walked out." The root of the problem, Bell said, was jealousy: "He can't bear that I've got a bigger personality than him, and I'm better at the job. He hates me." (Henderson declined to comment on his relationship with Bell.)

The discord intensified in 2014, after Bell published a memoir, "Right or Wrong." While promoting it, he spoke to the Financial Times and said, of bankers, "They're all complete criminals. The whole bloody lot." The reporter asked him if such opinions might sit uncomfortably with Bell Pottinger's financial-services clients. "That's the problem," Bell said. "You're not allowed to tell the truth. Isn't that disgusting?"

In Henderson's eyes, Bell had gone from being a flashy figurehead to being a threat to the company. In a series of meetings, Henderson pleaded with Bell to work part time. Bell was insulted by the idea, and rejected it. By early 2016, when Bell made the trip to South Africa, both men sensed that a brutal confrontation between them was inevitable.

When Bell won the Oakbay account, he didn't just secure a large monthly fee; he opened a front in South Africa that could lead to a significant amount of new business. Such a success would make Bell even harder to dislodge. Fortunately for Henderson, a large portion of the account was directed to the corporate-and-financial team, which was outside Bell's bailiwick. In the war between Bell and Henderson, fees were ammunition.

Perhaps because the top executives at Bell Pottinger were focussed on internal rivalries, nobody involved in the decision to represent the Guptas appears to have deeply weighed the risk of working for such toxic figures. Henderson told me that, for the first three months of the account, he was not adequately briefed on the Guptas' reputation. Yet the brothers were constantly in the news during this period.

In March 2016, an African National Congress politician claimed that Ajay Gupta had met with him and offered him the post of minister of finance, with an accompanying bribe of forty-four million dollars. The politician alleged that

Zuma's son Duduzane had engineered the meeting. (Representatives of the Guptas have denied that any such meeting took place.)

Henderson also could have sought the counsel of South African executives at Bell Pottinger. When Daniel Thöle, a partner from Johannesburg who mostly did PR work for mining companies, heard that the firm had signed the Guptas, he was appalled. Concluding that Bell Pottinger had become "morally and commercially untenable," he soon left the firm. Thöle recently told me, "People want to work for an ethical business, and be advised on their reputation by an ethical business."

The Oakbay account was initially split in two. Bell's geopolitical team would oversee the economic-emancipation campaign; Victoria Geoghegan and Nick Lambert, from the corporate-and-financial team, would work on countering public 'misperceptions' about Oakbay.

The work of the two teams often overlapped, however. They shared crisis-communications duties, addressing some of the more damaging allegations of corruption against the Guptas. The division of duties caused friction, with geopolitical-team members sometimes complaining of being 'frozen out' by the corporate-and-financial team.

According to two former partners, when Tony Gupta awarded the account to Bell Pottinger, he included a caveat: he did not want any more face-to-face meetings with Bell, having found him obnoxious. As a result, Bell oversaw the geopolitical team's work from London. Much of its work on Oakbay was performed by Jonathan Lehrle, a publicist who had grown up in South Africa.

Lehrle, a favourite of Bell's, had worked on many election campaigns, particularly in Africa. (Lehrle claims that the account was overseen by the corporate-and-financial side, and that he and his geopolitical colleagues acted 'solely in an advisory capacity'; internal e-mails and documents, however, show that he regularly participated in discussions about the account.)

Bell Pottinger's efforts went far beyond representing Oakbay. According to internal Bell Pottinger documents, the Guptas asked the firm to portray Duduzane Zuma as a "businessman in his own right." Bell Pottinger also began offering talking points about 'economic apartheid' to South African politicians, including Collen Maine, the leader of the A.N.C. Youth League. In a speech in February 2016, Maine said that "the two richest individuals in South Africa have fifty per cent of the economy."

The economic-apartheid rhetoric reflects an uncomfortable truth about South Africa: despite making progress since the end of apartheid, it remains a profoundly unequal country, and the financial divides among ethnic groups are stark. But Bell Pottinger laid mines in its own path by working on behalf of the Guptas. One of its other clients was Richemont, the Swiss-based luxury-goods business, which is controlled by Johann Rupert, South Africa's second-richest man.

Rupert became one of the targets of the economic-apartheid campaign. Notwithstanding the shaky ethics of a London PR firm inflaming a debate about racial and economic inequality in South Africa in order to benefit a rich family with government connections, the Oakbay work was a flagrant conflict of interest. Victoria Geoghegan had spun for Richemont herself, and Bell's relationship with Johann Rupert stretched back decades.

11 February 2016, a debate in South Africa's parliament, in Cape Town, descended into chaos. Members of the Economic Freedom Fighters, a radical party led by Julius Malema, disrupted the proceedings, and were ejected from the chamber. On their way out, they began chanting "Zupta Must Fall!" The conflation of 'Zuma' and 'Gupta' soon became commonplace in South Africa. The families' fates were politically and linguistically entangled.

That day, Bell Pottinger began what it called a 'front-foot campaign' to "get the Guptas' message out there to counteract negative and threatening press." Publicists on the account contacted a prominent South African journalist, Stephen Grootes, telling him that, if he agreed to sign a nondisclosure agreement, he could interview 'an important person'. Grootes complied, and was informed that the subject was Ajay Gupta.

Bell Pottinger insisted on recording the interview. A representative promised to hand over the footage to Grootes after a 'light edit'. Grootes agreed to the arrangement, but said that he would make a simultaneous recording.

The interview took place on February 16th. Gupta sounded defensive as he deflected questions about corruption. Grootes asked him if any of his family members had flown to Switzerland with the South African minerals minister, in the hope of securing a mining deal between a Gupta-controlled business and the mining giant Glencore. "Rubbish," he said.

(In fact, according to an investigation by the South African government, Tony Gupta met with the minister in Switzerland.) Bell Pottinger executives, likely aware that Gupta's performance was disastrous, shelved their footage; they also did not return Grootes's recording equipment. A digital copy of the interview was buried on Bell Pottinger's server in London. Grootes felt hoodwinked, but, having signed the nondisclosure agreement, he couldn't press his case in public.

That March, the South African bank Investec severed its PR contract with Bell Pottinger, because it objected to the firm's work for the Guptas. This caused alarm among some Bell Pottinger employees, but it did not unduly trouble the firm's senior management. On 22 March 2016, shortly before the trial contract with Oakbay was set to expire, Bell e-mailed Victoria Geoghegan, the publicist, in his characteristically loose style: "on your trip to Joberg and Cape Town this week you are not authorised to agree to go on handling the Gupta account nor to resign the account, merely to assess the situation and then report back."

According to several people at the firm, it should have been obvious that the only prudent choice was to resign the Oakbay account. At weekly meetings in the Holborn office, several partners and associates asked their managers why Bell Pottinger was representing the Guptas. "You don't mess with South Africa," one partner said. "Especially from London."

At a meeting that spring, the executive chairman of the corporate-and-financial division responded to internal questions about Oakbay by saying that the Guptas' companies were audited by KPMG, an international firm with stringent compliance procedures.

The chairman's argument, an attendee told me, was essentially this: "If they pass KPMG's sniff test, they should be fine for us." A few days after that meeting, however, KPMG dropped Oakbay. Other banks in South Africa, including Standard Chartered, began refusing to service Gupta-linked accounts. It was another signal for Bell Pottinger to discontinue its relationship with Oakbay.

On 24 March 2016, Victoria Geoghegan sent an e-mail to Bell, Henderson, and other executives, which summed up the company's choice: "As we have known from the start, we are in the middle of a civil war with the Guptas and allies on one side, and Johann Rupert and others on the other side. More mud will inevitably be thrown. However, it is difficult to turn down such a large retainer."

Bell told me that, around this time, he became opposed to renewing the Oakbay account after Johann Rupert left him a message expressing concern that Bell Pottinger was working for the Guptas. "I said it was the wrong thing to do,"

Bell told me. "Johann Rupert was a client. And I wasn't sure why we were doing something against his interests. I instructed everyone to stop working for the Guptas, and they completely ignored me."

The contract was renewed, on a rolling monthly basis. Henderson, however, told me that both he and Bell agreed to the terms. An 'anti-embarrassment clause' was attached, allowing Bell Pottinger to exit the contract if the worst allegations against the Guptas, such as the bribery accusations, were confirmed. Henderson's version of events appears to be borne out by e-mails. In a message from April 2016, Bell suggested that the Gupta brothers move their banking operations to Nigeria, in order to bypass the South African banking blockade.

After the account was renewed, Bell Pottinger continued to draft talking points on economic emancipation, including one noting that "inequality in South Africa is greater today than at the end of apartheid." It also commissioned advertisements claiming that South African banks had threatened the livelihoods of Oakbay employees. On April 18th, the Bell Pottinger team asked an Israeli digital-reputation service, Veribo, to help suppress negative Google results about the Guptas. (The company, which has changed its name to Percepto, has said, "We now regret our involvement.")

Bell Pottinger's efforts on behalf of the Guptas became increasingly ugly. I recently reviewed sections of a 2017 report about the Gupta affair, which Henderson commissioned from the law firm Herbert Jones Freehills. (The full text has not been released to the public.) According to the report, in the summer of 2016 a publicist on the Oakbay account set up a website, voetsekblog.co.za, with a related Facebook page and Twitter feed.

In Afrikaans, voetsek means 'go away'. The website's content which was mostly aggregated from other sources, highlighted racial and economic disparities in South Africa. Its home page read: "You know what they say, don't get mad get even so it's time to cause some havoc. For too long black South Africans have been left out of the economy... our economy."

The Twitter account, @Voetsek_SA, posted similar messages and many cartoons. Some of the drawings were produced by the Guptas' newspaper network; others were commissioned by Bell Pottinger. Many of them were offensive. One image that appeared on @Voetsek_SA shows a table of fat, rich-looking white people—one of whom resembles Johann Rupert—gorging on food while emaciated black people eat crumbs off the floor. An army of bots linked to the Guptas promoted the cartoons on Twitter.

The website, the Facebook page, and the Twitter feed have since been scrubbed from the Internet. Branko Brkic, the editor of the South African newspaper the Daily Maverick, whose reporters covered the Bell Pottinger story, told me that the firm's deployment of the Guptas' cynical strategy was 'beyond the pale'. He said, "Bell Pottinger literally stole the page from Goebbels and applied it to twenty-first-century South Africa. That's just plain evil. They were going well beyond their brief. It's almost as if they felt pleasure doing it."

When Henderson later apologised for the firm's work on the Oakbay account, he wrote that Bell Pottinger contained many "good, decent people who will be as angered by what has been discovered as we are." Indeed, most Bell Pottinger employees did ordinary PR work, often for such unimpeachably bland companies as the grocery chain Waitrose. But it is also true that the underhanded tactics used on the Oakbay account were part of the firm's DNA, particularly in the geopolitical division.

In 2011, during the Arab Spring, Bahrain erupted in protests against the royal family. At the time, Bell Pottinger was advising the Bahrain Economic Development Board, and on occasion its brief extended to advising the Bahraini government more generally. The government responded to the protests with a repressive backlash. Bell Pottinger's digital team prepared for its Bahraini clients a list of the most influential dissidents on social media.

Any employee involved in this work does not know the fate of the individuals on the list, but he remains troubled by the fact that Bell Pottinger performed this service at a time when Bahraini officials were imprisoning and torturing people who spoke out against the regime. The Bahrain account brought in three and a half million dollars annually.

In the same period, the firm also worked for Abdul Taib Mahmud, the chief minister of Sarawak, a state in eastern Malaysia. He had held the post since 1981, and was seeking his eighth term. Opposition figures frequently called Taib corrupt. One journalist who criticised Taib was Clare Rewcastle Brown, who lives in London but was born in Sarawak. She is the sister-in-law of Gordon Brown, the former Labour Prime Minister of the U.K. In 2011, Rewcastle Brown was subjected to a series of smears by a blog called Sarawak Bersatu, which described itself as representing a "group of Sarawakians who aim to protect Sarawak against the influences—and hidden agendas—of foreign political groups and activists."

Material posted on Sarawak Bersatu, and on a related Twitter feed, impugned the motives and the reporting practices of Rewcastle Brown and called her an agent of British socialism. The site promoted stories falsely claiming that one of her colleagues had engaged in sexual improprieties. According to a former Bell Pottinger employee with knowledge of the site, the firm generated Sarawak Bersatu's material. This was 'fake news' before it had a name. When I informed Rewcastle Brown that Bell Pottinger was behind Sarawak Bersatu, she said that she had "no idea this was being run out of London."

A former Bell Pottinger partner expressed shock when I described the Bahrain and Sarawak accounts. It was possible, he said, to draw a straight line between these episodes and the South African scandal. The partner said the Sarawak work suggested that certain people within Bell Pottinger had 'a playbook'.

One publicist who helped write the Bell Pottinger playbook is Mark Turnbull, who worked at the firm from 1995 to 2012, and often focussed on geopolitical accounts, including in South Africa and Iraq. He subsequently became a top executive at Cambridge Analytica, the British firm that advised Donald Trump's 2016 Presidential campaign. The company fell apart earlier this year, after its harvesting of Facebook user data was exposed. Shortly before Cambridge Analytica's collapse, undercover journalists at Channel 4 News, in London, secretly recorded Turnbull describing his modus operandi.

He bragged about the deployment of misinformation against a client's political opponents. "We just put information into the bloodstream of the Internet, and then, and then watch it grow, give it a little push every now and again," Turnbull explained. "It has to happen without anyone thinking, That's propaganda. Because the moment you think, that's propaganda, the next question is: Who's put that out?"

Until 2016, Bell and Henderson had an equal number of supporters on the company's board, but that summer one of Bell's oldest allies, Mark Jones, indicated that he could no longer support him, allowing Henderson to take control of Bell Pottinger. Bell resigned. As Bell sees it, Jones "turned on me and stabbed me in the back!" (Jones told me, "I do not want to talk about it.")

Bell threatened to sue the company for wrongful dismissal, and demanded a $6.7-million severance payment. Eventually, he told me, he settled for four million dollars. (Henderson claims that the payout was significantly lower.) Bell later sold company stock worth $1.3 million. Even though he had been given a soft landing, he was enraged by his ejection. A former colleague recalls Bell saying, "It's my company—it's my name above the door."

Publicly, Bell has told several journalists, including me, that he had resigned in protest, because Bell Pottinger had refused to drop the Oakbay account. When I questioned this claim, Bell clarified that he had resigned "not entirely over the Gupta crisis, actually over the challenge to my authority. But the Gupta thing was an exaggerated version of it."

It's hard to see how Bell's two stories—that he was stabbed in the back, and that he resigned in protest—can coexist. In any event, he left the company in August 2016. Later that year, Jonathan Lehrle, one of the geopolitical publicists on the Oakbay account, also left Bell Pottinger. He founded a new PR agency, Sans Frontières Associates, and named Bell its chairman. Within months, Sans Frontières had hired several other former Bell Pottinger publicists.

When I interviewed Bell at his town house, he told me that his departure had caused a catastrophic leadership vacuum at Bell Pottinger, which ultimately led to the failure of the business. He compared the company to the U.K. after Thatcher resigned as prime minister, in 1990. "The moment I'd gone, the grip went," Bell said. "They say that Thatcher had a grip on Britain when she was in power, and the moment she left the grip went."

Bell warmed to his theme: "Henderson doesn't understand the basic principle of running a public-relations company, which is money in, money out. Subtract one from another, and if you've got a red number, you're in shit, and if you've got a black number, you're fine. It took him a year to take it into complete loss-making."

This narrative, I told him, omitted the overwhelming reason that clients had dropped Bell Pottinger: the Oakbay scandal, in which he had played a significant role. Bell brushed this off, countering that Henderson "didn't get any new business." He added, "That's all to do with him, his leadership. Business was roaring in while I was running the place."

In October 2016, Thuli Madonsela, the Public Protector of South Africa, whose mandate is to expose threats to the country's democratic system, published a report titled 'State of Capture'. It described "alleged improper and unethical conduct by the president," and chronicled Zuma's corrupt dealings with the Guptas.

According to Madonsela, the Guptas had indeed acted as a shadow government, using cash bribes and promises of ministerial promotions to further their financial interests. In the report, a parliamentarian named Vytjie Mentor charged that, in a meeting, the Guptas had told her she could become the minister for public enterprises, as long as she agreed to make South African Airways drop its Johannesburg-to-Mumbai service.

The Guptas had links to the owners of a rival airline that coveted the route. When Mentor demurred, President Zuma himself emerged from a nearby room and escorted her out. (Representatives of the Guptas denied that the meeting took place.)

Around the time that 'State of Capture' was released, reports of Bell Pottinger's work for the Guptas appeared in the South African media. In response, Richemont, Johann Rupert's company, and Mediclinic, in which Rupert also holds a large share, cut ties with Bell Pottinger. That November, at Richemont's annual general meeting, Rupert denounced Bell Pottinger: "While they were working for us, they started working for the Guptas. Their total task was to deflect attention. Guess who was the target? A client of theirs—me!"

Rupert added that Bell Pottinger had described the white-owned businesses supposedly in control of South Africa's economy as 'white monopoly capital'. Rupert's accusation went viral, and it soon became a widespread notion in South Africa that Bell Pottinger had invented this term. In fact, academics have used the phrase for years, but Bell Pottinger certainly helped popularise it. The Twitter account that it launched to support the Guptas regularly promoted content referring to 'monopoly capital'. Shortly after Rupert's speech, a twenty-three-minute portion of Stephen Grootes's interview with Ajay Gupta leaked on YouTube. Evidently, someone had downloaded the video from Bell Pottinger's server.

Despite the negative press and the loss of accounts, Bell Pottinger continued working with the Guptas. Henderson says the Oakbay team reassured him that the allegations against the brothers had not been proved, and that Bell Pottinger's work was ethical. In any case, the firm began losing money in 2016; it was no time for a weak stomach.

Some former Bell Pottinger employees say that Henderson's decision to maintain the Oakbay account can be attributed not just to financial pressure but to his arrogant management style. (One of them said that he could be an 'aggressive little bully' who ignored contrary views.) Others believe that Henderson had been distracted by the feud with Bell and by his romantic life: he had recently divorced the mother of his four children and begun dating Kerzner.

Henderson told me that the explanation was simpler: "I made an error of judgment."

In March 2017, a twenty-one-page dossier titled "Bell Pottinger PR Support for the Gupta Family" began circulating in South African government circles. Although its author was anonymous, it had an oddly personal tone, citing seemingly irrelevant details about people on the Oakbay account, such as the fact that a wedding venue in Tuscany where Victoria Geoghegan had been married rented for twenty thousand dollars a week.

The document also contained explosive accusations, including that Bell Pottinger employees had created Twitter bots on behalf of the Guptas and had colluded with Jacob Zuma on messaging. Henderson vigorously denied these claims, and the Herbert Jones Freehills report later found them to be false.

The dossier's author seemed intent on associating the Gupta account with Geoghegan, who was described as 'leading the project', and with Henderson, who was said to 'not care one bit' about criticism of Bell Pottinger's decision to work with the Guptas. In one passage, a 'former partner' pointedly exculpates Bell: "When the Gupta project first arose, senior members of the Geopolitical team, including Bell, were quite outspoken that we should not do it."

Henderson and Geoghegan, the dossier alleges, saw the account merely as 'a lucrative contract', and never "appreciated how divisive the project would be and the implications it might have, specifically on the Geopolitical team, who were seeing the immediate impact of the company's decision to work with the Guptas in their marketing meetings."

To some Bell Pottinger partners, the sudden appearance of the dossier, along with the earlier leaks of sensitive material and the Stephen Grootes interview, suggested that Bell and his allies at Sans Frontières were attempting to destroy Bell Pottinger. One partner considers it an 'open-and-shut' case.

Many details that leaked to South African journalists in November 2016, including the fee structure of the Oakbay account, were known only to Bell, Henderson, and the four people working daily on behalf of the Guptas. The Grootes interview, meanwhile, was uploaded to YouTube with a comment referring to a nickname for the account, Project Biltong, that was known only to the publicists who had worked on it.

South African government officials handed the dossier to other journalists, who were told that its findings came from former Bell Pottinger partners with 'operational' knowledge of the Oakbay account. A South African media source told me that he understood the dossier's sources to be former Bell Pottinger employees who wanted to "exact as much hurt as possible on Bell Pottinger itself."

On 19 March 2017, the Sunday Times of South Africa ran a long article based on the dossier, which suggested that Bell Pottinger had been hired by the Guptas to 'divert public outcry' from 'state capture' to 'white monopoly capital'. The report cites a former Bell Pottinger 'insider' saying that Bell left the firm because he disapproved of its work for Oakbay.

Two weeks later, the entire dossier was published on the South African Communist Party's website. Solly Mapaila, the Party official who posted it, told me that an anti-Zuma group had given it to him. According to a former South African government official, among the document's sources were 'insiders within Bell Pottinger'; he declined to name the insiders, but reminded me that some people at Bell Pottinger had worked for President de Klerk. The only partner or senior manager who had worked for de Klerk was Bell. (Bell has repeatedly denied any involvement with the dossier or its distribution.)

The dossier had its desired effect. South Africans were outraged by the revelation that a British PR firm had meddled in their nation's politics. To many of them, Bell Pottinger's actions felt not just irresponsible but colonial. On social media, a campaign was launched against Bell Pottinger and its staff. In April 2017, thousands of South Africans marched against Zuma's government, and some protesters carried posters denouncing Bell Pottinger.

One poster showed Victoria Geoghegan's photograph along with the slogan 'Gupta's Girl'. That month, Bell Pottinger issued a statement claiming that many assertions in the dossier were 'wholly untrue', and that a 'politically motivated' campaign was being waged against the firm. But it conceded that the campaign had worked—Bell Pottinger could no longer be an 'effective advocate' for Oakbay. It was dropping the account.

Henderson told me that, on reading the dossier, he realised that forces were conspiring "against Bell Pottinger, and, to a certain extent, me."

Relinquishing the Oakbay account did not contain the damage. In South Africa, Bell Pottinger had become inextricably linked with the 'Zupta' project and with the insidious propagation of the 'white monopoly capital' theme. The Guptas, for their part, continued their aggressive tactics. According to a newspaper investigation, one of their employees built a website that promoted false stories about critics of the brothers.

Peter Bruce, a South African journalist who had called the Guptas corrupt, became the subject of a smear campaign claiming that he'd cheated on his wife. (Bruce and two other journalists targeted in this fashion recently filed suit against Bell Pottinger's insurer, A.I.G. Europe, for defamation and breach of privacy.)

In May 2017, more than a hundred thousand e-mails relating to the Guptas were leaked to the media. Among them were messages detailing Bell Pottinger's work for Oakbay. The e-mails appear to have been obtained from a server at Sahara Computers, one of the Guptas' companies. The hashtag #bellpottingermustfall became popular on Twitter, and Bell Pottinger employees received a stream of hate mail. The South African Tourist Board, a Bell Pottinger client, severed ties with the agency.

The 'optics', as publicists like to say, could not have been worse. Henderson attempted to stop the firm's tailspin by ordering the Herbert Jones Freehills review of the Oakbay account. However, while the company was handing documents to the law firm's investigators, Henderson says, he learned about the Voetsek site. He was taken aback. He called Victoria Geoghegan on a boardroom speakerphone, and asked her to explain how the site had been created. I obtained a transcript of the exchange.

Geoghegan told Henderson that Jonathan Lehrle, the South African-born publicist, had come up with the site. He had advised the team to create something that captured the gossipy feel of the British blog Guido Fawkes, a pro-Brexit, Thatcherite site that the Guardian has described as "a cross between a comic and a propaganda machine." The idea was that Voetsek would host content on economic emancipation from other news sources. (Lehrle told me that Voetsek was a group creation, not his alone, but he admitted that he thought up the name. Moreover, a briefing document from March 2016, written by Lehrle, proposed creating a blog that contained 'emotive language' and 'powerful imagery'.)

"The whole site is racially motivated," Henderson told Geoghegan, adding, "We've denied that we did this!" Geoghegan explained that the Oakbay team had commissioned a cartoonist to create work for the site. "I could never put our company's name to this, do you accept that?" Henderson asked.

"It wasn't branded 'Bell Pottinger'," Geoghegan said. She then noted that "the creation of the website was under Tim Bell." "You allowed me to keep denying the allegations, and losing clients, when we were actively using this website!" Henderson said. "We have lied." "The allegations that we were asked about we did not lie about," Geoghegan said. She repeated that Bell had signed off on the Voetsek site, but told Henderson that, as CEO, he needed to take responsibility. "Everyone knew that economic emancipation was the campaign!" Geoghegan said. "I don't believe you can say you were unaware."

That day, Henderson fired Geoghegan and suspended three other people who'd worked on the Oakbay account. He then issued an 'absolute' public apology for the firm's work on a 'social-media campaign' in South Africa that was 'inappropriate and offensive'.

The next day, Bell told the Financial Times that Henderson "knew all about it from the very beginning."

By July 2017, Bell Pottinger was hated by many South Africans, but the scandal did not gain traction in the United Kingdom until the Herbert Jones Freehills report was commissioned and Geoghegan was fired. Soon after British journalists took note of the Gupta account, the Democratic Alliance, a liberal South African opposition party, organised protests outside Bell Pottinger's headquarters. The Democratic Alliance also filed a complaint with the Public Relations and Communications Association, a U.K. trade group to which the firm belonged.

On September 4th, the association concluded that Bell Pottinger had violated its code of conduct. Henderson, who knew of the verdict in advance, resigned the day before it was announced. At that point in the scandal, he recalled, the loss of clients had caused a drop in revenue of about eight per cent—a 'survivable amount', as he put it. His resignation, he hoped, might stanch the bleeding.

Bell Pottinger was expelled from the Public Relations and Communications Association for five years, the harshest possible sanction. At a press conference, Francis Ingham, the group's chairman, declared that Bell Pottinger had "brought the PR-and-communications industry into disrepute." In media interviews, Ingham called Bell Pottinger's work for Oakbay "the most blatant instance of unethical PR practice I've ever seen," and declared that the firm had "set back South Africa by possibly ten years."

Ingham's outrage struck some observers as hypocritical. George Pitcher, a former publicist who is now a priest, wrote, in Politico, that the association looked "like a bunch of pimps throwing up their hands in horror at the moral turpitude of their highest-earning whore." Senior figures at Bell Pottinger speculated that Ingham's tone had been influenced by Bell, with whom Ingham is friendly. Only a few months earlier, Ingham had inducted Bell into an international PR hall of fame, saying that Bell had 'created modern PR' and 'elevated our work'. Three days after Bell Pottinger's expulsion from the association, Ingham and Bell were spotted having lunch together.

Herbert Jones Freehills, meanwhile, published a skeleton account of its findings. It reported, "While we do not consider that it was a breach of relevant ethical principles to agree to undertake the economic emancipation campaign mandate per se, members of BP's senior management should have known that the campaign was at risk of causing offence, including on grounds of race. In such circumstances, BP ought to have exercised extreme care and should have closely scrutinised the creation of content for the campaign. This does not appear to have happened."

That evening, a former managing director of Bell Pottinger, David Wilson, who left the firm in 2015, learned that Tim Bell was shortly to be interviewed on the BBC program 'Newsnight'. Wilson was an investor in Bell Pottinger, and had friends who still worked there. Believing that Bell could fatally damage the firm, Wilson sent him a text urging restraint: "Tim please remember some of us shareholders… This is dire for us."

Bell did not reply.

The 'Newsnight' interview was widely perceived as embarrassing. Bell, who was wearing a suit with a polo shirt underneath, had left his phone on, and it rang twice during the segment. On the first occasion, Bell fumbled with the device before turning its screen toward the interviewer, Kirsty Wark, with a puckish grin. "Look who it is!" Bell stage-whispered. The caller was Johann Rupert, the founder of Richemont.

Bell said of Oakbay, "I had nothing to do with getting this account!" He continued, "Of course, James Henderson is to blame."

Wark asked Bell, "Do you think this is curtains for Bell Pottinger?"

"Almost certainly," Bell said. "But that's nothing to do with me."

"It doesn't strike anyone as possible that you could be the innocent in all this," Wark said.

"Well, I'm sorry, but I am," Bell said.

Wilson, like many former and current Bell Pottinger employees, watched the interview with dismay. To outsiders, Bell had come across as a floundering old man. But many former colleagues, who knew how skilled he could be with the media, saw a calculated performance, down to the ringing cell phone. "Tim doesn't do very much by accident," one of them said. Despite the seemingly amateurish display, Bell had delivered two messages with clarity: Bell Pottinger was in grave trouble, and Henderson was at fault.

The next morning, the headline of the London newspaper City A.M. was 'BELL ROTTINGER'. All day, the firm haemorrhaged clients. Chime Communications, which had been attempting to sell its stake in Bell Pottinger, announced that it was simply giving up its shares.

Crisis communications was one of Wilson's specialties—he had steered Rebekah Brooks, the former editor of the News of the World, through the infamous phone-hacking scandal—and he tried again to reach Bell. He felt that if he could persuade Bell to stop talking to reporters the firm might survive.

Bell met Wilson for coffee the next morning at a restaurant in Sloane Square, arriving in a chauffeur-driven town car, which idled in a no-parking zone as they spoke. They sat outside, so that Bell could smoke. (Bell says that he has no recollection of the meeting, but text messages confirm that he and Wilson met at the restaurant.)

Wilson asked Bell to keep quiet, for the sake of his former colleagues. Bell refused, noting that journalists were calling him. Wilson recalls his saying, "I can't lie!" Bell admitted that he was also determined to get back at Henderson for pushing him out of the company. As Wilson remembers it, Bell used the word 'revenge'.

"I was trying to protect the business," Wilson told me. "He was intent on murdering it."

As the difficult exchange drew to a close, Bell said, "Today's a big day for them with Bahrain." The Bahrain account was Bell Pottinger's largest, and without it the firm would implode. Bell mentioned teasingly that his friend Lord Chadlington advised the Bahrainis on communications matters. Wilson realised that Bell was signalling his awareness that Bell Pottinger was already doomed.

The Bahrain account was indeed lost, and the next day Bell Pottinger was declared insolvent. Many of the firm's employees and partners lost their jobs immediately; some stayed on to help administrators wind down the business. Operations ceased within weeks. Henderson lost both his fortune and his fiancée. Kerzner had invested heavily in Bell Pottinger—she'd bought shares in 2017—and when the business collapsed so did her relationship with Henderson. They postponed a wedding planned for November.

Earlier this year, the couple reconciled. Henderson established a new PR firm, J&H Communications. It has signed a few clients, but even former allies of Henderson's worry that his name will forever be tainted by the Oakbay scandal. "A PR firm that can't manage its own reputation isn't worth much in the marketplace," one said. In April, the Daily Mail reported that Kerzner and Henderson had split up for good, and that she was "on the look-out for love again."

Bell's public image, meanwhile, has suffered little damage, and Sans Frontières appears to be prospering. Bell recently represented the Russian reality-TV star Ksenia Sobchak, who ran against Vladimir Putin in the 2018 Presidential election. Bell's new firm has also bid for a large account in Bahrain. His recent media appearances have felt like a victory lap. The Mail on Sunday noted, in a sympathetic interview, that Bell's 'fame—or notoriety—has gone skywards' since he left Bell Pottinger.

An article in the New York Times described him as having 'stepped directly out of an Evelyn Waugh novel' and made note of his 'ingratiating candour'. On his seventy-sixth birthday, a month after Bell Pottinger's collapse, Bell married Jacky Phillips. The headline in the Daily Mail: "BELL POTTINGER FOUNDER BEATS HIS RIVAL JAMES HENDERSON BY MARRYING FIRST." The feud, by its own petty terms, has ended decisively in Bell's favour.

The legacy of a boardroom tussle between two privileged white businessmen in London will have a longer effect in South Africa. After the firm collapsed, Thuli Madonsela, the official who published 'State of Capture', said that, in a democracy as young as South Africa's, Bell Pottinger's PR campaign had been 'reckless and dangerous'. By hijacking a legitimate debate about economic inequality on behalf of mercenary aims, the firm had poisoned political discourse in South Africa.

In mid-February, an arrest warrant was issued for Ajay Gupta, on corruption charges. But he and his brothers had apparently gone abroad. (Their whereabouts are unknown.) South Africa's national prosecutor now considers Ajay Gupta to be a 'fugitive from justice', and other South African prosecutors wish to bring Atul and Tony Gupta back to South Africa to face charges. In addition, the Financial Times has reported that the F.B.I. is investigating the brothers' allegedly corrupt business dealings in the United States.

On February 14th, Jacob Zuma stepped down as the President of South Africa. In his resignation speech, Zuma—who had previously said that to resign would be to 'surrender' to 'white monopoly capital'—suggested that he had been a victim of a conspiracy. As if repeating Bell Pottinger's talking points about economic apartheid, he framed his ouster—which was primarily about his incompetence and dishonesty—as the result of racism. "I respect each member and leader of this glorious movement," Zuma said. "I respect its gallant fight against centuries of white-minority brutality, whose relics remain today and continue to be entrenched, in all manner of sophisticated ways." [95]

[95] Ed Caesar is forty years old. He lives in Manchester, and writes for the *New Yorker*. He has won eleven major journalism awards—including a British Press Award, PPA Writer of the Year and the 2014 Foreign Press Award for Journalist of the Year. *https://edcaesar.co.uk/googlebooks*

Notes

"White Privilege," speech given by the deputy principal, Kevin Leatham, at the alma mater of the writer, Jeppe High School for Boys, 2018: *We imagine excess, ease and extravagance. And that is simply not the experience of all white South Africans. Many (if not most) of the white people come from working-class or middle-class families, who have had to work hard for what they have. And so, when we hear the words 'white privilege' we become defensive because we think that our hardships and hard work are being dismissed.*

But the word 'privilege' has nothing to do with wealth. Privilege simply refers to a right, advantage, or immunity that only a particular person or group get to enjoy. So, for example, in our school, the first-team players are allowed to wear white scarves. That's a privilege they enjoy. It doesn't mean that they are wealthy—it simply means that they get to enjoy something that the rest of the pupils do not. My mum grew up dirt poor. She was one of eight children; her father lost his leg fighting in World War 2 and the family had to get by on a meagre government railways pension. My dad was the son of Irish immigrants who arrived in this country with absolutely nothing to their name. Not a cent.

They worked hard. All of them. And I'm sure that they would argue that they were never given a hand-up or a hand-out. They worked themselves out of poverty. But here's the thing: the only reason they were able to, was because they were white. Their whiteness meant that their hard work was allowed to amount to something. You see, no one is saying that white people don't work hard.

But what I am saying is, their hard work was and is allowed to amount to something because the pool was rigged in their favour. Would my mother have been able to achieve what she did if, instead of competing against the 20 or so other white applicants, she was competing against 10,000 applicants just as qualified as she was? I doubt it. It was because of her whiteness that we, as a family, were allowed to accumulate wealth and improve our lives. Imagine playing a video game where the save function was disabled and you were unable to accumulate experience points. That's what it was like being black during apartheid.

No matter how hard you worked, or how much money you earned, you couldn't own land, businesses, or homes. You couldn't buy your kids a safer suburb to grow up in or buy them a better education. Every generation started back at zero. Being white was like being the only one with a save function. Everyone was working through the game, but only white people got to accumulate an advantage.

I want to make this crystal clear: saying that white people enjoy a privilege is not saying that their lives are easy or that they haven't worked hard. White people are not immune to the human condition, they suffer loss and hardship like everyone else. So then what is it? What is white privilege? For me, it's simply a preference for whiteness that saturates our society. I guess if you are white, it's sometimes hard to see the privilege because you're in it and it's all you've ever known. It's like asking a fish to notice water.

I'll give you an example: kids love plasters. They will have the tiniest scratch, and act like they're about to bleed out—just so that they can get a plaster. I am relieved that these days there are plasters available with cartoon characters on them like Lightning McQueen—because plasters are one of many products that have been designed just for white people. The so-called flesh-coloured plasters only match a white skin tone. More than 80% of our population is black.

That's well over 40 million people in our country (and another 38 million in the States—so don't tell me there's no market) and yet pharmaceutical companies are specifically catering to the needs of less than 10% of the population... white people. It's a privilege to have your needs acknowledged; your needs catered for; your needs addressed. When you go to a hotel, and get a complimentary bottle of shampoo, whose hair do you imagine it is designed for?

As a white person, when I get a job or make a team, I enjoy the privilege of people assuming I earned it. People do not assume that I got where I am professionally because of my race or because of affirmative action programmes. When I walk in to teach a new class at the beginning of a school year, my accent and name are unlikely to result in my pupils questioning my credentials or my competence. White people also have the privilege of options. Go into any toy store. You will see a wall of blond and blue-eyed dolls. Ten years ago, there were no black dolls, but they have recently introduced a handful into the mix. But only a few.

It's the needs of white little girls that are clearly their priority. Look at superheroes. We all got very excited about the recent Black Panther film, and the first black superheroes. The film took in more than $1.3-billion worldwide, proving once again that there is a huge black market. Some people argued that it wasn't a big deal. There were always black superheroes. What about Blade, Hancock, Cyborg and Iron Man's sidekick? Black people should stop being greedy, I mean, there are at least five black superheroes. How many do you they want? Well, do you know how many there are in total? Marvel lists 7,000 official characters. DC Comics claims to have more.

So, five out of a possible 14–15 thousand?! Yes, black people, you should be satisfied with that. Know your place. Now, these are just examples of the millions of ways that whiteness is valued and given priority in our society. Some might argue that the examples amount to nothing more than an inconvenience, but I would argue that constant and daily messages that you are somehow 'less-than' because of the colour of your skin, shapes your sense of self, and does serious damages to your sense of the possibilities for your life.

When you are black you do not have the privilege of being presumed innocent. These examples are pretty close to home for me. Literally. Sometimes it's easier to take a step back and look at cases from overseas. And on this issue, there are plenty to choose from. Just this month, two black men were arrested in a Starbucks, after a white female employee called the cops. Their crime? Sitting at a table and waiting for their friend.

A couple of weeks ago, at Yale University, a black student who is studying for her master's degree was working on an assignment and fell asleep in the common room of her own dormitory. A white student called the police claiming there was an intruder. She told them she was a student and even used her key to unlock her bedroom, but the three officers were not satisfied. She was still questioned and had to produce identification papers to prove she had a right to be there. Is anyone here going to claim that if a blonde girl fell asleep in her own res, the police would be called? Just an inconvenience?

Tell that the mother of Michael Brown, the innocent and unarmed black teenager who was shot six times by police. Or Trayvon Martin's family, just 17, gunned down for looking suspicious. Or explain to the four-year-old girl, who watched from the back seat as her father, Philando Castile, was shot seven times in the chest after being pulled over by the police. The video of the murder was caught on tape and it's one of the most heart-breaking things I've ever seen. I'll say it again: when you are white, you enjoy the privilege of being presumed innocent.

As a white man, I benefit daily from the colour of my skin. Daily. And let's just remember what that privilege comes from. I benefit because crimes against humanity were committed. Torture, murder, rape, humiliation, oppression... that's the source of my advantage. Now how am I supposed to feel about that? What do we do with that?

Making you feel bad about yourselves is certainly not my intention here today. You have no reason to feel ashamed. After all, none of you were born when the crimes that have created your advantage were committed. But I will tell you what I feel is an appropriate way to respond. Stop denying it. Stop pretending that it isn't real. Stop throwing your hands in the air at the very mention of it. As a start, I am going to ask you to be grateful for your privilege, and realise that through no fault of yours, or their own, millions of people are worse off and don't deserve to be. The best thing to do is just acknowledge it.

You have been given an unfair advantage. So, use it. Do something meaningful with it. Or don't. But whatever you do, don't deny it. Your denial is not harmless. In my mind, it should be a crime. I think Tom Eaton put it pretty well when he said: "If you can look out of your car window and still genuinely believe that white people and black people start from the same base and enjoy the same economic and social opportunities, then you are like someone walking into a blood-spattered room and not seeing anything amiss. You are unable to see that a crime has been committed, and you are likely to dismiss appeals for justice because you don't think an injustice has been done. No matter how kind and generous you might consider yourself, if you deny that a crime has occurred then you are subtly working to defeat the ends of justice."

FIN

www.ingramcontent.com/pod-product-compliance
Lightning Source LLC
Chambersburg PA
CBHW060453290526
45791CB00001B/105